Migration Narratives

Also available from Bloomsbury

Identity, Culture and Belonging, Tony Eaude
Issues and Challenges of Immigration in Early Childhood in the USA,
Wilma Robles-Melendez and Wayne Driscoll

Migration Narratives

Diverging Stories in Schools, Churches, and Civic Institutions

Stanton Wortham, Briana Nichols, Katherine Clonan-Roy and Catherine Rhodes

BLOOMSBURY ACADEMIC
LONDON • NEW YORK • OXFORD • NEW DELHI • SYDNEY

Bloomsbury Academic
Bloomsbury Publishing Plc
50 Bedford Square, London, WC1B 3DP, UK
1385 Broadway, New York, NY 10018, USA
29 Earlsfort Terrace, Dublin 2, Ireland

BLOOMSBURY, BLOOMSBURY ACADEMIC and the Diana logo are
trademarks of Bloomsbury Publishing Plc

First published in Great Britain 2020
This paperback edition published in 2022

Copyright © Stanton Wortham, Briana Nichols, Katherine Clonan-Roy and Catherine Rhodes, 2020.

Stanton Wortham, Briana Nichols, Katherine Clonan-Roy and Catherine Rhodes
have asserted their right under the Copyright, Designs and Patents Act, 1988,
to be identified as Authors of this work.

Cover design: Charlotte James
Cover images: © Katsumi Murouchi/ Getty images
and © Oleksii Liskonih iStock / Getty Images Plus

This work is published open access subject to a Creative Commons Attribution-NonCommercial-NoDerivatives 3.0 licence (CC BY-NC-ND 3.0, https://creativecommons.org/licenses/by-nc-nd/3.0/). You may re-use, distribute, and reproduce this work in any medium for non-commercial purposes, provided you give attribution to the copyright holder and the publisher and provide a link to the Creative Commons licence.

Bloomsbury Publishing Plc does not have any control over, or responsibility for,
any third-party websites referred to or in this book. All internet addresses given
in this book were correct at the time of going to press. The author and publisher
regret any inconvenience caused if addresses have changed or sites have
ceased to exist, but can accept no responsibility for any such changes.

Names: Wortham, Stanton Emerson Fisher, 1963-author. | Nichols, Briana, author. | Clonan-Roy, Katherine, author. | Rhodes, Catherine Rebecca, author.
Title: Migration narratives: diverging stories in schools, churches, and civic institutions / Stanton Wortham, Briana Nichols, Katherine Clonan-Roy and Catherine Rhodes.
Description: London; New York: Bloomsbury Academic, 2020. | Includes bibliographical references and index. | Summary: "Migration Narratives presents an ethnographic study of an American town that recently became home to thousands of Mexican migrants, with the Mexican population rising from 125 in 1990 to slightly under 10,000 in 2016. Through interviews with residents, the book focuses on key educational, religious, and civic institutions that shape and are shaped by the realities of Mexican immigrants. Focusing on African American, Mexican, Irish and Italian communities, the authors describe how interethnic relations played a central role in newcomers' pathways and draw links between the town's earlier cycles of migration. The town represents similar communities across the USA and around the world that have received large numbers of immigrants in a short time. The purpose of the book is to document the complexities that migrants and hosts experience and to suggest ways in which policy-makers, researchers, educators and communities can respond intelligently to politically-motivated stories that oversimplify migration across the contemporary world. The study has been documented in a short film which can viewed here: www.adelantethefilm.com"– Provided by publisher.
Identifiers: LCCN 2020023058 (print) | LCCN 2020023059 (ebook) |
ISBN 9781350181311 (hb) | ISBN 9781350181328 (ePDF) | ISBN 9781350181335 (eBook)
Subjects: LCSH: Mexicans–United States–Social conditions–Longitudinal studies. | Immigrants–United States–Social conditions–Longitudinal studies. | United States–Race relations–Longitudinal studies. | African Americans–Relations with Mexican Americans.
Classification: LCC E184.M5 W68 2020 (print) | LCC E184.M5 (ebook) | DDC 304.8/73–dc23
LC record available at https://lccn.loc.gov/2020023058
LC ebook record available at https://lccn.loc.gov/2020023059

IS BN: HB: 978-1-3501-8131-1
PB: 978-1-3502-1274-9
ePDF: 978-1-3501-8132-8
eBOO K: 978-1-3501-8133-5

Typeset by Integra Software Services Pvt. Ltd.,

To find out more about our authors and books visit www.bloomsbury.com
and sign up for our newsletters.

Contents

List of Figures		vi
Preface		vii
1	Intersecting Migrant Histories	1
2	Schools: Three Diverging Individual Mexican Pathways	37
3	Churches: An Emerging Irish-Mexican Community	75
4	Neighborhoods: Diverging Stories of Decline	109
5	Public Spaces: Victims, Revitalizers, and Competition	147
6	Community Organizations: Three Imagined Mexican Pathways	199
7	Powerful, Limited Stories	237
References		255
Index		266

Figures

1.1	The sun rises over downtown Marshall	9
1.2	The commuter train connecting Marshall to the region	18
2.1	Marshall Middle School	52
2.2	Bilingual sign outside of a Marshall elementary school	67
3.1	Church in Marshall	75
3.2	Early morning celebration of the Virgen de Guadalupe	83
3.3	Mexican and Irish food, side by side, at a St. Joseph's celebration	97
3.4	Parishoners entering St. Joseph's carrying the Mexican and American flags	107
4.1	For rent sign in Marshall's East end	113
4.2	Parked cars along a downtown residential street	127
5.1	Mini-Mall catering to Mexican shoppers	162
5.2	A storefront on Main Street advertising money transfer services to Mexico	174
5.3	Polling station during municipal elections	190
6.1	Mexican folkloric dance exhibition	232
7.1	An aerial view of Marshall at sunset	237
7.2	Clouds parting after summer rain	254

Preface

This book describes experiences of and stories about migration in one American town that became home to thousands of Mexican migrants between 1995 and 2016. Across those two decades the town's Mexican population increased by over 1,000 percent, and Mexicans constituted almost a third of the town by 2016. The Hispanic population in the United States grew from 9 percent in 1990 to 18 percent in 2016 (Flores, 2017; Pew Research Center, 2017), and 23 percent of all schoolchildren in America in 2016 were Hispanic (Bauman, 2017). Because of their large numbers and relative youth, migrants from Latin America and their descendants will continue to play a crucial role in America's future. Some expect that many of these migrants and their children will travel pathways similar to those imagined for previous migrant groups, like the Irish and the Italians, ultimately assimilating to the American mainstream (e.g., Gans, 2012; Levine, 2004). Others predict that they will face challenges similar to African Americans, facing racial injustice and ongoing struggle (Behnken, 2016; Jones, 2012; Manning, 2000). Both these predictions, and others, will surely turn out to be true in some cases—because migrants from Latin America are traveling divergent pathways (Alba & Nee, 2003; Portes & Rumbaut, 2001; Pew Research Center, 2008).

In order to understand the likely futures of Mexicans and other migrants from Latin America, and in order to establish policies that will allow the United States to benefit from the advantages of ongoing migration, we need careful, empirically grounded accounts of Latin American migrants and the communities where they live in twenty-first-century America. Such accounts are particularly needed in the current political climate, which includes powerful but oversimplified and often inaccurate stories about migrants and their futures. The ascension of Donald Trump, Jeff Sessions, Stephen Bannon, and Stephen Miller in 2017 brought a formerly extremist, aggressively anti-migrant position to the center of American discourse, policy, and action. This position contrasts with the familiar, sympathetic story about America as a country largely composed of current and former migrants that has benefited from their energy, cultural traditions, and economic successes. America's history is not that simple, of course, as African Americans and Native Americans can attest. But the country's relative openness to migrants has yielded vibrant technologies, traditions, and businesses, as well as a younger, more entrepreneurial population than in many comparable nations (Fairlie, Reedy, Morelix, & Russell, 2016; PennWharton, 2016; Trevelyan et al., 2016; Vandor & Franke, 2016). Despite failures along the way—including stereotyping and the racist mistreatment of migrants that have occurred throughout American history—the familiar, positive story about American migration concludes that the nation has succeeded by allowing smart, energetic people from around the world to mix and create in ways that benefit everyone. We will argue that this story is too simple, but that it nonetheless accurately describes some migrants' aspirations and experiences.

There has always been another vision of the country, one that considers newcomers a threat and tries to exclude them. On this view, migrants threaten "us." They take "our" jobs, claim "our" money, and threaten "our" communities with crime and dangerous habits. This view of "others" has appeared throughout human history, in almost all times and places, although it waxes and wanes. This darker vision misrepresents some realities of migration, but not completely so. Migrants willing to work for lower pay can depress the wages of longstanding residents, for example, at least over the short or medium term (PennWharton, 2016). The longer-term consequences of migration are positive for the vast majority of residents (Bove & Elia, 2017; Nunn, Qian, & Sequeira, 2017a, b; Smith & Edmonston, 1997), but the US government has nonetheless recently justified cruel treatment of migrants and their families by telling stories that cast migrants as a threat to the nation.

It is important to see that both these visions of migration in America oversimplify. They are stories that we tell about migration, stories which are true in some respects but false in others. Migrant communities and individuals move along diverging historical pathways. These varied pathways intersect with historical changes already underway in the communities that receive migrants, with varied outcomes for migrants and longstanding residents (Alba & Nee, 2003; López-Sanders, 2009; Smith, 2014). Changing host communities receive changing migrant communities, often yielding unexpected futures for newcomers and hosts. These more complex outcomes are not adequately captured by the triumphant story of migrant success, or by the pessimistic story of migrant-induced decline. We accept the strong scientific and ethical arguments that America will be most successful by welcoming migrants, instead of closing itself off in the cruel, cramped, self-defeating vision advanced by contemporary anti-migrant activists. We are not arguing that the two stories are equivalent. However, based on our empirical research, we claim that both these stories fail to describe the facts. The stories told by advocates on both sides of the political debate must be interrogated and compared to the more complex reality.

In order to move beyond simple stories and make warranted empirical, political, and moral judgments, we need scientific accounts both of the realities of migration and of the influence our simple stories have on those realities. In this book, we trace the historical development of the town we call "Marshall," describing how longstanding residents—themselves descendants of prior migrants—interacted with Mexican migrants over the first two decades of the Mexican community from 1995 to 2016. We describe how experiences of and stories about migration unfolded both for newcomers and for longstanding residents, across various institutional spaces. We emphasize the ongoing evolution of prior migrant communities and the relations these groups developed with heterogeneous Mexican migrants, showing how interethnic relations played a central role in Mexicans' diverse pathways. We intend our account of this town as a resource for more complex thought and action as Americans and others around the world struggle with increasingly consequential debates about migration.

Before turning to our analysis, we would like to explain our use of terminology for racial and ethnic groups. We understand that race and ethnicity are socially constructed and differentially experienced, and all terminological choices obscure potentially relevant differences. When we describe "Black" or "African American" residents, we are referring to non-Hispanic Black residents with African ancestors. We met no Black Caribbean or African immigrants in Marshall. Our interlocutors, including African Americans, used the terms "African American" and "Black" interchangeably, and we adopt this practice. When we describe "White" residents, we are referring to non-Hispanic people of European descent. On many occasions, we refer to Irish Americans and Italian Americans more specifically, but we also sometimes refer to members of these groups as White. We are aware that some Mexicans consider themselves White, but most Mexican, other Hispanic, Black, and White residents of Marshall did not refer to Mexicans as White. When we describe "Mexicans," we are talking about residents who had migrated from Mexico or whose parents were Mexican and who self-identified as Mexican. Mexicans in Marshall almost never identified themselves as Hispanic or Latino, so we use these terms only when we include other Latin Americans. Throughout the book, we document the heterogeneity of Mexican residents. Despite this heterogeneity, virtually all Mexican and most other residents used the term "Mexican" to refer to the varied individuals who were first- or second-generation Mexican migrants. We have made these terminological choices in order to follow our interlocutors' own usage. We recognize that these terms are sometimes used to stereotype and racialize people in both advantageous and disadvantageous ways, but there are no neutral terminological choices available. We use the term "host" to refer to residents from ethnic groups that have lived in Marshall for generations. Black, Irish, and Italian residents were in earlier historical periods "migrants" and not "hosts," but by 1995 they were established populations in town while Mexicans were newcomers. Finally, a note on translations. Many of the passages we quote were originally spoken in Spanish. We have translated these in the following text, with the help of native speakers. In order to save space, we do not include the extensive Spanish originals.

For eleven years our research team conducted an ethnographic research project in Marshall. Twenty researchers spent thousands of hours in schools, churches, restaurants, businesses, government offices, homes, and community organizations. We talked to hundreds of White, Black, and Hispanic residents with Irish, Italian, English, Polish, German, African, Mexican, Puerto Rican, Venezuelan, and Peruvian ancestors. This book would not have been possible without the contributions of the sixteen other researchers who worked with us. We would particularly like to thank Elaine Allard, Katherine Mortimer, Carlos Martínez, Sarah Gallo, Noam Osband, and Holly Link for their extensive contributions. We also acknowledge important assistance from Kathy Lee, Yomara Arroyo, Kimberly Daniel, Emilce Santana, Julissa Ventura, Krystal Smalls, Ian McDiarmid, Elias Arellano, Gideon Dishon, and Carmen Delgado. In addition, we thank Ian Bennett, Amitanshu Das, Jay Lemke, Mary Lou de Leon Siantz, Sofia Villenas, and Aaron Walters for help collecting data, planning the project, or reviewing drafts.

We owe a great deal to the Marshall residents who took time to speak with us and in many cases welcomed us into their lives. Given the demands of research ethics and the charged climate around migration, we cannot identify the town or any of its residents. In what follows, we have changed many facts about the town and about individuals in order to maintain confidentiality. We regret not being able to thank these friends, acquaintances, and colleagues by name, but we are grateful to them for allowing us into their lives.

Across our eleven years in Marshall, some of us used to joke that the project seemed to encourage members of the research team to get married and have children during their time in Marshall. We would like to dedicate the book to our children and the many children of other research team members, as well as to all the unnamed children in Marshall with whom we have worked. As they grow, may they be blessed with the same kinds of human connection and insight that we have gratefully received from our friends and acquaintances there.

1

Intersecting Migrant Histories

○✤○

[Each Mexican migrant] is a fellow human being ... They are coming to the country for a real need, to provide for their children and their family. They are not trying to get one over on us. I see good, hard-working people trying to make a better life for their kids just like my grandparents and some people's great-grandparents ... My grandfather and grandmother were both from Ireland, and my grandfather would say how it would be nice to go back to Ireland someday. My grandmother would say "You can go back, but I won't." ... [Like my grandparents, the Mexican migrants are likely to stay in the US and not go back to Mexico] because their children and wives are here ... While some do go back, the vast majority stay. Some move out of Marshall, but since I've been here it has been more permanent as well. They get jobs and some open their own businesses, so they won't just up and leave. (Father Kelly of St. Joseph's parish)

This book describes residents' experiences with and stories about migration across two decades in a town that recently became home to thousands of Mexicans. The town we call Marshall was shaped by five groups of migrants over its 200-year history. English, Irish, Italian, African American, and Mexican migrants moved to the town in large numbers, and many of their descendants remained and continued to influence its path. Mexicans have been the most recent migrant group, with a rapid increase starting in 1995. The population of the Mexican community increased from about 100 in 1990 to just under 10,000 in 2016. By 2016, Mexicans, together with a few other migrants from Latin America, comprised almost a third of the town's population, and their children were approaching a majority in half of the town's elementary schools. The Mexicans entered a complex setting dominated by Irish American, Italian American, and African American residents, a town whose character and practices continued to change as formerly migrant groups traveled intersecting pathways in school, work, and community life.

Longstanding residents—members of formerly migrant groups whose families had been in Marshall for over a generation—often told stories that compared their own families' migrant histories with Mexican migrants'. Many of these stories described similarities between the narrators' migrant ancestors and contemporary Mexicans. In the passage above Father Kelly described similarities with his Irish migrant ancestors. Both Irish and Mexican migrants came for a better life, pushed out of their home countries by hardship and drawn by perceived opportunities in America. Both struggled at first, but many members of both groups made better lives for their children over time. In his work as the Spanish-speaking priest of the largest parish in town—the traditionally Irish Catholic church, which welcomed Mexicans starting with his arrival in 2002—Father Kelly had many opportunities to interact with Mexicans and appreciate similarities between his family and theirs. He consistently characterized the migrants as good, hardworking people who built better lives for their families and in the process revitalized his church and the town. Stories like his were one important resource that residents used to evaluate Mexican migrants in Marshall, and these narrative evaluations (Wortham, 2001) helped shape Mexicans' pathways over time.

છ৪০

> I think Hispanics are coming here to get a better life also, same thing my parents did—came here for a better life from down South. The only difference is that it's not that much difference for real, 'cause when they came here, years ago, they used to do the same thing—have a lot of people in the house, know what I mean? And then, as they got older, people trickled out and moved to different houses ... the same thing the Spanish [speakers] are doing, for real. Come to think of it, like you said, they got all the people in the house, they all live there, so they can get a better life, have what they want, you know what I mean? And that's the same thing our people did when they came here. (Doreena, an African American senior citizen)

Doreena's parents came from the South in the "great migration" of African Americans to Northern cities and towns that took place across the first half of the twentieth century (Tolnay, 2003). Because their ancestors traveled from the South, we consider Blacks in Marshall to be another migrant group, although—as we discuss below—their ancestors' enslavement makes their situation different in some important ways. Doreena was born in Marshall and lived there until 2014, and her daughter-in-law and granddaughter both continued to live there in 2016. She described how early African American migrants had to live with many people in a house, just as Mexicans were doing, because they could not afford more space. Over time, her parents and many other African Americans worked hard and were able to achieve better lives for their children. She expected that today's Mexican migrants may do the same. However, Doreena also had an ambivalent relationship with Mexican newcomers. After living in Marshall her whole life, she had recently moved out of the East side of town—home to both African American and Italian migrants across much of the twentieth century— because the influx of Mexicans had changed the character of the neighborhood and she no longer felt welcome there.

ଔଡ଼

> In twenty, twenty-five years mostly all the business is going to be Mexican, because right now they work with all the contractors. They all learn the trade. Because the way they work in Mexico, they don't work, so they're a little slow. But when you put them to work, they work. The Black people, you employ the Black people, the boss leaves, they sit down, they doesn't work. But these Mexicans, you put them to work and they work. They want to better themselves. You can see it. It's just like the Italian people. The Italian people, when they come from Italy they just work like slaves because they want to better themselves. (Marco, a business owner and child of Italian migrants)

Thousands of Italian residents came to Marshall in the first half of the twentieth century, leaving southern Italy and bringing their skills as tradesmen to a rapidly developing America. Like many other Italian and Italian American residents, Marco saw similarities between his parents and the Mexican migrants. The Italians were determined to succeed, and most worked hard to achieve better lives for their children. The Mexicans, he told us, were just the same. Like Father Kelly and Doreena, Marco characterized Mexicans as hardworking, upwardly mobile migrants following a pathway similar to his own ancestors'. This optimistic story about migrant struggle and ultimate success was common in Marshall, and it led many Irish and Italian American residents to empathize with the Mexicans, at least some of the time.

Marco's comments add an additional dimension to our picture of migrant life in Marshall, however. He compared Black residents unfavorably to Mexicans, claiming that Mexicans are like hardworking Italians but Blacks are allegedly lazy. We do not agree with or condone the racist stereotypes in his story, but it is important to document how these stereotypes and evaluations played an important role in positioning Blacks and Mexicans with respect to each other and with respect to White residents. Mexicans were on the same upward pathway as

English, Irish, and Italian migrants, Marco claimed, but Black residents were not. From the perspective of Doreena and other African Americans, Black migrants did the same things as other migrant groups. African Americans migrated from the South for a better life; most worked hard and provided opportunities for their children. But non-Black residents did not see or acknowledge this history. As we will describe in Chapter 4, the successes of many African Americans have been erased from other residents' stories about Marshall's history. This represents one way in which migration in Marshall did not simply follow the familiar story of migration, struggle, and ultimate success for each successive group. Mexicans entered an environment in which—sometimes in fact, but more often in others' imaginations—many Black residents had not followed the classic migrant pathway from struggle to success. Thus Mexicans' migrant experiences in Marshall were different than they would have been in a town without Black residents. In Chapters 4 and 5, we describe how the experiences of many Black residents were in some ways the same but in other ways different than those of other migrants. We show how this made Black-Mexican relations more complex and how these complex interethnic relations influenced many Mexicans' pathways.

☙❧

> We got other people coming in here, the next wave of immigrants, we gotta … make it easier for them so they don't have to struggle, so that they don't have to go through the problems that we went through … We can't lay back and worry about not getting along because this person's a different color or this person comes from a different country … Marshall is unique. We've got a mixture of everybody, of all cultures, of all races, of all religions in this town. We've got a mixture of everything here … [Among the Mexicans] you're gonna get some bad apples, as in anything, you know, any group. But if people are willing to work hard—you know, Italians when they came here, they worked hard, Irish when they came here they worked hard, the Polish when they came here they worked hard, the Chinese, the Koreans, the Japanese, when they came here, they worked hard. And now they own their own businesses. They own their own home; some of them are living in mansions from working hard and it's the way you have to do it. (James, a lifelong African American resident)

James Smith's parents migrated to Marshall from the American South in the middle of the twentieth century. His parents worked hard, and he and his wife both became high-ranking public servants in town before retiring. He repeated the familiar story of migrant struggle and success that appeared in the three earlier passages, describing how each migrant group in turn followed a pathway upward. This story overlooks systematic exclusion of various kinds, but it was nonetheless very commonly told and it accurately described many migrants' experiences. James Smith added two new elements to the familiar story. First, he described more than just his own experience as a successful child of African American migrants. He also claimed that "Marshall is unique," a mixture of people from many backgrounds. Second, he said that earlier migrants, including people like him, ought to overcome their negative stereotypes of Mexican migrants and be more open to the newcomers. James' comments suggest that Mexicans and their descendants in Marshall might travel a pathway not captured by simple positive stories of struggle and success or by simple negative stories of threat and decline. James imagined that Marshall might be a new kind of town, one in which migrants were welcomed and diversity was considered a strength.

Alba and Nee (2003) describe more complex outcomes of migration, in which both migrants and longstanding residents are changed by migration and in which ethnic boundaries are constituted in various ways not described by the familiar stories. Their account accurately captures migrants' and longstanding residents' diverse experiences in Marshall, because longstanding residents' pathways were altered as Mexican and preexisting Marshall communities influenced each other. Sometimes these changes involved positive interethnic rapprochement like that imagined by James, and sometimes they did not. In the second decade of Mexican migration to Marshall, some Mexicans, Irish, Italian, and African Americans began to build connections in optimistic, mutually supportive ways. Chapter 3 describes how this happened in the Irish Catholic church, and Chapter 6 describes how it happened in two community organizations created by African Americans. But in some other spaces interethnic relations were tense.

The familiar positive story about migration that recurred in the comments by Father Kelly, Doreena, Marco, and James does in fact describe some aspects of Mexicans' experiences in Marshall. Many Mexicans, as well as many Irish, Italian, and African American migrants who preceded them, experienced elements of the classic positive American story about migration—in which migrants came looking for a better life, worked hard, and provided greater opportunities for their upwardly mobile children. In the early stages of migration for each group, however—and sometimes throughout their experience in America—most migrants also experienced the hostility and exclusion voiced by anti-migrant activists. Many longstanding residents in Marshall felt that migrants threatened to undermine "our" country because they were different and allegedly beneath "us." Mexicans had to struggle against racialized stereotypes and deliberate exclusion. A somewhat more complex but still familiar story of migration in America would include both these aspects, as if they were separate phases: first, migrants struggle against poverty and racism; longstanding residents see them as disrupting an idealized past and ushering in a bleak present; over time, however, migrants work hard, prove their worth, and provide better lives for their children; these children's successes then benefit the larger community.

This story is still too simple to capture the full reality of migration in Marshall, but it does accurately describe aspects of real life for many migrants. Many Irish, Italian, and African American residents in Marshall narrated an idealized but partly accurate history in which their ancestors came as migrants and traveled pathways from struggle to success—"up and out" of the less desirable downtown neighborhoods, as one resident described it—to better jobs, wealthier surrounding towns, and arguably brighter futures. Many Mexicans followed this same pathway in some respects over the first two decades of Mexican presence in Marshall. During the first decade, most Mexican migrants—largely single men—were stereotyped as invasive, dirty, and easily victimized, and many of them struggled. In the second decade, however, more and more young, intact Mexican families settled in town, more Mexican-owned businesses were established, and Mexican children often succeeded in school. Many Mexican migrants in Marshall faced challenges but nonetheless traveled pathways that are described well by the familiar story about migrants struggling and then moving "up and out."

We are aware that this positive migration story is sometimes unjustly used to blame unsuccessful migrants, as if their failure to succeed in conventional terms is their own fault (see the compelling critique in González, 2016). But this unethical use of the story does not change the empirical reality that the classic positive migration story does accurately describe both the aspirations and the experiences of many migrants. Instead of embracing or condemning the story, we document its accuracies and inaccuracies by examining empirical evidence about actual migrants' lives in Marshall. In addition, we document empirically how this and other migration stories themselves shape migrant experiences. We must assess stories both as potentially accurate descriptions of the human world and also as facts that partly constitute that world (Gergen, 1973; Silverstein, 1985).

All migration stories oversimplify. Individual migrants travel diverging pathways, sometimes because of systematic differences in their situations (Portes & Rumbaut, 2001; Wimmer, 2008) and sometimes because of contingent factors like features of the particular towns they migrate to or aspects of their individual family situations. In addition, each migrant group changes the community into which new migrants arrive (Alba & Nee, 2003). As Marshall changed over historical time—with the arrival of new groups and other socioeconomic shifts— the pathways of each migrant group intersected with other groups to create a situation that cannot be captured by a simple model of migrant integration where successive generations assimilate to an allegedly stable American culture. For Mexicans, two contingent facts about prior migrant groups in Marshall were particularly important. First, many descendants of prior migrants—especially Irish Americans and Italian Americans—remembered their own ancestors' struggles and this made some of them more sympathetic to Mexican migrants than residents of similar towns. Contrast, for example, the hostile host reaction in otherwise similar towns described by Flores (2014) and Jones (2012). Second, African Americans were in some respects not a typical migrant group, and they did not simply move "up and out" in the years before Mexicans arrived. Thus Mexicans entered a complex setting of interethnic struggle.

Individual Mexicans in Marshall traveled many different pathways across the first two decades of their community, only some of which are described by classic positive and negative migration stories. This book describes both stereotypical and less familiar Mexican migrant experiences in Marshall, across two decades and five institutional spaces—schools, churches, neighborhoods, public spaces, and community organizations. In this chapter, we introduce our argument and describe the town and its history. Chapters 2 and 3 describe schools and churches, where we observed Mexicans moving from the substantial challenges that faced the more transient migrants in the first decade to fewer challenges and more successes experienced by the increasingly more settled Mexicans in the second decade. Chapters 4 through 6—on residential spaces, public spaces, and community organizations—introduce more complexity, providing an account of complex interethnic relations and diverging migrant pathways.

In fact, Irish and Italian migrants themselves had not uniformly enacted the "up and out" story. Many continued to face hardship of various sorts. Both in reality and in the popular imagination, however, Irish and Italian Americans tended to experience many aspects of the classic story. Overall, the Irish replaced the English, and the Italians replaced the Irish, despite some divergence within each community. African Americans, however, were different. Even though they began arriving only a decade or two after the Italians, African Americans did not replace the Irish and the Italians. Many African Americans remained poor and were unjustly prevented from moving to more desirable neighborhoods and jobs. Blacks had different experiences than Irish and Italian migrants for several reasons: the later decades of Black migration happened to overlap with the town's economic decline, which meant fewer resources to go around; there was a second wave of already-disadvantaged African American migrants who came to Marshall in the later twentieth century from nearby inner cities; and Black residents faced more entrenched racism and disadvantages than other groups, like ongoing housing and workplace discrimination.

When Mexicans arrived in Marshall, then, they confronted a complex ethnic landscape. Some Black residents held powerful positions in town, and we will describe how Mexicans had to reckon with this. But many Black residents also continued to be disadvantaged. In this situation, Mexicans could have traveled various pathways: moving "up and out" faster than African Americans, following Irish and Italians while leaving many Black residents behind (Gans, 2012; Lee & Bean, 2007); joining African Americans in solidarity and fighting against White racism (Jones, 2012); or positioning themselves in other, less familiar ways (e.g., Smith, 2014). The book describes how some Mexican residents followed each of these pathways, as well as others, while navigating the complex ethnic situation in town.

In order to analyze Mexicans' pathways and prospects in Marshall and elsewhere, we make three theoretical claims—about diverse, contingent realities, simplified but powerful stories, and solidifying pathways across time. First, the real experiences of any individual migrant or group are always complex, with pathways shaped by multiple possibly relevant resources (Latour, 2005; Rodríguez, 2012; Wimmer, 2008). Many factors could influence particular migrant experiences and outcomes. In practice, different resources become important for different individuals and communities at different times. In order to understand the pathways actually traveled by migrants, we must attend to the *diverse, contingent realities* that make their heterogeneous pathways possible. We need an account of how, despite the presence of various resources that could have yielded diverse pathways, particular migrants ended up traveling in one direction or another. Second, migration stories are facts in the world (e.g., Haviland, 2005). Ordinary people outside of academia give accounts of migration and other human phenomena (Gergen, 1973; Silverstein, 1985). Migrants and longstanding residents tell stories to themselves and to others, and these stories shape people's ideas and actions. Migration stories are always incomplete, and many are inaccurate. But the normative evaluations embedded in people's stories (Wortham, 2001) nonetheless influence the realities of migrant life. Stories always contribute to but rarely determine the pathways migrants end up traveling. In order to understand the pathways actually traveled by migrants, we must attend to the *simplified but powerful stories* that influence those pathways. Third, both individual and community pathways emerge over time. Particular resources—from among many possibly relevant ones—become important across an event, a developmental phase or an era in a community's development (Agha, 2007; Silverstein, 1992; Wimmer, 2008). These realities include simplified stories, which can foreground certain resources and background others, but they always include other resources like prevailing attitudes among longstanding resident groups, the economic opportunities in a town, the availability and location of housing and employment, systematic discrimination against members of certain groups, etc. At some point relevant resources coalesce, creating a recognizable event, identity, or direction. In order to understand migrants' experiences and prospects, we must attend to their *solidifying pathways across time*. Migrants' lives take shape as contingent configurations of simple stories and other resources coalesce to guide them onto one pathway out of the many they could have traveled. In this book, we show how this happened in Marshall for individual migrants and for the Mexican community as a whole over its first twenty years.

Figure 1.1 The sun rises over downtown Marshall.

Allie

In order to elaborate what we mean by these three theoretical claims, we introduce here a girl we call Allie. Allie came to Marshall from Mexico as a toddler in 2003 and began school there in kindergarten. The following three sections describe some of the diverse, contingent realities, simplified but powerful stories, and solidifying pathways across time that shaped her experiences.

Diverse, Contingent Realities

Allie's educational pathway was different than those traveled by older migrants who arrived in Marshall as teenagers. She learned English as a child; she learned academic English at the same time as her native English-speaking peers; and institutional features of the American educational system were familiar to her, though not to her parents. Allie also started school more than a decade after the beginning of the Mexican community, at a time when educators in Marshall had become familiar with Mexican students, and she had many Mexican peers in her classes. Latour (2005) would say that contingent, heterogeneous "resources"— like Allie's fluency in English, her comfort in the American school system, her teachers' familiarity with Mexican students, and the relatively large population of Mexican migrants in the second decade of the community—constituted her situation. She could have arrived in Marshall later in her ontogenetic development and struggled to learn academic English. She could have arrived in Texas or California, instead of a town with little history of Mexican migration. She could have arrived in a town that did not remember its own migrant history and was more hostile to migrants. She could have arrived during the early years of the Mexican community in Marshall, when she would have been more of an anomaly. Each of these resources or realities of her situation influenced her, and they formed what Latour calls a "network"—a configuration of interacting people, objects, ideas, stories, and settings that together make possible the phenomenon or process in question. Networks are configurations of diverse, contingent resources. Configurations of resources constitute particular individual and group experiences and pathways.

For any given object we are trying to explain—like Allie's pathway in school or the reception Mexicans received in Marshall—we must determine which of various possibly relevant resources in fact made a difference. A central claim of Latour's (2005) actor-network theory is that, while various resources can play a central role in the network that constitutes any particular object of inquiry, no one resource plays a central role in all cases. No general theory that foregrounds one or a few resources can explain the experiences and pathways of all migrants, all Mexicans, or all residents of Marshall. Social class, skin color, age on arrival, historical era, parental aspirations, religious institutions, peer group, personality, neighborhood, committed teachers, and many other resources could have been relevant to Allie's pathway, but none of them were crucial in all aspects of her life or for all Mexican migrants. Different phenomena, even apparently similar ones, will often be constituted by contingent, emerging networks that contain different relevant resources and thus lead in different directions.

Our account of Mexican migrant pathways in Marshall describes resources and processes that often play an important role in contemporary migrants' lives in America. But we do not propose a general theory. Instead, social scientists must describe how resources come together in contingent networks at particular points in time, and then we must compare the somewhat different configurations of resources that may play a role in different situations. In this book, we model how to explore potentially relevant resources and how to determine which become central to networks that constitute individual and community pathways. Those interested in other migrant communities should look for the kinds of resources we describe in their own settings and examine how they might play important roles in the networks that constitute migrant pathways elsewhere. Instead of simply accepting or dismissing simple stories about migration, and instead of adopting universal theories that claim to explain all instances, we must recognize both similarities and differences among migrants and their communities and we must examine empirically how different configurations of resources lead to different pathways in various cases.

One important kind of diversity among the resources relevant to Mexicans' pathways in Marshall involves their different "scales" (Blommaert, 2007; Carr & Lempert, 2016; Lemke, 2000; Wortham, 2005, 2012). The interconnected processes that made possible Allie's pathway had different spatial and temporal extents. First, Marshall had a distinctive history, including the settlement of Irish, Italian, and African American migrant groups, and it mattered that Allie did not arrive either in an area of longstanding Mexican settlement like California or in a town that had not seen migrants for many decades. In an area of traditional Mexican settlement she might not have had as much flexibility in how she could become socially identified, because in these settings accounts of Mexicans can be more rigid (Hamann & Harklau, 2010; Hamann, Wortham, & Murillo, 2002; Millard, Chapa, & Crane, 2004; Wortham, Murillo, & Hamann, 2002). In a town with little recent history of migration she might have been seen as more alien (Flores, 2014; Murillo, 2002). Second, the Marshall Mexican migrant community changed significantly across two decades, and it mattered that Allie arrived after the community was well established (Hamann, Wortham, & Murillo, 2015). If she had been one of the first Mexicans to arrive in town, she would likely have been treated as more unusual and local service providers would have had less experience with people in her situation. Third, various institutions and spaces in town—like schools, churches, and community centers—had their own divergent, changing histories of interacting with Mexicans, and it mattered both whether and when Allie experienced these spaces. School played a central role in Allie's life, and she aligned herself with highly valorized school activities. If she had spent more time in some other institutional spaces, she might have been pulled toward different values and outcomes. Allie's pathway emerged through the intersection of processes and resources from these and other scales. In order to understand how she came to be who she was, we must trace objects and processes across the various relevant scales to identify which resources in fact played a role in making her pathway take the shape that it did.

Our analysis of Allie, other Mexicans, and the broader community attends particularly to processes at four scales that influenced the experiences and pathways of migrants and longstanding Marshall residents as they adjusted to the new demographic realities in town: the history of the town across two centuries, including its incorporation of various migrant groups; the history of the Mexican migrant community in Marshall and its relations with other groups in town as it changed across its first two decades, including the history of different spaces that Mexicans frequented and the institutions that anchored them—educational, religious, residential, commercial, political, and nonprofit; the ontogenetic development of individuals and families that came to the town at different stages in their own pathways through life; and pivotal events that took shape across hours and days. In Marshall it turned out that processes at each of these particular scales provided important resources that migrants and longstanding Marshall residents drew on as they interacted with each other and traveled along their pathways. An adequate account of migrant experiences and pathways in Marshall requires attention to resources at least at these four scales. Realities from other scales were also relevant in Marshall, and we discuss some of these in the analyses below. Nationally circulating discourses about Mexicans, about immigration, and about race in America, for example, were often relevant to individual and community pathways in Marshall, and we incorporate these resources into our analyses where appropriate. But realities from four scales—the town's history, the Mexican community's history, individuals' ontogenetic development, and pivotal events—were consistently relevant to shaping individual and community pathways in Marshall, and we attend particularly to them.

In order to explain how Allie and other Mexican migrants in Marshall both followed and diverged from the classic positive migrant story "up and out," we must examine diverse, contingent resources from various scales, and we must identify which ones contributed to the networks that constituted their actual pathways. In doing so, we build on recent work that takes similar approaches to migration. Portes (Portes & Zhou, 1993; Portes & Rumbaut, 2001) and Alba and Nee (2003) have shown that unilinear assimilationist accounts of migration do not suffice. Contemporary research has extended this and emphasized the importance of contingent local settings in shaping migrant pathways (e.g., Jones, 2012; López-Sanders, 2009). Rodríguez (2012) and Wimmer (2008) provide comprehensive, multi-level accounts of migrant pathways that draw on processes at several scales to explain migrant outcomes. These theories are compatible with our Latourian approach, because they acknowledge the role that contingent, heterogeneous resources play in shaping sometimes-unexpected migrant pathways. We go beyond this work by combining Latour's ideas about contingent resources and networks with descriptions of the scales from which resources come and, as described below, by adding an account from linguistic anthropology of how individual and community pathways emerge and solidify over time.

Simplified but Powerful Stories

One particularly important resource that helps to constitute migrant pathways is the migration stories told and heard by migrants and longstanding residents. Stories are powerful means for communicating evaluations of individuals and groups, because storytellers cannot help but position themselves with respect to the characters they narrate (Bakhtin, 1935/1981; Wortham, 2001; Wortham & Reyes, 2015). Migration stories can shape people's evaluations of and actions toward migrants and others, even when those stories are false or oversimplified. Allie's prospects, for example, were influenced by the stories Marshall educators told about Mexican students' abilities and potential futures (Wortham, Mortimer, & Allard, 2009). Our approach to explaining migrant pathways pays particular attention to oversimplified stories about migration. Whether they are proposed by local residents or scholars, we should recognize both the truth in and the limitations of these stories, and we must account for the roles they play in constituting migrants' actual pathways and experiences.

Silverstein (1985) explains how stories and other resources can intersect to produce historical change. He analyzes how English lost the formal and intimate second person pronouns that still exist in German (*du/Sie*), French (*tu/vous*), and related languages. English used to have two second person pronouns, *thee/thou* and *ye/you*—with *thee/thou* the nominative and accusative forms used to refer to addressees in intimate or informal speech and *ye/you* used for more formal occasions or to refer to social superiors. In seventeenth-century

England the Quakers became notorious for refusing to use *ye/you*, as part of their protest against social hierarchies. At that time a person would normally call social superiors "you" and intimates or social inferiors "thou," but the Quakers objected to this social distinction. The Quakers called everyone "thou," even social superiors, to make an ethical and political point. Non-Quakers began to think that the exclusive use of "thou" made a speaker sound like a Quaker. Stories were increasingly told in which the use of *thee/thou* identified speakers as Quakers, as non-mainstream, heterodox people. Over time, non-Quakers stopped using *thee/thou* altogether, for fear of being identified as members of a stigmatized group, and eventually the linguistic form disappeared.

Historical development in cases like this emerges from an intersection between people's stories—what Silverstein calls "ideologies"—and the heterogeneous realities construed by these stories. From a scientific point of view, the association between Quakers and "thou" is an oversimplification. Others besides Quakers in seventeenth-century England used "thou," in various ways, and the Quakers advocated other linguistic and non-linguistic changes in their efforts to undermine social hierarchy. The grammatical distinction between intimate and formal second person pronouns also does more than just index social status—it facilitates complex interactions involving intimacy, revulsion, respect, and other moves (Friedrich, 1972). The Quakers' fixation on one function of one form was partly correct, but it oversimplified. The story or ideology about Quakers nonetheless contributed to the loss of *thee/thou* for all subsequent speakers of English. Silverstein's account of language ideologies illustrates how oversimplified stories can play powerful roles in social change.

Allie entered school in an environment full of stories about Mexicans and their prospects. Educators and longstanding residents sometimes told stories that positioned Mexicans as academically unpromising, as fit for the trades but not professional jobs (Mortimer, Wortham, & Allard, 2010; Wortham, Mortimer, & Allard, 2009). These stories had less impact on Allie but significantly influenced Juan and Nancy—two other Mexican students described in the next chapter. Stories about the larger Mexican community were also important sites for struggle over the appropriate place of migrants in town. In Chapter 5, for example, we discuss "payday mugging" stories that positioned Mexicans as victims and African Americans as perpetrators of street crime. These stories influenced relationships between and stereotypes about Black and Mexican residents, and they contributed to a Mexican pathway "up and out" that was unavailable to many African Americans. As we trace Mexicans' pathways across their first two decades in Marshall, we attend closely to these and other oversimplified stories that influenced both individual and community development.

Solidifying Pathways across Time

Given that various stories, together with other potentially relevant resources, could have become central to the network that constituted the pathways Allie and other Mexicans actually traveled, how did she end up in one place and not another? How are the contingency and indeterminacy in individual and community pathways overcome in practice? When Allie entered school at age five, she could have ended up dropping out, she could have been swept into the school-to-prison pipeline (Winn, 2011), she could have been steered toward lower-status vocational training, she could have persevered but ended her schooling after high school, she could have attended college and dropped out, or she could have graduated from a four-year college and gone on to future professional success—and in doing any of these things she could have been fulfilled or unfulfilled, and she could have identified as Mexican, Mexican American, or simply American. In order to understand what actually happened, we have to trace the emergence of durable configurations of resources that made a particular pathway solidify. Pathways are initially more fluid—meaning that individuals and communities could move in various directions and experience different outcomes—but they become more rigid as particular resources become more constraining. Sometimes pathways change direction, as configurations of stories, objects, habits, and practices shift, but eventually they settle into new directions and resolidify (Wortham, 2005, 2006, 2012).

Social life is navigable because certain configurations of ideas, habits, objects, and behaviors become taken for granted. When Allie first went to school, for example, she was positioned as a struggling English-language learner. She spoke English with an accent, and teachers were prone to identify her using widely circulating national stereotypes about poor, migrant Mexicans who have difficulties in school. Over time, however, stable models and habits can dissolve, and new ones can solidify. Networks change as different resources come into play. Right before Allie started school, many intact young Mexican families began settling in Marshall. More and more Mexicans started businesses and planned to stay in town so that their children could have opportunities in America. More educators, especially in the elementary schools, began to expect that Mexican children would become fluent in English and succeed academically (Gallo, Allard, Link, Wortham, & Mortimer, 2014). At the same time as all this was happening in the community, Allie began to love reading. This passion was fostered by her own talent and inclinations, by an individual teacher who encouraged her, by the availability of book fairs at her school, and by Catherine Rhodes, who spent substantial time with her family and supported Allie's reading. The changing Mexican community in Marshall, together with these other resources, made possible a shift in Allie's pathway—she went from experiences as and stereotypes of a struggling English-language learner to being an avid reader and "promising" student.

Silverstein (1992, 2013) and Agha (2007) provide general, linguistic anthropological theories of how resources come together to create durable pathways over interactional and historical time. When Allie entered kindergarten, her teachers and peers could have taken her accented English as a sign that she was an unpromising student, or as a sign that she was an emergent bilingual whose language skills would provide advantages in the job market, or as a sign that she was transient and likely to return to Mexico, or as a sign of various other possibilities. Silverstein (1992) describes how such initial indeterminacy in identifying an individual is overcome in practice when a set of signs lock together in what he calls a mutually presupposing "poetic structure," a configuration of resources that support each other in establishing one outcome as most likely. For example, Allie's teacher might have emphasized how she wished she could speak Spanish because it was so useful—as in fact some elementary school teachers in Marshall did (Allard, Mortimer, Link, Gallo, & Wortham, 2014). Non-Mexican students could have started to use Spanish words and intonations in admiring ways, acting as if Spanish fluency was desirable for everyone, as some in fact did (Link, Gallo, & Wortham, 2014). If cues, realities, or resources like these accumulated, they could have come collectively to indicate that Allie's fluency in Spanish was an asset and not a liability. Over minutes in an interaction, or over months and years in an ontogenetic or historical trajectory, resources like this reinforce each other such that one interpretation or direction becomes most likely. Silverstein (1992) and Agha (2007) describe how events and pathways solidify and become rigid—coming to have clearer meaning and direction—as cues or resources link together and more definitively establish one pathway or another. In the next chapter, we will see how this happened to Allie in school, as she did homework diligently and successfully, became an avid reader, joined the Reading Olympics team, and was more often positioned as a promising student by her teachers and as a "nerd" by her peers.

Pathways solidify as a network of heterogeneous resources coalesces and becomes stable, at least provisionally—in this case, when parents, educators, students, and Allie herself began more consistently to tell stories about and position her as a "good student" and when other resources like the teacher's attention and her nomination for the Reading Olympics team coalesced with the stories to establish a more definite pathway for her. Not all resources are equal, however. As Blommaert (2005) and Silverstein (2013) explain, there are various centers of gravity or "emanation" which have authority and give some resources and configurations coercive force. This emphatically does not mean all Mexicans, or all poor people, or all migrants, experience certain outcomes because of omnipresent, homogeneous "structures" (Latour, 2005). The social world is constraining, with certain people more likely to occupy certain positions. But such constraints take hold through contingent networks, and the centers from which authority emanates are varied and often in conflict. Allie was perceived as a Mexican migrant and sometimes subject to stereotypes about dangerous, dirty Mexicans that circulate through national media (Bonilla & Girling, 1973; Herrera Lasso & Pérez Esquivel, 2014; Solorzano, 1997). But she was also an excellent student, and her teachers usually focused on her academic promise. Instead of assuming "structures" as our starting point, we describe how social constraints were produced and became relevant to individuals and groups in Marshall—as networks solidified and made possible the pathways actually traveled by people like Allie.

Our analyses trace the migration stories and other diverse resources that shaped Marshall residents' ideas, habits, and actions toward migrants and each other. Simple stories sometimes misconstrued but also combined with heterogeneous resources to constitute the pathways taken by individual migrants and the larger community. We describe how configurations of stories and other resources sometimes facilitated familiar migration pathways and at other times constituted unexpected ones. Some migrants, like Allie, traveled pathways that seemed to be taking them "up and out," while others did not. The Mexican migrant community as a whole moved from being a group of single men hoping to return to Mexico to a group of settled migrants who planned to stay. But this pathway was uneven and more complex than the simple, familiar positive migration story imagines it. Mexicans in Marshall benefited in some ways from stories told about their imagined similarities to earlier Irish and Italian migrants, but their relationships with these groups were not always positive and Mexicans did not simply follow in earlier groups' footsteps. They helped create something new, instead of assimilating to something old. Mexicans also navigated complicated relationships with African American residents, who had only partly moved "up and out." In the rest of this chapter, we sketch the origins of these interethnic dynamics through an overview of Marshall's first two centuries.

Marshall's History

Marshall's history—both facts about what actually happened and residents' often-inaccurate stories—provided important resources for both Mexican migrants and longstanding residents as they experienced the Mexican migration that accelerated in 1995. We draw part of the following account from published histories and government documents. We also rely on the memories and perspectives of many people we met during our eleven years in town. We do not claim to know everything about Marshall's history, but we have systematically gathered evidence from diverse sources. We have been careful to speak with residents from different backgrounds, and we describe the social positions of individuals whom we quote—thus offering the reader an opportunity to assess the evaluations implicit in the following historical narratives. Some of the stories we tell here represent the most accurate account we have been able to compile about Marshall's past. Others are clearly interested stories that are useful not for their accuracy but because they nonetheless influenced people's beliefs and actions. Together, they give a sense of both material and ideological resources that were available to Mexicans and longstanding residents when the Mexican migration accelerated in 1995.

Figure 1.2 The commuter train connecting Marshall to the region.

The Town's Early History

Marshall was incorporated about 200 years ago, with a population of approximately 500 mostly English settlers. From the beginning it was a transportation hub, which facilitated the development of government, commerce, and industry. The town lies on a major body of water, and by the mid-nineteenth century rail lines also served the town. Within a few decades of its founding, the town had industrial, retail, banking, and government enterprises. There was fabric, beer, and iron manufacturing, for example. Appropriate to the town's beginnings, its official motto celebrates labor. The following two descriptions come from official accounts of the town written around the turn of the twentieth century. In order to preserve confidentiality, we do not cite the sources of these comments. One commentator wrote of the town's motto:

> [We] give dignity to labor and significance to life. Labor gives satisfaction to him who labors only as the laborer puts a purpose into his labor ... It was the thought of the [town] Fathers that this laborer should see himself in his labor and find his highest joy in achievement. Thus and thus only, should Marshall become the Home of the Happy.

Another town booster extolled the town's virtues:

> its low tax rate and cheap rents; its police protection; its churches, schools and newspapers, public amusements, and the charm of its location, make this locality one of the most pleasant and desirable for the home of the laborer, the mechanic, the merchant, the professional man, the manufacturer and the retired gentleman.

Because of these and other attractive features, downtown Marshall became a shopping and entertainment destination from the late nineteenth century through the mid-twentieth century, with multiple department stores, music halls, movie theaters, government offices, and other institutions. The first school opened before incorporation, and Marshall residents voted to fund a public school system twenty years later.

The first church in Marshall was Anglican, and it was built the same year the town was founded. The first Catholic parish was founded by Irish migrants about twenty-five years later. Father Kelly described the parish's history:

> We just finished celebrating our 175th anniversary. The parish ... started with Irish migrants who were going to mass in the [nearby] city. They decided the church was needed here in Marshall for primarily Irish migrants who were working on the railroads and, since that time, to serve everyone in Marshall,

which was heavily Irish Catholic—but there was also a mix of everything, some German Catholics, Slovak Catholics. Down a few blocks there is a church built specifically for the Italian community, and so the Italians moved there.

The Italian Catholic parish was founded by Italian migrants at the turn of the twentieth century, with a sister church in Italy and masses offered in Italian into the twenty-first century. The African Methodist Episcopal church was founded about thirty years after the incorporation of the town. The First Baptist Church was a stop on the Underground Railroad, with parishioners supporting abolition before the Civil War. Both Frederick Douglass and Lucretia Mott spoke there late in the nineteenth century.

Several Waves of Migration

Marshall was initially settled by people of English origin, with a few Germans, Scots, Dutch, and Swedes arriving early in the nineteenth century. A couple of decades after the incorporation of the town, Irish migration began. Irish migrants came mostly to work on railroads and canals, and large numbers lived in Marshall—where rent was relatively cheap and they avoided some ills of city life. This was the first large-scale migrant group to settle in town after its founding. Irish migrants continued to arrive, in smaller numbers, until the middle of the twentieth century, and many of their descendants still live in Marshall. The Protestants who initially settled Marshall did not welcome the Irish Catholics, who were segregated and stereotyped (Ignatiev, 1995). But by the end of the nineteenth century, the Irish played a prominent role in town commerce and politics.

Italian migrants began settling in Marshall at the end of the nineteenth century, with rapid growth at the beginning of the twentieth century and another wave of arrivals after the Second World War. Most of the Italians in Marshall came from two towns, one near Naples and the other on Sicily. We occasionally saw posters for sports teams or other paraphernalia from one of these towns in local businesses and homes. During our time in Marshall, the Italian church still had a social club where Italian was spoken by a few longstanding migrant residents. Many Italian migrants had originally been masons or other skilled laborers, recruited to work in quarries and the building trades. Italian migrants constructed most of the factories and mills that provided employment for Marshall residents until late in the twentieth century. James Smith, a lifelong African American resident of Marshall, recalled experiences with Italian migrants from fifty years earlier, during his childhood:

> The Italians were pretty resourceful … because a lot of those guys came over here with skills, you know. They were bricklayers, masons, and they used their skills to be able to make a good living for themselves. They started businesses. We had a lot of Italian businesses … And of course they hired people, laborers and other skilled workers, and this is the way Marshall evolved.

Many Italian migrants became entrepreneurs, opening businesses in town. More than half of the major landlords and business owners in town during our decade of fieldwork were Italian or Italian American, at most two generations removed from migrant ancestors.

Carlo Faccone was an Italian American plumber typical of the Italian migrant and Italian American community. He described how his father migrated from Sicily to Marshall in the 1920s.

> So my father sent his two sisters, who married here, and his brother, who married here. And then he came … He was 32. And he was a blacksmith. And his trade was making rod iron railings and things like that. But when he came it was the Depression, and there wasn't any work.

Carlo's father initially worked in the federal government Works Progress Administration program, sharpening picks and shovels. Carlo's mother was born in Marshall, the daughter of Italian migrants. She worked in a mill during the Depression to make ends meet. Through Carlo himself, the Italian community in Marshall played a central role in creating the Mexican community. Carlo married a Mexican woman named Juana and brought her to town in the 1970s. It was the subsequent arrival of Juana's siblings, cousins, and friends that started Mexican migration to Marshall.

Leo Ciccone was another child of Italian migrants whose family moved to Marshall when he was very young. He had a long and eventful life in town, as a policeman, boxer, businessman, media host, and more recently as the officially appointed "ambassador of Marshall" charged with reaching out to current and potential residents as a town booster. He shared positive memories of his childhood in town:

> I would say growing up in Marshall, growing up going to the movie theaters, having movie theaters, bowling alleys; we had the different clubs that we went to. We had the baseball team. There was Friday night football, baseball; there was the Park. It was a place everybody would go. The swings, the carousel. The carousel was free; it didn't cost anything. And everybody knew everybody.

Leo also recalled an ethnically diverse population during his childhood.

> There was the Italians, there was Irish and Germans, there was English. There was not a lot of Blacks. They were in certain areas. Down on Maple, Maple and Pine Street. They called it the "Hollow" there. They had Ash Street … And we didn't have any prejudice in our family; my father didn't call anybody names. We had a problem with the Irish, you know. They turned out to be later in adult life my good friends.

As Leo's comments illustrate, interethnic relations have been fraught in Marshall throughout its history. Leo claimed that things worked out for him across his lifetime. Despite substantial ethnic tensions between Irish and Italian residents in the early and middle twentieth century, for example, Leo eventually became friends with some Irish former antagonists.

Leo was incorrect about the situation of Black residents during his childhood, however. Census data show that African Americans were about 10 percent of the town's population in 1950. At that time there was roughly the same number of Black residents as European migrants, with 80 percent of the population being American-born citizens of European ancestry. As mentioned above and described extensively in Chapter 4, White residents often did not know about the upwardly mobile Black community that existed in Marshall during the middle of the twentieth century. Facts about Black presence and successes had been erased from White residents' stories. Many Black migrants followed pathways similar to Irish and Italian migrants, but non-Black residents did not know this. The stories told about Black migrants by everyone except African Americans themselves left out their successes. These inaccurate stories about Black residents played an important role in constructing difference between African Americans on the one hand and Irish and Italians on the other. As we will describe below, this illustrates the power of stories, together with other realities, to disadvantage one group systematically.

Leo was not alone in telling inaccurate but powerful stories about other migrant groups, and inaccurate stories were told about groups besides African Americans. Like people everywhere, Marshall residents positioned themselves with respect to various ethnic and racial others through the stories they told about one another (Wortham, 2001; Wortham & Reyes, 2015). Throughout the book we describe these varied stories about and actions toward each other, and we will show how both accurate and inaccurate stories influenced residents' beliefs and actions. Incomplete, misleading stories about African Americans failing to move "up and out" provide one example. Many other stories positioned ethnic groups as homogeneous entities in ways that had causal effects on beliefs, policies, and actions, even though the groups were in fact internally diverse. The following chapters describe the interplay between oversimplified but powerful stories about race and ethnicity and the more complex realities we observed in Marshall.

Italian migrants settled in the East end of town, which became known as the "ethnic" side, in contrast to the West and North, where the Irish—who had become "White" (Ignatiev, 1995)—and the remaining White Protestant residents lived. As we will illustrate in Chapter 4, Italians were racialized and often considered non-White in early twentieth-century America (Barrett & Roediger, 2008). Irish Americans and other residents of Northern European origin worked to keep them out of the West and the North sides of town by steering them away from real estate there. The other group that began moving into the East end a decade or two after the Italians, and also made it "ethnic," were Black migrants from the American South. For several decades in the early and middle twentieth century, many Black and Italian residents lived in the same neighborhoods.

James Smith grew up in the East end and lived his whole life in Marshall. He received a bronze star and a purple heart in Vietnam, and after his return he became a policeman and rose high in the department.

> Well like I said, back in the day ... the East end was predominantly Italian and Black, you know. They were homeowners; it was a proud community. The Italians were proud of their heritage. Some of them came over from Italy. They sent for their families to come over and they were able to start businesses, increase some of the industry here in Marshall. And of course you know the Black community we had our heritage. We were proud people, you know. A lot of us came up here from down South to start a new life. We moved into some of the communities. Some communities didn't want to accept you and, you know, you tried to make the best of it. I think the Italians and the Blacks got along quite well in my neighborhood.

In the first half of the twentieth century, many of the surrounding towns would not allow Black migrants to settle. Marshall accepted them, although they were steered to certain neighborhoods. The East end was the most important of those, and there they lived side by side with Italian migrants. In an era when both groups were racialized and stereotyped by Irish, English, and other longstanding residents, many Black and Italian residents had cordial relations.

The first African Americans came to Marshall around 1910, in search of mill and factory jobs and to escape challenging conditions in the South. James described his family's history:

> My father ... and my mother got married when they were young. [Their families] all worked in the fields. There were really no jobs in the South back then ... [My mother got tired of the South and] my father got a job at Amalgamated Iron and Steel ... We were able to save up money and between my father and my uncle, they bought a house together on Pine Street ... My uncle and his family lived on the 1st floor and my father and my mother and my brothers and I we lived on the 2nd floor. We shared the house together with the kitchen and the bathroom and we managed to make it work. And when my father was able to save up enough money between working in the steel mill and my mother doing day work and working little part-time jobs as the cashier at one of the local restaurants here in town, they were able to save up enough money to buy their own home.

Like many other African Americans, James' parents endured residential and workplace discrimination and persevered to raise their families and give their children opportunities to be upwardly mobile. African Americans from the South continued to arrive in Marshall until the 1960s, with another influx happening after the Second World War. Many Black residents had positive memories of their childhoods in town, as James did:

> Back in the day it was a booming town. Everybody looked forward to the weekends. Friday night, Saturday, we went downtown, downtown Marshall ... We liked to dress up a little bit, put on nice clothes, go down Main Street with mom, do some shopping. ... It only cost you maybe 35 cents back then to go to the movies, and that was one of the things we liked to do on a Saturday afternoon, go to the movies at the Maple Theater. And then we would meet afterwards and go off to Woolworths and play the games over there and the penny machine games and sit at the counter and order sodas, beer floats and ice cream.

Doreena also grew up in the East end. Like James, she described her childhood in Marshall positively. "It was wonderful ... You could go to stores from one end of Main Street all the way down."

Despite James' and Doreena's positive memories, there was pervasive racial discrimination during the Jim Crow era. Until the 1960s there was only one racially integrated theater in Marshall, located in the East end. African Americans were not allowed to enter the YMCA/YWCA until after the Civil Rights Movement, so they had no swimming pool available and on hot summer days were forced to swim in a creek. This exclusion had tragic consequences in the late 1950s, when two Black children drowned at a popular swimming spot. Members of the Black community responded by building a community center with a pool which still existed during our time in Marshall. We will discuss this center more extensively in Chapter 6 when we describe how community organizations developed to address the unmet needs of the various populations in Marshall.

Narratives of Decline

Largely because of Irish, Italian, and African American migration, the population of Marshall rose from 500 at its founding, to 30,000 in 1900, then to 50,000 in the middle of the twentieth century. At that point, the town began a population decline that accelerated in the 1960s and 1970s. This decline reversed with the arrival of Mexican migrants, and the town's population was moving up by 2010. Leo, James, Doreena, and other longstanding residents described Marshall as a great place in its heyday in the mid-twentieth century. But several factors around 1970 began to reverse Marshall's fortunes. It is important to note that members of different ethnic groups placed the beginning of this decline at different historical moments, with White residents generally placing it decades earlier than African Americans. But everyone agreed that a decline occurred in the late twentieth century.

James Smith described its beginning:

> Well, back in the early days ... we had a lot of corner stores, little corner grocery stores that you can go to ... Everybody got along. We would have a running tab—Louis, one of our stores, we called him Louis, he had a store up on Ash Street. He would run a running tab, you know for the families ... You need bread, Ma would say "well, go get some bread." We went to the store, grab a loaf of bread, "Louis, Ma wants the bread, just put it on the tab." He would put it on the tab for Smith ... My dad, when he got paid on Friday, he would go and settle up with Louis, you know pay his bill, tab for the week. That was the good thing back then, you know, you didn't have to worry about going to the malls because they weren't in existence then. But as soon as the malls came along, it kind of changed everything, you know, a lot of the local corner stores, they started drying up.

Stories told by members of all groups described this sort of social cohesion and trust in the middle of the twentieth century—as if it had been a golden age—but then stories turned to the town's subsequent decline. Leo Ciccone, for example, told a similar story:

> I think after the war people were still, people were still together. Soldiers were coming home from the service. There were parades and parties and all. And then they started, they didn't want to stay in Marshall. For what reason? Then the movie theaters start closing down. The marquee on the most beautiful movie theater, they sold it ... [and] it's down in Florida.

America developed a suburban car culture, a new interstate highway bypassed Marshall, and more people moved out of town and found the limited parking in downtown Marshall inconvenient. Two malls were built in the 1960s, and this led many retail businesses to close. This all reflected larger national trends in this historical period (Hanchett, 1996). Leo explained how large shopping centers fundamentally changed social relationships:

> If you want to meet somebody, the only time you meet them may be at the ... mall. And then they're not going to stay there and talk because they're busy. They parked their car, they had a hard time getting into the shopping center. They get in there, they want to shop, get home before the traffic gets bad. You know everything is in movement. In Marshall, when people shopped they would go to the corner store. There weren't any big shopping centers. I think that's what changed Marshall.

At the same time as the malls went up, deindustrialization and the movement of manufacturing overseas led to the closure of plants and the loss of jobs in town (Bluestone & Harrison, 1982). With the decline of both retail and manufacturing, people moved out of Marshall. This led to a decline in homeownership and an increase in rental properties. By 1980, half of the government "Section 8" rent support vouchers given to poor county residents were being used in Marshall—even though the town had less than 5 percent of the county's population. Town government was at best ineffective and at worst corrupt in responding to the decline in businesses and owner-occupied housing.

This created fundamental material and ideological changes in Marshall. The town went from being what members of every group saw as an attractive place to live and raise children—a place that offered decent jobs, shopping opportunities, entertainment, and a sense of community—to being seen as a relatively depressed, empty, and perhaps unsafe town. Doreena described the sadness and confusion that the decline brought to many longstanding residents.

> [Before, it was] friendly, a lot of people was friendly, and everybody worked together, kept the neighborhood up and stuff. But then everybody started drifting, going different places ... so it changed quite a bit. It was very good before it changed. But then everybody started moving in and people started moving out ... It feels strange for real 'cause I went down to the old neighborhood and some of the people that used to be there, they gone now, and I couldn't believe they moved. They gone. Only three families left down there.

All narrators agreed that this decline included the loss of retail stores and jobs, the decrease in homeownership and increase in rental properties, and the loss of community and trust as residents became more transient.

But residents from different groups disagreed about when and why the decline occurred. Irish, Italian, and other White narrators pointed to the 1970s, citing the malls, the loss of manufacturing, and the arrival of a new wave of

Black migrants moving out from inner cities. Black residents acknowledged that the loss of local businesses did some damage in the 1970s and 1980s, but for them the decline accelerated in the 1990s with the arrival of Mexican migrants. White residents often identified Black residents as the cause of the decline, in part because they did not recognize the ongoing sense of intact community experienced by African Americans in the 1970s and 1980s. According to most Black residents, however, the real decline started when Mexicans moved into the rental housing, taking over neighborhoods and spaces formerly occupied by middle-class Black residents who had moved "up and out" (Santiago, 1996). Mexicans also opened stores where Spanish was spoken and Blacks did not feel welcome. As Doreena said:

> It has changed quite a bit ... A lot of Spanish people have moved in, and the whole neighborhood just changed. I mean, there's not that many Black people there no more on the East end ... A lot of them had businesses. They used to have second hand stores, and different shops. A lot of them people moved on. So, and now it's a lot of, downtown Spruce Street now it's mostly all Hispanic people and stuff like that down there.

James Smith offered a similar account:

> We had you know a majority of businesses, they were owned by Americans. And when the Latinos started moving up there and started coming in, it started changing. And if you go up there now you'll see probably 90% of the businesses up on Main Street are Latinos.

By "Americans" James probably meant African Americans, and he contrasted them with the Mexican migrants who began arriving and starting businesses in the 1990s.

Most Black residents from longstanding Marshall families told a similar story about how the town's decline accelerated in the 1990s, although there was some variability across generations. Doreena's granddaughter Tiffany, for example, grew up in Marshall. She had Mexican friends in school. She felt some solidarity with them, but she also felt displaced by them.

> Maybe [it's] the language barrier? Or like, kind of, you know when I'm walking down Spruce Street and then, and I'm older now, different than before. The new Spruce Street is very Hispanic. And it's like, it's not that I'm like, you know—look, I feel neighborly with them, you know what I mean. In a way, I see your struggle, you see my struggle. We're both struggling. But it's kind of like I can't really talk, it's like I can't really relate, like that's as far as it goes right there.

Younger Black residents were more likely than their elders to envision solidarity with Mexicans and to empathize with the challenges Mexican migrants faced. We will describe this further in Chapter 6 when discussing two community organizations founded by young Black residents that served Mexican youth and created interethnic connections. But Tiffany and many younger African Americans nonetheless felt displaced by the Mexican migrants who began arriving in the 1990s. Like their parents and grandparents, they looked back nostalgically to an earlier era of robust Black community life in Marshall.

This divergence between White and Black stories stems from a difference between Black residents and earlier migrants. As many have argued (e.g., Massey & Denton, 1998), African Americans are in important respects not a typical migrant group. Mexicans did not simply follow Irish, Italian, and Black migrants in a typical migration story with cycles of struggle and ultimate success, in part because many Black residents who preceded them in migrating to Marshall did not follow a pathway similar to Irish and Italian migrants. Both in their material situations and in the stories told about them, African Americans did not make the imagined transition from struggle to success as quickly or as completely—in significant part because of the more intense racism that they faced. Chapters 4 and 5 describe how Mexicans encountered and navigated this complex situation. Black residents sometimes reacted to the arrival of Mexicans in ways that echoed earlier migrant groups, with stereotypes and exclusion, but some African Americans also built solidarity with Mexicans. Irish and Italian Americans also influenced Black and Mexican pathways, through the stories they told about the two groups and through their control of material resources.

Mexican Revitalization

In 1995, right after the Mexican currency crisis, large numbers of Mexicans began coming to the United States (Chiquiar & Salcedo, 2013). Many of these migrants settled in places that had not traditionally been home to people from Latin America, like small towns in the Great Plains, the Southeast, the Midwest, and the Northeast (Zúñiga & Hernández-León, 2005). In Marshall, Mexicans were originally drawn to work in landscaping and restaurants, and shortly thereafter they began to work in construction and retail. In 2010, Father Kelly told us about the "explosion" in the Mexican population in the church:

> It was about 20 years ago that there was a small influx of Hispanics, mostly Puerto Rican, but there was never a really big group here at the time. About 15 years ago the Mexican community started to come here and again it was small, but almost overnight it just exploded. So we have a lot of Mexican families who

are here. And of course they are predominantly Catholic. The parish started a mass in Spanish about 15 years ago … And I've been here for eight years and I would say that coming to church we have about 1000 different Mexican families.

The Mexican population in Marshall went from about 100 in 1990, to 2,500 in 2000 to almost 10,000 by the time we ended our research in 2016.

As described in the last section, Black and White residents tended to diverge in their evaluations of Mexican migration. African Americans often blamed Mexicans for the decline of the town at the end of the twentieth century. Residents like Doreena and Tiffany felt pushed out of their neighborhoods and excluded from Mexican businesses and other spaces. On the other hand, almost all White and Mexican narrators characterized Mexican migrants as helping Marshall reverse its decline. Some Irish and Italian American narrators agreed with Black residents that the Mexican community was relatively closed, and some shared a sense of being excluded from Mexican neighborhoods and businesses. But most White residents nonetheless gave Mexicans credit for bringing life back to downtown churches, businesses, and neighborhoods. They characterized Mexicans as family-oriented, hardworking people whose efforts were revitalizing the town (Wortham, Mortimer, & Allard, 2009). St. Joseph's church, for example, was thriving because of Mexican parishioners. In 2010, this traditionally Irish Catholic church had twice as many Mexican families as English-speaking ones. "This past year we had 250 baptisms, and about 248 of them were Mexican," Father Kelly told us.

The first Mexican to settle permanently in Marshall was Carlo Faccone's wife Juana, in the late 1970s. They lived a romantic story. Carlo took a cruise that stopped in Mexico, and Juana and her sisters performed Mexican folk dances on the cruise ship. Carlo was quite taken with Juana, and he returned to Mexico seven or eight times over the next ten months to court her. Juana described the first time she met him:

> He didn't talk to me directly. He said to the person who was working in the store, he told him, in English, please tell the young lady that he would give her a piece of the pineapple that he was eating. He did not imagine that I spoke English, but from there he followed me and we chatted. We went along and we arrived at the boat, and I introduced him to you [her sister Martha], and you said, "Who is that man?" [laughter]. I introduced him to Martha. So that day, Carlo was going to return to the US the next day. He only wanted, um, he asked me for my telephone number; he asked me for my address. But I, being very on the alert, I did not give him my phone number [laughter]. I only gave him my address. So upon writing it down, he read the address, and he said, "Someday I'm going to look for you." Three weeks later he looked for me.

After Carlo returned several times and her family saw his dedication to Juana, they accepted him as her suitor. The cultural similarities between Italians and Mexicans helped. Because he spoke Italian, Carlo was able to understand some Spanish. Mexicans' strong commitment to family was familiar to him, and they were both Catholic. Many months later, he said to Juana: "Honey, I don't have no money to travel anymore, so we're going to have to get married." She told us that she "didn't think twice" before agreeing to marry him.

At their engagement party in Mexico, one of Juana's uncles asked Carlo whether he thought she would be happy living in Marshall. Carlo said, "Of course she will—we're in love, I have a good job and I'll take care of her." The uncle pointed out that it was cold up there, she would have no friends, and she did not speak English that well. Carlo was chagrined, and he asked what he could do to make his new wife happy. The uncle had a simple answer: Take some of her sisters with you. So Carlo did. He told us:

> We settled into a place in the Hills. We were there for ten years I guess. We had a one bedroom. And in the meantime we brought a few people from Mexico. Martha came, and Alma, your other sister came. And her brother Manuel, he came. He went back because he was married and had a little baby. But Martha came first. And then she stayed a couple weeks. And then she went home. And then Alma came. And then Martha came back. And Alma and Martha stayed. And then we worked.

Juana had five sisters and five brothers, and over time seven of the siblings moved to Marshall. All living siblings now make their homes in and around the town. They are professionals and business owners who have children and grandchildren born in the United States. Father Kelly presided over the funeral for their mother, who lived at the end of her life with Juana's oldest sister in Marshall. Twenty of Juana's American-born nieces and nephews stood beside the casket during the ceremony.

Juana's sister Martha credited her mother with instilling the determination that she and her siblings needed to successfully navigate their lives as migrants:

> And that is what has made us strong, it has made us brave, and without fearing anything. When we came to this country, she always had a positive attitude in saying ... just work hard, then you will achieve your goals. Because when she found out that we had to do whatever we had to do to survive [including at one point Juana and her sisters cleaning toilets], she said, that is what you have to do ... Don't think about ... what other people will say. Dedicate yourself to what you have to do.

This attitude is characteristic of migrants in classic positive stories of migrant struggle and ultimate success. Many Mexicans, including most in Juana's family, described themselves in these terms. Many Irish, Italian, and African American residents also respected Mexicans' determination and hard work. We have already seen how they often compared Mexican migrants to their own migrant ancestors—describing similar effort, sacrifice, and devotion to family. In fact, Juana had an advantage over some other residents, as she was married to an American citizen and had access to some material and symbolic resources. But she nonetheless struggled in many ways, and we should not disparage her embrace of the (in her case) largely accurate classic migration story.

Not all White residents evaluated Mexican migrants positively, of course. Around town we heard disparaging comments about Mexicans that echoed some national discourses about Mexican migrants being "illegal," parasitic, and dangerous (Chavez, 2008; Dick, 2011). One longstanding downtown resident summarized the complaints:

> Somebody will say, oh what is the person doing on my steps, or why do I have trash that doesn't belong to me, or why does the place next door have seven and ten cars when there are just two apartments … There is no way that the city will pick up all the trash from all those people. We have houses with sometimes twenty, thirty people live in a house, a single-family home. We don't have enough police to police all this. All the services, the quality of services came down, but our taxes are higher.

Father Kelly claimed this was not the dominant discourse, however.

> I don't have a lot of English-speaking people complain to me directly about the fact they're undocumented. I hear little murmurings here and there at events I go to. There is also a good number of people that acknowledge they are here and hardworking and are trying to do what our families did years ago, to come here and have a better life and financial security. Definitely there is some tension, but I'm not hearing a whole lot of it from our parishioners.

We heard many negative comments about Mexicans in Marshall, but positive stories were more common. We argue that this relatively positive reception resulted in part from the migrant history of the town. Many residents remembered their own migrant ancestors and were sympathetic to Mexicans as a similar migrant group. In this way, the relatively recent and salient history of migration to Marshall made it different than some other towns that have been more hostile to Mexican migrants (Flores, 2014; Jones, 2012; Murillo, 2002). Most White residents credited Mexicans with bringing energy and effort that brought revitalization and reversed the town's decline. Both scholarly work and popular media about similar towns often credit Hispanics with revitalizing small-town America in this way (Grey & Woodrick, 2005; Gordon, 2015, 2016; Jordan, 2012; Sulzberger, 2011; Zúñiga & Hernández-León, 2005). In subsequent chapters, we will describe in more detail the conflicting stories that circulated about Mexicans in Marshall—many that characterized them as upwardly mobile migrants, but also some that cast them as dangerous interlopers.

Juana said that until about 1990 she could stop other Mexicans in Marshall, ask where they came from, and then almost always successfully trace their presence back to someone connected to her. After 1990, however, the population began to increase more rapidly and she was no longer able to find such connections. Several central members of the Mexican community nonetheless came to Marshall because of her. The owner of the first Mexican store and the first Mexican restaurant, which opened in the early 1990s, was a cousin who slept on her couch for months when he arrived in town; her brother, nephews, sister, and another sister's husband opened four Mexican stores during the first decade of the Mexican community, all of which still existed in 2016; her nephew was the first Hispanic resident to run for political office in Marshall, in the early 2010s; and a successful landscaper who ran the local soccer league—which provided a crucial point of contact for many new arrivals—came from her home state in Mexico and had learned about Marshall through her cousins.

Although Juana and her family were central to creating the Mexican community in Marshall, they themselves were not typical Mexican residents. Because of their arrival a decade or two before the community began to grow, because of their hard work and accumulation of assets over those intervening years, because of their relationship with a financially stable American citizen in Carlo, and because of their middle-class origins in Mexico, they had significant symbolic and economic capital. The typical Mexican resident between 1995 and 2005 came from a state in central and not western Mexico, had only recently arrived, came from a rural working-class background, and had much less capital.

Juan Castro represents this group. We will describe his experiences in more detail in the next chapter. He grew up in a small town in Querétaro, where he stayed until he was fifteen. He migrated to the United States around 2000 because his family needed financial support and he could not earn enough in Mexico. He came to Marshall because an uncle lived there. He started working as a dishwasher in a restaurant, then he got a job in roofing. He had a cousin who had arrived in the United States a couple of years earlier, and Juan's parents kept reminding him that the cousin had already saved enough money to start building a house back in Querétaro. Juan told us that Mexican families are not like American ones, where you work for yourself. In Mexico you have a responsibility to work for your family, to take care of your parents, and he felt a need to work and send them money. After a couple of months Juan's father did not want him to be alone in the United States, so he came to Marshall and they moved in together. Then his brothers came from California, where they had been working, and some of his sisters came from Mexico. Unlike Juana and her siblings, Juan and his family were working-class people from a rural area in central Mexico, and most Mexicans in Marshall were like Juan.

Marshall has been what Enrique Murillo and Sofia Villenas (1997) dubbed a "New Latino Diaspora" community—a town that had not historically been home to migrants from Latin America, but where such migrants settled in large numbers starting in the mid-1990s (Hamann & Harklau, 2010; Wortham, Murillo, & Hamann 2002; Zúñiga & Hernández-León, 2005). By 2016, however, Marshall was no longer a "new" Latino diaspora community. As the Mexican migrant community in Marshall developed, it changed in various ways—in the ideas migrants and hosts had about themselves and their town, in the opportunities migrants found and created, in the characteristic activities migrants engaged in both among themselves and together with longstanding residents. The most significant shift was from a community dominated by single men who planned to work, make money, and return to Mexico, to a community dominated by young families with children who planned to stay in the United States (Passel & Cohn, 2008). Most towns in the "Latino Diaspora" are maturing, and we need additional, careful descriptions of what these towns have become after two decades with Mexican residents (Hamann, Wortham, & Murillo, 2015).

The rapid growth in the Marshall Mexican migrant community brought dramatic changes to the town. Juan, as a younger single male, was typical of Mexican migrants who arrived in the ten years after 1995. By 2005, however, the typical Mexican in Marshall was like Allie—part of an intact, young nuclear family with small children. The number of new migrants declined after the US economic crisis in 2008, but the community continued to grow through births and migration from elsewhere in the United States. In some ways, the transition from single men to intact families marked the start of a transition to work, sacrifice, and success, as described in archetypal positive migrant narratives (Massey, Alarcón, Durand, & González, 1987). But this story oversimplified a more complex reality. Often, up to the present day, Mexicans were still positioned as "illegal" invaders. Mexicans' relationships with African Americans were complex and produced divergent, unexpected pathways. Mexicans' own activities also changed the town, such that longstanding and migrant communities became something new as they grew together. This book describes how residents' migration stories and other diverse realities came together to create the divergent, solidifying pathways along which different migrants traveled.

The Central Argument

We make several core claims about migration in general and about Mexican migrants' pathways over their first two decades in Marshall.

- Simple stories about migration accurately describe some migrant pathways, but individuals and communities follow diverse pathways that often diverge from familiar stories.
- Both typical and unexpected pathways could have happened differently. They are contingent—emerging and taking shape across developmental and historical time.
- A pathway solidifies over time as a network of diverse, contingent resources establishes a particular direction for an individual or community.
- The resources that constitute any pathway come from various scales. In Marshall, four relevant scales were: cycles of migration across centuries, changes in the community over two decades, divergent pathways of individuals across years, and contingent events that took place across hours and days.
- Residents tell oversimplified and sometimes inaccurate stories about migration, but many stories nonetheless become resources that shape actual pathways.
- Relations between ethnic groups, and stories about those relations, are important resources that influence migrant pathways. In Marshall, Mexicans' relations with Irish and Italian Americans differed from their relations with African Americans. The complex, three-way relationship among Mexicans, Irish/Italian Americans, and African Americans facilitated diverse pathways.

We have introduced each of these claims in this chapter, but we cannot elaborate all components of our account at once. In the next five chapters, we describe various pathways traveled by individual migrants and segments of the Mexican migrant community in Marshall over its first two decades. Each chapter describes one space in the community—with Chapter 2 on schools, Chapter 3 on churches, Chapter 4 on residential neighborhoods, Chapter 5 on public spaces, and Chapter 6 on community organizations. Each chapter illustrates some of our core claims, and together the chapters provide empirical descriptions that support the entire argument.

All of the chapters describe heterogeneous pathways that Mexicans traveled in Marshall. Chapter 2 presents diverging individual pathways traveled by young Mexican migrants. The chapter focuses on schools, where we trace the ontogenetic development of three Mexican students and describe how their positions in the changing Mexican migrant community shaped the pathways they followed. Chapters 3, 4, and 5 describe relations among and stories about different ethnic groups in Marshall, as well as the influence these had on Mexicans' pathways. Chapter 3 focuses on churches, especially relations between Irish Americans and Mexicans at St. Joseph's parish. Chapter 4 focuses on residential neighborhoods, describing both facts and stories about Black-Mexican relations in downtown Marshall. Chapter 5 focuses on public spaces and provides a more comprehensive account of how individual and community pathways were shaped by relations among Black, White, and Mexican residents. Chapter 6 uses descriptions of diverse community organizations to bring together the claims in our argument and summarize the major pathways attributed to and traveled by Mexicans in Marshall.

Schools, churches, neighborhoods, public spaces, and community organizations in Marshall varied in the resources they provided, the people who interacted within them, and the migration stories that circulated in each. We trace how the pathways traveled by longstanding residents and migrants were constituted in each space by networks of stories and other resources that changed across the first twenty years of the Marshall Mexican community. We also follow individual characters from Irish American, Italian American, African American, and Mexican communities, illustrating diverse pathways by describing their experiences and perspectives. We have introduced several of the central characters in this chapter: Father Kelly, Carlo, Leo, James, Doreena, Juana, Juan, and Allie. Through our accounts of these individuals and the broader Marshall community, we trace how Mexicans' pathways intersected with the heterogeneous, changing town—sometimes in ways that resembled familiar positive and negative migration stories, and sometimes in unexpected ways. As claims about reality, the migration stories told pervasively in this historical moment were oversimplified but often contained elements of truth—although some stories were truer than others. In addition to assessing their truth value, however, we must also explore how these stories partly constituted the realities that they imperfectly described.

2

Schools: Three Diverging Individual Mexican Pathways

This chapter describes the pathways three Mexican students took in school. These students came to Marshall at different ages and at different moments in the development of the Mexican community. Juan came as a teenager and started high school early in the community's development, Nancy came as a young child and was in middle school in the middle of the community's development, and Allie came as a toddler and started elementary school in the second decade of the Mexican community. Through these cases, we illustrate how ontogenetic and community development interconnected, with resources from each contributing to the solidification of both individual and community pathways. While interethnic relations were important in Marshall schools, and this chapter does describe a few stories that Black, White, and Mexican students told about each other, here we do not focus on the relations among migrant groups that arrived over the past two centuries. We focus more explicitly on cycles of migration and interethnic relations in Chapter 3—where we describe Mexicans' relationships with Irish Americans in church—and in Chapters 4 through 6, which describe Black-Mexican relations.

Schools have substantial influence over young people's life prospects because they have institutional authority to certify students' competence and to provide credentials that open or foreclose future opportunities (e.g., Mehan, 1996). Like schools everywhere, Marshall schools sometimes empowered students and facilitated upward mobility, while in other cases they disadvantaged students by deploying ethnic stereotypes and foreclosing opportunities. Stories about educational capacity and school performance also influence individuals' conceptions of themselves and groups' perceptions of each other. In Marshall, students, educators, and town residents from all backgrounds characterized students variously with respect to their academic performance, their work habits, the relationships they had with members of their own and other groups, and their career trajectories. In our accounts of the three focal students in this chapter, we describe how schooling both opened and closed opportunities for them and how stories that circulated in and about schools influenced their pathways.

Across our eleven years in Marshall, members of the research team visited every school in the Marshall School District. We conducted detailed, multiyear observations in one elementary school, one middle school, and one high school. We observed English as a Second Language (ESL) classes in the high school for more than two years starting in 2006. We got to know about two dozen individuals, including Juan, and we followed several outside of school to their homes and community activities. In one middle school Katherine Clonan-Roy convened and ran girls' groups—extracurricular meetings devoted to open discussion about issues of personal concern (Clonan-Roy, 2018)—for five years, starting in 2011. These groups served seventy-two girls in total, including Nancy and a dozen peers whom we got to know both inside and outside of school. In one elementary school, members of the research team gathered data for over five years, starting in 2009, following one cohort of students across their elementary school careers and regularly visiting other classrooms (Link, Gallo, & Wortham, 2017). Allie attended this school, and members of the research team spent at least 200 hours with her and her family outside of school.

Juan, Nancy, and Allie represent Mexican students' experiences in Marshall schools at three levels of schooling. Their pathways diverged because of diverse, contingent resources of several kinds. First, it mattered when a student arrived in the history of the Mexican community. Students who started school during the first decade entered schools that had little experience with Spanish-speaking students. At the high school, these students tended to be segregated into "sheltered" ESL classes, and at all levels Mexicans were unfamiliar to other students and to Marshall educators. Students who arrived in the second decade of the Mexican community entered schools that enrolled large numbers of Mexicans, and educators had some experience with Spanish-speaking students. Second, the age at which a student entered school in the United States made a difference. Students who began their schooling in the United States as teenagers encountered an academically demanding curriculum delivered in unfamiliar academic English (Allard et al., 2014). They usually struggled to learn English while keeping up with a rapidly moving curriculum (Clonan-Roy, Rhodes, & Wortham, 2013), and they often joined Mexican peer groups that mixed infrequently with others (Clonan-Roy, Rhodes, & Wortham, 2016; Silver, 2015). Students who began their schooling in elementary school learned English at a younger age and often mastered academic English at the same time as their native English-speaking peers (Oropesa & Landale, 1997). They also tended to form some friendships across ethnic lines. Third, we found divergent attitudes toward Spanish and Spanish speakers at the elementary and secondary levels—with elementary school teachers much more likely to consider Spanish fluency a resource and high school teachers more likely to consider it a barrier (Allard et al., 2014). Taken together, these configurations of resources meant that Mexican students who began in Marshall elementary schools were more likely to make academic progress and develop positive images of themselves as students.

Individual students' ontogenetic pathways thus intersected with the development of the Mexican community and with teachers' and other residents' reactions to Mexicans, leading to divergent student experiences and outcomes. Depending on the configuration of these resources in a particular case, individual migrant students followed different pathways. In Marshall, Mexican migrant students also entered a town with no history of Mexican settlement, and this often made a difference (Wortham, Hamann, & Murillo, 2002). If they had started their US schooling in areas of traditional Mexican settlement like Texas or California, they would have encountered more familiarity with but also more entrenched stereotypes about people like them. Finally, as mentioned above, Marshall was somewhat more welcoming to Mexican migrants than many similar towns (Flores, 2014; Jones, 2012). The history of migration to Marshall made some longstanding residents more sympathetic than in other places (Wortham, Mortimer, & Allard, 2009).

In order to describe how these diverse resources came together in different configurations to shape the school experiences of Mexican students in Marshall, we trace the pathways traveled by Juan in high school, Nancy in middle school, and Allie in elementary school. Juan entered Marshall High School in the early 2000s when he was fifteen. He had come to Marshall to work, but he chose to attend school also. Nancy arrived in Marshall as a young child about the same time as Juan, but at a much younger age, and she began elementary school in Marshall. We met her as a middle school student in 2011. Allie also came to Marshall as a young child, about five years after Nancy, and she began school there. We met her at the beginning of her elementary school years in 2010. These three students' pathways represent three clusters of Mexican students who entered Marshall schools over the two-decade history of the community. In the first decade, many older Mexican youth came to Marshall and entered high school. In the second decade, most Mexican schoolchildren came from intact families and began in elementary school, although children in Nancy's cohort—

who started school earlier in the Mexican community's development—often followed different pathways than those in Allie's. The divergence between these three clusters of Mexican students shows one way in which migrant children's experiences differed despite their demographic similarities. Within each cluster, individual children also followed different pathways, as we mention below when contrasting Juan, Nancy, and Allie with their peers. In addition, some migrant students in Marshall did not fall into any of the three groups. Juana and Carlo Faccone's children and other early arrivals, for example, went to elementary school in the 1990s, and at the other end of the spectrum some teenagers continued to arrive directly from Mexico into the 2010s. Not all Mexican students had experiences like the three we describe here, but these three clusters provide insight into common pathways.

In Marshall schools during the first decade, Mexican students mostly encountered stories that cast them as good workers but not good students (Wortham, Mortimer, & Allard, 2009). Educators and peers typically assumed that Mexican youth were in Marshall to work and not to study. If they went to school at all, people often said that it was "only to learn English," without an expectation of further academic success. This story unjustly discouraged some students, who might have persevered in the school if there had been a little more encouragement. As the numbers of Mexican students increased, and as they began to start their schooling at younger ages in Marshall elementary schools, the stories became more varied. Some educators and longstanding residents continued to identify Mexican students as academically unpromising, but we less often heard that Mexican students just wanted to learn English and find blue-collar jobs. As we will see in Allie's case, later in the second decade it became easier for Mexicans to be seen as diligent students who were expected to do well in school. In our analyses of Juan, Nancy, and Allie, we describe these common stories about Mexican students' academic prospects and how migrant students' experiences both diverged from and intersected with the stories. We also show how the stories themselves became important factors that facilitated and constrained students' opportunities.

Juan in High School

The first large group of school-age Mexicans that arrived in Marshall were high school students—adolescents who migrated to the United States in search of jobs and who worked and attended school simultaneously. We begin this chapter with Juan, who arrived in Marshall shortly after 2000. We met him in 2006, in an ESL class at the high school, and three members of the research team interacted extensively with him both inside and outside school. We spoke with him in restaurants, social service agencies, and while he was working on landscaping jobs. He became comfortable enough with us that, when he was summoned to court in a landlord-tenant dispute at one point, he called us for advice and support.

Childhood and Migration

Juan grew up in a small town in the Mexican state of Querétaro called Jalpan de Serra. He was born in the city of Querétaro, but his parents moved to this small town when he was little and he remained there until migrating to the United States at age fifteen. In Mexico he attended elementary and middle school, and he helped his parents with the animals and the crops. He told us that school in Mexico "isn't the same as it is here. [There they] don't teach you. They don't care if you learn or not." When he was in middle school, his father migrated to the United States and got a job in construction. He sent back money that his mother used to open a general store. Two of his brothers also migrated to California and sent money back. By this time Juan was no longer going to school. He was helping his mother with the small farm and with the store, but he felt that he was not contributing enough to the family. His parents had debts, and he knew that his mother worried about money. So he decided to migrate to the United States by himself. He went to Marshall because his uncle was living there and because he had heard there were good opportunities for earning money.

Juan's migration was in part a result of poverty and lack of economic opportunity in Mexico. It was also facilitated by his familiarity with migration to the United States (Newland, 2009). Many other Mexican men he knew, including his father and brothers, had traveled to the United States to work. This made migration to the United States seem feasible. The economic situation in Juan's family was similar in many ways to Nancy's and Allie's families. These girls' parents were also rural, working-class people who migrated in search of economic opportunity. But there were two crucial differences. Nancy and Allie came with intact families or traveled with their mothers and reunited with their fathers in the United States. Nancy and Allie also started elementary school in Marshall. Juan's experience differed significantly because he was an adolescent when he migrated, because his mother remained in Mexico, and because he entered Marshall High School earlier in the development of the Mexican community. His pathway resembled many adolescent migrants in early New

Latino Diaspora towns like those described by Wortham, Murillo, and Hamann (2002) and Zúñiga and Hernández-León (2005).

Unlike Nancy and Allie, Juan vividly recalled the trauma of crossing the border. He agreed to pay a "coyote," someone who helped migrants move to the United States. He and a group of people whom he mostly did not know first took a truck from his town to Mexico City, then they traveled on a bus to Nogales where they crossed the border. They walked all night through the hills. The first time he crossed, US border patrol caught them and returned them to Mexico. They waited until about 2:00 a.m., and it was really cold. He was afraid because people said that if you fell asleep you could freeze to death. There was one person he knew in the group, but he couldn't wake him up. He just wouldn't wake up and they had to leave him. It turned out that he was fine, however, because later Juan saw him in the United States. After a long drive shut in a truck, he arrived in Marshall and his uncle was waiting for him. He paid the money Juan owed, which was $2,500. Juan had to work to pay this money back. Initially he got a job with a roofing company, tearing off roofs, and then jobs in two different restaurants washing dishes. It took him about six months to pay his uncle. The obligation to pay this debt, as well as his desire to send money to his mother in Mexico, meant that Juan focused on work from the beginning. The need to make money was central to his life at this stage. Unlike many of his peers, however, he did not let work divert him completely from school.

Work and Plans to Return

After several months Juan's father moved to Marshall, largely because he didn't want Juan to be by himself. Then his two brothers, who had been in California, moved to town. Then one of his older sisters came, although she returned to Mexico eventually. Then another older sister came, and she remained. His father and siblings all came to work. His sisters cleaned offices and houses. The third sister came, and she worked in a Mexican store. Juan's father worked in construction, eventually being promoted to run a team. He knew how to do "anything related to bricklaying and ironwork." His father started working for a guy who paid him $60 for twelve hours of work. "This was not a good wage," Juan felt. Then his father and brother figured out how to get jobs directly, instead of working for the contractor, and they subsequently made a lot more money. His father did good work and so he got more clients and became his own boss. At that point they had less financial pressure than before.

It was nonetheless "really hard work, a slog day after day." Juan occasionally went to work with his father, and he had to break concrete with big hammers and his hands got all calloused and hurt, and "in the winter you still have to work even though it's really cold." When he spoke with us in 2006, he was working at a Mexican store, four hours a day. They paid him six dollars an hour, and he told us that it was "not enough." He worked there four days a week, went to school, and worked construction with his dad on Saturday. Sunday was his day off—"time for me." Later in his schooling, he worked as a busboy in a restaurant in the evenings, forty hours per week, until midnight, then went home and got about six hours of sleep before getting up for school the next day. During his first five years in the United States, he worked as a roofer, dishwasher, busboy, cook, landscaper, cashier, and construction worker. Despite all the work he had "very little money." He had to contribute to the family's rent, pay for his cell phone and internet, plus car expenses, as well as send money to his mother. The money he made "wasn't enough by any means."

In addition to financial challenges, Juan and his family encountered other sorts of dangers. He told us about an incident when someone tried to assault one of his sisters. In the United States, he said, you can't really tell if people are friends or enemies. "People here are false, but in Mexico you really know people." There was a woman whom his sister Gabi worked with who tried to sell her to a man. A man paid this woman to bring Gabi to him so that he could see her. Gabi did not realize what the woman was doing. One day Gabi forgot her sweater in the car on the way to work and the woman called her and said, "Listen, you forgot your sweater. Mr. So-and-so is waiting in some place and he wants you to go there and get your sweater." His sister said "What? What? How am I going to go there just for my sweater? Tomorrow I can go get it." But the woman said, "No. He wants you to come get it because if not he's going to throw it away." She said "No. I'm not going for my sweater." Later she realized what this woman was trying to do. And this woman was from the same state in Mexico as Juan's family. In the United States, he told us, even a fellow Mexican can say that she is your friend, but in reality you never know.

In part because of experiences like this, Juan planned to return to Mexico once he saved some money. Despite having relatives in Marshall, Juan was homesick. When his mother told him on the phone about the upcoming festival in his home town, he promised her and himself that he would be there the next year. When he told us about the food they typically ate at the festival, he became animated and happy. But when he talked about life in Marshall, he became somber. Some of his old friends from Mexico lived in Marshall, but it was not the same because he had no time to see them. In 2006, he was planning a trip back to Mexico the following August. He planned to leave school around February and work full time, because he needed to make enough money to return to the United States after his trip. "Maybe I'll make it back here and maybe I won't," he said. Some people didn't make it crossing the border, he told us. Those who crossed the water sometimes drowned. Those who crossed the desert sometimes died of thirst. For those, like him, who crossed through the hills, it could be a snake or a bad fall, because the hills are very steep. There was a lot of danger no matter where you crossed. He did not know at this point what pathway he would follow, whether he would make it back from Mexico or not. As he said, "I don't know what my luck will be."

In his desire to return to Mexico, Juan was different from Nancy and Allie. He had grown almost to adulthood there and found Mexican culture familiar and appealing. He spoke English relatively well, but he was more comfortable in Spanish. His mother and extended family still lived in Mexico. He did not in fact make it back to Mexico to visit his mother as he had planned—in significant part because he feared the increasing border security that made the trip risky—but he desperately wanted to go. Nancy and Allie, in contrast, considered Marshall their home. They spoke Spanish relatively well, but they preferred English. They had few or no memories of life in Mexico. Quite rapidly, within a decade after the Mexican community began to grow in Marshall, most Mexican schoolchildren were different than Juan and his peers: he felt much more Mexican than American, and he had more intense emotional attachments to Mexico.

School

At this point in his life, Juan was seventeen years old and his future pathway was uncertain. A small number of Mexican migrants in Marshall worked hard, earned money, and returned to Mexico. Juan had wanted to follow this path, but he gave up this idea in 2007. He could have traveled various other pathways from this point. Within Juan's cohort of adolescents who had migrated to Marshall to work, there was significant variation. Some Mexican migrant youth in Juan's position attended school, and some did not. The school district truant officer tried to find those under sixteen and make them attend, but this was a difficult task given the language barrier and the transient population. Some peers never attended school or dropped out to work. Juan, however, decided on his own that he wanted to attend school. His father initially wanted him just to work so that they could save money and go back to Mexico as a family. But Juan had been interested in English even when he lived in Mexico. So, he said to himself, "No, I have the opportunity to study. I'm going to study here." One of his brothers agreed that this was a good idea. This older brother encouraged Juan to continue in school, and he offered to help Juan financially. The contingent fact of having his brother's support made a significant difference in Juan's pathway—without it, he would almost surely have dropped out of school to work full-time.

Despite his father's request that he not attend school, Juan had great respect for him. His father worked hard and was "a good father," always available to give advice. Nonetheless, Juan did not want to do hard labor his whole life. He liked to work, but not in the sort of physically demanding job he saw his father and brothers doing. His father was often sick from breathing dust and from working outside in the cold. Juan told us that he did not want to work like that. He wanted to have a secure job. He told us that as a child he used to ask his father for many things, but the family could not afford them. He didn't want his own children to ask him for things and for him not to be able to provide. He decided to do something to secure a good job. Maybe he could own a business. If he couldn't study computers, or be an English teacher—two jobs he told us he would really like to have—maybe starting a business could help him make money.

Juan, like virtually all the Mexican students in his cohort who persisted in school, worked hard both in school and in their after-school jobs, and they were often exhausted. Most did not get to sleep until after midnight on weekdays. But they aspired to careers, and they wanted to speak English well, so they continued with school despite the hardship. Many educators and other residents saw these Mexican students as hardworking and well behaved, but longstanding residents also tended to characterize them as academically unpromising. We have described this as a modified version of the "model minority myth" (Wortham, Mortimer, & Allard, 2009). This myth inaccurately presents all members of "successful" minority groups as the same, and it contrasts them with a false, stereotyped version of "unsuccessful" minorities. A model minority is "the 'good' minority that seeks advancement through quiet diligence in study and work and by not making waves; the minority that other American minorities should seek to emulate" (Lee, 1994; National Commission on Asian American and Pacific Islander Research in Education 2008:1). Like the Asian migrants who are stereotyped as the prototypical model minorities, educators and other longstanding Marshall residents told stories about Mexicans as diligent workers who contributed to the local economy, who did not expect special treatment and did not complain.

Stories about Mexicans diverged from those about Asian migrants, however, because educators and other longstanding residents typically did not expect Mexican students to succeed in school. After saying positive things about Mexicans one day, for instance, one teacher claimed that "the people who really progressed were the Koreans" because "they're big on education." She then claimed that Koreans "did so well because they all learned English," even those who migrated later in life, while "older Mexicans are not learning English." Another high school teacher was more explicit, telling us that some of the Mexican students were "unmotivated, lazy and have no desire to do work." She went on immediately to sing the praises of Ming, a Chinese ESL student she characterized as "ultra-motivated." In drawing this false, racializing contrast, she failed to acknowledge that Juan and other Mexican students in her own class were working hard and getting good grades. A third educator described how, about a decade earlier when the Spanish-speaking population began to increase, the principal of an elementary school with both Asian and Mexican students "kept all the Asian students and sent all of the Spanish-speaking students to another school [laughing] and ... her reasoning was, who are the kids who are going to help me most on the test?"

When speaking about students like Juan, who started their US schooling in high school, educators often told us, falsely, that Mexican students were not academic, that they came only to learn English, that they didn't speak good Spanish, and that they were wild and unsupervised. One educator repeatedly characterized the Mexican ESL students as "over-age"—meaning older than the norm for their grade level—and "lacking in academic skill." Both he and the high school principal also claimed that there were similarities between Mexican migrants and special education students, saying that it was "unrealistic" for teachers to expect English-language learners to "learn like everyone else." The principal confirmed that the ESL program followed a special education model: "The model for upper functioning Special Ed. kids works for the upper functioning language kids," he explained. This was a particularly pernicious analogy, because it inappropriately allowed educators to have low expectations for the Mexican students.

Strikingly, several educators—most of whom did not speak Spanish at all—told us that Mexican students spoke "bad Spanish." The principal even lamented that they were trying to teach "English to kids who can't read, write or speak their native language." These claims were ludicrous, because Juan and all of his friends were native Spanish speakers who could also read and write Spanish. One educator described the students' Spanish as "Tex-Mex" and another called it "hillbilly Spanish" (Allard, Mortimer, Gallo, Link, & Wortham, 2014), revealing a stereotype about the students' rural, working-class backgrounds. Some educators also claimed that most Mexicans in Mexico did not aspire to schooling beyond ninth grade, and so argued that it was unrealistic for American schools to have high aspirations for them. Some worried about declining academic standards. As one high school teacher said, "if you have a group who is highly unmotivated and they're absent a lot and … you start giving them open book tests, or take-home tests, or projects instead of tests and replacing a lot of the harder curriculum. … I think some teachers feel that we are starting to do that and we're not holding our standards high enough." Another teacher said that "there isn't much hope" for older Mexican students. She told us a story about a student whose parents claimed falsely that he had moved out of town so that he could work and not be truant. A while later, she said, someone saw him in town "just sitting on some stoop." Other research has shown that these sorts of false, racializing stories about migrant students can play an important role in pushing them out of high school (Behnke, Gonzalez, & Cox, 2010).

Some of the stories we heard were ridiculous—for example, Juan and his peers spoke perfect Mexican Spanish and were literate—and in other respects the stories oversimplified. Many students like Juan were intelligent, worked hard, and aspired to academic success. The stories were also hard for members of the research team to hear. Although we continue to believe that most Marshall educators cared about their Mexican students, we also knew that many of their stories were false and damaged Mexican students' prospects. We did speak to some teachers about their false stereotypes, and we ran professional development sessions during in-service days that presented more accurate portrayals of Mexican students to Marshall educators (Gallo & Wortham, 2012). While in the schools, however, we sometimes could do no more than document stories about Mexican students that—together with some educators' low expectations—unjustly created high barriers for Juan and others who came to Marshall as teenagers. These migrant students were generally welcomed by Marshall residents as laborers, but they were not expected to succeed in school. The stories that were told about Mexican migrant students were one important resource that pushed them toward the working-class pathways they ended up following. Juan himself struggled against some of these stories and was able to graduate from high school, but many of his peers did not.

Mexican children in the next generation, like Nancy and Allie, rarely had to juggle work and school. They were not expected to work outside the home, although they did significant work helping their families with translation, navigation, childcare, and other duties (Orellana, 2009). The girls' families were similar to Juan's economically, but they were different in three crucial ways. First, Nancy and Allie came to Marshall as children too young to work, whereas wage labor was for Juan a primary goal from the beginning. Second, they were female, and male children were more often expected to earn income in support of the family (Stanton-Salazar, 2001). Third, Nancy and Allie's families were in fundamentally different positions than Juan's. His nuclear family was partly back in Mexico, where he, his father, and his siblings hoped to return. The family goal was to save money and improve their situation back home. The girls' nuclear families were focused on building a life for themselves and their children in the United States, although Allie's family periodically considered a return to Mexico. In these three crucial ways, the networks of resources that constituted the girls' pathways differed from Juan's.

Some Mexican teenagers in the first decade of the Mexican community chose not to attend school and instead worked full time. Those who did enroll in school had difficulty juggling their school and work responsibilities. Allard (2013:271) collected data on absenteeism in the Marshall High School ESL class she observed:

> Another recurring issue was chronic absenteeism. Of the nineteen students for whom I was able to collect attendance data, fifteen had double-digit absences, ranging from a modest ten (out of 180 days enrolled) to an unbelievable ninety-six (out of 176 days enrolled). No student had fewer than seven absences. Related to both absenteeism and low engagement was withdrawal from school. Of the twenty-two students who came through the beginner ESL classroom, ten withdrew during the year of my fieldwork and several more withdrew during the following year.

In addition to the demands of their jobs, Mexican students often withdrew from school because of struggles with the subject matter. One high school educator spoke with Allard (2013:264–5) about this:

> What [the teacher] thinks is really hard is when a student comes in with little education from Mexico or when the student comes in and the last grade that they've been in was the sixth grade, which is really grade school, and maybe they finished when they were 12 and now they're 16 and they've been out of school for all that time. For that student, school is really difficult and [the teacher] feels for them. Especially in math, if they haven't been doing math for all these years and maybe even struggled with their multiplication and division or can't really remember how to do it, having them start in algebra is really a challenge.

For any student, having missed or forgotten foundational content and being thrown into a more advanced class would be difficult. For students with limited academic English, the difficulty was often insurmountable. Because of the many challenges—from financial to linguistic to academic—it was very common for Mexican students in Juan's cohort to leave high school before graduation. Many educators unfortunately came to consider that the expected outcome.

Juan himself followed a pathway different from his peers who left school to work. Despite being older than the usual age for ninth grade, with his brother's financial support he enrolled at Marshall High School and started in the ESL program. For him and other English-language learners, this initially involved a sheltered experience—with both ESL classes and some subject matter classes taught in Spanish. Because of the significant challenges finding certified bilingual teachers in math, science, history, and other subjects, it was not possible for the district to offer all classes in Spanish. In a normal year, they offered a few, and for other subjects the Mexican ESL students attended mainstream classes and received some support from bilingual paraprofessionals. In the ESL class itself, where students learned English from certified bilingual teachers, Juan told us that he felt well supported. He also had Mexican friends in the class. They supported each other and sat together in the cafeteria. ESL class sessions included friendly banter. On many occasions we observed students translating for each other, helping others who did not yet understand academic English.

During his first two years in high school, Juan passed key courses like algebra and business math. As his English improved, he transitioned into mainstream classes. By his junior year, he was taking academic classes at the high school in the morning and vocational tech classes in the afternoon—before going to work in the evening. He became interested in appliance repair as a possible career, because one of his brother's friends made a good living in that field. This aspiration provided motivation for him, as he confronted challenges posed by full-time school and part-time work. He spoke to us earnestly and optimistically about his prospects for greater economic success and a more comfortable life, if he could learn the skills and work in a trade. Juan's aspirations were not as ambitious as those that came naturally to many longstanding residents, nor were his goals as ambitious as those Allie and some of her peers could embrace only a decade later. But he did graduate from high school with skills for a career that his father and brothers did not have access to.

Juan was in many ways typical of the young Mexican migrants who enrolled at Marshall High School during the first decade of the Mexican community. He struggled to manage both work and school. He faced the challenge of learning English at the same time as he was responsible for learning subject matter. He was homesick. He was concerned about money, having to cover his expenses and wanting to contribute to his family back home. He was a victim of crime and worried about violence. He did not have much time to spend with friends, and his life included relatively few moments of joy and relaxation. He nonetheless worked hard and learned English, mastered high school subject matter, and developed vocational skills. He did not go on to higher education, but in challenging circumstances he obtained credentials to pursue a trade that required a high school diploma. Many of his peers who did not finish high school were also able to pursue stable, rewarding lives as entrepreneurs or craftsmen, but his high school diploma opened a few other possible pathways.

In this section, we have described various resources, from various scales, that contributed to Juan's pathway—for example, his arrival as a teenager with very limited English, his arrival early in the Mexican community's history when educators had few experiences with Mexican students, the financial situation of his family that forced him to work, but also the emotional support from his father and financial support from his older brother. Stories about Mexican students like Juan were also important resources shaping his pathway. Among educators and longstanding residents, the dominant story about Mexicans in Juan's generation was that they came to work. These stories largely characterized them as hardworking contributors to the community but (falsely) also as people who had limited academic capacity and poor prospects in school. Juan struggled against this to some extent, but he nonetheless felt its impact when he was guided onto the vocational track. Many of these resources have been described for Mexican students in similar situations (Behnke, Gonzalez, & Cox, 2010). But Juan did not simply follow a standard trajectory. Several of the resources available in his situation were somewhat distinctive, like his brother's financial support and his location in a relatively welcoming New Latino Diaspora community. His pathway was also contingent and emergent. At age seventeen, he could have moved in several other directions—returning to Mexico, dropping out of school, moving to California, pursuing higher education. Some of his peers did each of these things, but given the particular configuration of resources that in fact came into play his pathway emerged and solidified as it did.

Nancy in Middle School

Many in the next cohort of Mexican students in Marshall encountered a different set of resources than Juan. They learned English as young children, they attended US schools starting in kindergarten, and they thought of Marshall as home. Like Juan, however, many faced challenges from poverty, racism, and fear of deportation. Stories about Mexican children and youth that had been applied to Juan's generation also persisted into the second decade of the Mexican community. Many educators and longstanding residents continued to assume that younger Mexican children would face linguistic and cultural challenges that made academic success unlikely. This story misrepresented students' actual capacities and experiences, but Mexican schoolchildren nonetheless confronted the story as they moved forward in school. Mexican children in Nancy's cohort followed pathways that were constituted by this set of resources that were in some ways similar to and in some ways different from those relevant to Juan's cohort. As in all cohorts, however, individuals in Nancy's group sometimes diverged from the norm because of contingent events or processes that became relevant to their particular situations.

In this section, we describe how Nancy and her friends navigated school. We met Nancy in 2011 when she joined an after-school program for Latina girls at Marshall Middle School (MMS) created and run by Clonan-Roy (2018). From 2011 to 2015, Clonan-Roy spent time with Nancy in the after-school program, in middle and high school, in the community, in her home, and on social media. Through girls' group activities, interviews over dinner, and informal trips to the mall or downtown Marshall, Clonan-Roy learned about Nancy's personal story and her family's pathway. Nancy had moved to Marshall from Mexico when she was three, with her parents and three older brothers. While she was in middle school, Nancy lived alone with her parents. Extended family members moved into their home periodically, including her mother's sister-in-law and one brother's girlfriend and children. Two of her brothers were deported to Mexico when she was in fifth grade. Her third brother lived with his girlfriend and children nearby in Marshall. The deportations were traumatic for the family, both because of the loss of regular contact with loved ones and because of the ongoing fear that they created. One of Nancy's older brothers was subsequently killed in a car accident in Mexico. Nancy never saw him after he was deported.

Because of her gender and her position as the youngest member in the family, Nancy was not expected to earn money (Zambrana & Zoppi, 2002). Her brothers came to the United States when they were older, and they lived lives more like Juan's. They did not focus on school, but instead did physical labor to make money for themselves and their family. Nancy's parents were happy for her to attend school, learn English, and pursue a job that education could make available to her. Many families like Nancy's were mixed—with some children arriving later in life and pursuing pathways that looked more like Juan's, while

Figure 2.1 Marshall Middle School.

younger children had more educational opportunities like Nancy. Many of these families were also mixed status, with some younger children being US citizens (Mangual Figueroa, 2016).

Interethnic Relations

For kindergarten Nancy attended Archibald Elementary School. She had been in the United States for a couple of years before going to school, and she told us that she already spoke English relatively well at that point. But she struggled with reading and was placed in ESL. All Marshall elementary schools had pull-out programs for ESL students. Students attended mainstream classes, but they were pulled out occasionally for lessons with certified ESL teachers. These ESL classes brought together Mexican students, who generally enjoyed seeing their peers and having an opportunity to speak Spanish during the school day. Mainstream classes at all the elementary schools were ethnically mixed. During Nancy's years in elementary school, starting in 2003, Mexican students represented between 20 and 40 percent of the population at these schools. Several of the elementary schools were majority Black, but Archibald was further away from downtown and had a smaller population of Black students than the district as a whole. At that time Archibald had many White, some Mexican, and a few Black students. By the time Allie went to elementary school about five years later, three of the elementary schools had become or were approaching majority Mexican. But this had not yet happened when Nancy attended Archibald. As they still did five years later, Mexican students formed a demographic pyramid in the Marshall School District—with many more in the early grades and relatively few at the high school. This was changing by 2016 and will continue to change as the large group of Mexican elementary school students (including Allie) moves up to middle and high school. But during Nancy's time and beyond, stories about and treatment of Mexican students established during Juan's generation often persisted at the middle and high schools and were applied to Nancy and her peers.

Nancy told us that she had many Black friends in elementary school because "when you are little, you don't think about color." Peer groups were ethnically mixed, in contrast to Juan's experience at the high school around the same time—where ethnic segregation in the cafeteria and in friend groups was the norm. When she moved to middle school, however, interethnic relations changed. The Marshall School District had three middle schools: Wesson, Cox, and MMS. Nancy reported the typical student view—that Wesson had mostly Black and Mexican students, Cox had mostly Black students, and MMS was mostly White. As we will see, this perception of MMS was no longer accurate by the time Nancy arrived there. She began middle school at Wesson, then switched to MMS in eighth grade when her family moved to a different part of town.

Nancy told us that Wesson was "full of Black people" and that many of her acquaintances there in sixth and seventh grade had been African American. Nancy was still in ESL classes at that point, and she explained that ESL often sheltered Mexican students such that they did not have friends from other ethnic groups. But she said that this did not prevent her from making Black friends because she was "an open-minded person." We did not meet her until she arrived at MMS, so we have limited data on actual interethnic relations at Wesson. From the data we have, Wesson was apparently similar to many middle schools—with students beginning to form the ethnically based cliques that characterize secondary schools (Bucholtz, 1999; Eckert, 1987; Mendoza-Denton, 2008; Shankar, 2008).

An educator at MMS told us about the history of the middle schools, starting back when even Wesson was mostly White.

> My girlfriend is the principal at Wesson. Her and I taught together way back in the day ... She tells me that she has 50, 60, 70 percent Latinos. That's her breakdown in school ... So it really has changed, because the West end in Marshall [where Wesson is located] used to be you would have- I had a good

amount of White kids. And, not that I care. I don't really care what I get, but you could have anywhere from like [Field Street] on up. And then past Main Street ... You would have a lot of, like, really nice families that were predominantly White. And that has all changed. The dynamics have changed drastically.

Before Mexicans began to arrive in the mid-1990s, some White families remained in the West end and their children attended Wesson. These were "very nice families," according to this teacher's racial stereotype, in contrast to the poorer, non-White students who came later. Once the student population at Wesson became mostly Mexican and African American, the school became stigmatized, as the teacher went on to recount:

And there's this stigma, even within the kids. I hear it here [from MMS students in 2010] ... "Oh, I have to go to Wesson. Oh, I gotta go to that ghetto school. Ew." And kids want to stay here. And I don't know why. Because it's newer looking? Yeah, it's nice looking from the outside. But a school's a school, you know what I mean, as long as you have good teachers ... But that's not the way they think.

Whether she was just repeating these attitudes or subscribed to them herself, this teacher communicated the widespread racist view that Wesson was poorer and less nice, while MMS was higher status.

MMS, where Nancy spent her eighth-grade year, had a complex racial history. The building was renovated and expanded in the late 2000s. Students from downtown areas were bused to the expanded building. MMS was in a more affluent section of town. Educators referred to it as the "country club school" and youth often referred to it as "the White people school"—despite the fact that White students were a minority after the expansion. Black and Mexican students were transferred from their neighborhood schools to MMS, and this brought some racial tension. Teachers, as well as Mexican students, described conflict that had happened in school and on buses—sometimes involving Black youth saying that Mexican youth did not belong in the school and community, and sometimes involving White students making racist comments about Black and Mexican students. These tensions declined somewhat over time.

One teacher we spoke with had transferred to MMS right after the expansion.

So I was at Wesson for thirteen years, and then they made this the big middle school. Then some of us got transferred over, because we could quote unquote "handle downtown kids." ... [Back then] they really only had all the [White North Side] kids. And very, very little of the East end of Marshall ... We called this the country club school.

Here she mapped town social distinctions onto the middle schools. MMS was the "country club" school, for White students who lived on the North Side—the area least likely to have Black or Mexican residents. Wesson was for "downtown kids," meaning Black and Mexican students who lived in the downtown areas in the South and the East sides. These downtown kids required teachers who could "handle" them, because they were allegedly more challenging. This racist story about the neighborhoods and the middle schools circulated widely in Marshall.

Nancy began at MMS about five years after the expansion of the school. By that time the initial ethnic conflict had receded. The school had sizable Black, White, and Mexican populations, and students had to position themselves with respect to other groups. In one conversation at an after-school program, for example, Nancy and her friends described racial conflict and stereotypes at their school. They claimed that "we're not racist," but at one point in the conversation her friend said "I'm racist. Well, at points I will be racist because Black ... boys are always checking out my butt." A few minutes later, after some conversation about Black girls having expensive clothes Nancy claimed "that's why they're poor as shit." Her friend added, "That's why they are poor and can't afford a good house. But I have a good house and a lot of electronics." She went on to say that African Americans "are racist because they're always the ones that say I should go back across the border. They just do that because we're the easiest ones to target since we're already on the news, we already have the drug cartel, and all that other stuff. We're just really easy to target." Another friend added "and we come here because we want a good education and want to work, unlike them." Already in eighth grade, then, these Mexican girls repeated several common racist stereotypes about African Americans: they are poor, they are lazy, and Black males are sexually predatory. Nancy and her friends also described Mexicans as victims of Black racism. These stories about Black peers were inaccurate, but they circulated widely in Marshall as well as in the larger country.

Another educator at Nancy's school described interethnic relations in the school district. He confirmed the difference we have described between Mexican students who arrived later in life, starting in middle school or high school. "You'll find the Mexicans who, by and large, who have come later, all sit together and speak very little English. They get into clubs and they play soccer" together. For students like Nancy who arrived earlier, in contrast, "this is their country, and more and more of our students were born here ... It's very different growing up in the context of the United States." He claimed that residential segregation led White students to be somewhat removed from interethnic politics. "The White students just feel that they're detached in some way from all of this, that it doesn't affect them ... In other towns, there's a lot of racism on the part of White students, but we don't have as much of that in this district." As we have noted, White Marshall residents voiced some racist opinions about Mexicans and Blacks, but they did this less than White residents in many similar American towns. This teacher also added that, nonetheless, "there are definitely [interethnic] tensions. The kids are harassed on the buses." We heard many stories from Mexican children and parents about bad behavior by Black students on school buses in particular—with African Americans said to force Mexican children out of their seats and tell them to go back to Mexico. We heard enough first-hand reports of such events from Mexican parents and children that such incidents likely did occur, although we do not know how common they were.

Interethnic relations, then, were complex and shifted over time in MMS. When students were first bused in from downtown, familiar stereotypes about difficult "urban" students circulated widely. Black-Mexican tensions also surfaced. These stereotypes and tensions persisted at the time of Nancy's arrival, but during her time there Black and Mexican students also began to form friendships and even date each other. Widely circulating stories thus changed more slowly than and failed to capture the complexity of students' actual behaviors and experiences. As she completed her final year of middle school and prepared to transition to high school, there were various resources related to race that could have influenced Nancy's pathway—tensions between Mexicans and African Americans, emerging friendships between Mexican and African American students, some teacher's stories about Mexicans as difficult and unpromising, but also other teachers who were more encouraging.

Language

Nancy was still enrolled in the ESL program when she began sixth grade. This was a pull-out program in which she primarily attended mainstream classes but went to the ESL room for occasional lessons. Her ESL teacher, Mrs. Grayden, provided crucial support after her brothers were deported. This teacher was available to talk, and they discussed Nancy's sadness and fear. In seventh grade Nancy no longer needed ESL services, but Mrs. Grayden was still available for emotional support. In eighth grade Nancy switched to MMS, where she was no longer in ESL. This unintentionally removed sources of support—both the ESL teacher and Mexican peers who attended ESL classes. Nancy's route out of ESL was typical for Spanish-speaking students in her cohort. Most spoke Spanish but became fluent in English after several years and transitioned out of ESL into mainstream classes.

The fact that Nancy and other Mexican students sometimes spoke Spanish in school separated them in some ways from their White and Black peers. Elementary school teachers generally considered Spanish proficiency neutral or positive—either as a language that students had to use because they were still learning English or as a potential resource for staying connected to their families and providing career opportunities. Middle school and high school teachers more often considered Spanish a liability, as if the use of Spanish impeded students' growth in English or signaled a lack of English proficiency (Allard et al., 2014; Valenzuela, 1999). Educators at the middle and high schools often inappropriately characterized Mexican students as "at risk," and use of Spanish was often interpreted as an indicator of risk (Allard et al., 2014; Clonan-Roy, Rhodes, & Wortham, 2013; Clonan-Roy, Rhodes, & Wortham, 2016; Rosa, 2019).

The use of Spanish also sometimes caused interpersonal problems. Both educators and non-Mexican students often suspected Mexicans speaking Spanish were talking about English speakers who could not understand (Allard et al., 2014; Clonan-Roy, Rhodes, & Wortham, 2013; Clonan-Roy, Rhodes, & Wortham, 2016). Outside of elementary school, many White and Black residents complained that Mexicans made fun of them while speaking Spanish—even though they had no idea what the Mexicans were actually saying. Mexican students admitted that they did speak about others in Spanish at times, but they said it was relatively rare for them to speak in Spanish about a non-Spanish speaker who was present. Everyone agreed that English was the appropriate language of official schooling and that Mexican students should speak English while doing schoolwork. But they disagreed about the use of Spanish for other purposes while at school. For native Spanish speakers, it was natural to use their language when talking together, but others often found this threatening.

Among themselves, Mexicans sometimes accused other Mexicans who often spoke English of "acting White" and being "gringos." Nancy and her friends told us that these English-speaking Mexicans "act annoying and make corny jokes like White people" and are in higher-level classes than Mexicans who have lower English proficiency. Many Mexican students acknowledged that it was important to use English as the primary language at school but also believed that knowing and speaking Spanish were important. Among other things, their language established ethnic solidarity. When teachers disciplined Mexican students for speaking Spanish, the students often called the teachers "racist." Nonetheless, stories told by Black and White residents often positioned Mexicans as deficient, and these led some Mexicans to avoid Spanish in school, while other Mexican students labeled their peers as sell-outs when they used English too well (Clonan-Roy, Rhodes, & Wortham, 2013). As her pathway through school emerged, Nancy had to navigate these various beliefs and practices about race and language. She could have refused to speak Spanish in school, or she could have embraced Spanish and treated English as the language of the oppressor. In fact, she used both languages and did not adopt either of these positions.

Stories about "Hypersexual" Mexican Girls

From the beginning of our project in 2005, many Marshall educators spoke to us in ways that we have labelled a "moral panic about promiscuity" among Mexican girls (Clonan-Roy, Rhodes, & Wortham, 2016). In the early years, most of the stories presented Mexican girls as victims of predatory older Mexican men. Sometimes these stories contained derogatory characterizations of "Mexican culture," which allegedly permitted younger girls to become sexually involved with much older men. Toward the end of our time in Marshall, the stories tended to follow widespread discourses and more often unjustly blamed Mexican girls themselves for being provocative and promiscuous. For example, around the time when Nancy began at MMS, one day Stanton Wortham was translating for Mexican parents at parent-teacher conferences. All schools in the district had parent-teacher conferences twice a year. Because of the limited number of staff who spoke Spanish, members of our research team volunteered to translate for parents on these days as they met with their children's teachers.

On this occasion, a sixth-grade family came in with their daughter Geraldine to talk with the team of teachers. The teachers said some positive things about her academic work, and they shared a few minor concerns. Her mother asked several questions, but both parents were respectful and did not challenge the teachers. Her father asked about discipline, and the teachers assured them that Geraldine was not disruptive. At this point, the lead teacher turned to Geraldine and asked that she step out for a minute. The teacher then told her parents that Geraldine had been engaging in sexualized behavior with older boys. The mother was mortified, and Stanton Wortham felt terrible, fearing his Spanish was not good enough to communicate this shameful information in a tactful way. The mother asked for specifics—what exactly did Geraldine do, and with whom? The teachers were infuriatingly vague. Stanton Wortham tried to get them to be more specific. The teachers described an incident in which Geraldine was swaying her hips and flirting with an eighth-grade boy in a side hallway. The mother disagreed that this constituted the sort of sexual behavior the teachers initially described, and Stanton Wortham supported her interpretation. But she was also staring across the room at her daughter, who looked scared. The conference ended with both sides unsatisfied.

The teachers in this case were likely influenced by many resources—including both nationally and locally circulating stereotypes of Latina women and girls as hypersexual (García, 2009; Lundström, 2006; Rolón-Dow, 2004) and stories about Mexican adolescent girls in Marshall who allegedly engaged in sexual relationships. Several educators told us—inaccurately—that Mexican girls were more likely to date older boys, engage in sex, and suffer sexual abuse at younger ages than Black and White girls. As a result, educators claimed, Mexican girls became less academically engaged during middle school. Girls' experiences were in fact diverse, and our data indicate that very few middle school Mexican girls were sexually active, but this inaccurate story about promiscuous Mexican girls nonetheless circulated widely among educators.

We collected the following comments from MMS educators when we asked them open-ended questions about Mexican girls' sexuality.

> Mexican families are out of touch with US culture, customs, and laws, and because of this they allow their daughters to date much older men. Mexican girls assimilate too quickly, which causes them to initiate sexual activity at earlier ages. (A school district administrator)
>
> Mexican family parties cause problems because they allow older men to interact with younger girls and there is a lack of supervision. Crowded living conditions lead to girls' interactions with older men and can be causes of sexual abuse. (An ESL teacher)
>
> Early sexual activity and pregnancy are modeled in Mexican families by mothers, aunts, and other female family figures who have had babies at young ages. Many families are uneducated and do not value education as much as families who have experienced success through education. (A school district community liaison)

Educators supported such claims by telling stories about female Mexican students who had been dating older boys, having sex, dealing with pregnancy scares, or surviving sexual abuse. After extensive research with Mexican girls themselves, we have substantial evidence that this stereotype of hypersexual and sexually abused Mexican girls was not accurate and that this moral panic came from inaccurate overgeneralizations from a few girls' experiences.

One girl whom we have written about elsewhere (Clonan-Roy, Rhodes, & Wortham, 2016) did date an older boy and engage in sexual behavior, and she became publically identified as hypersexual. This girl was an acquaintance of Nancy's named Sara. Sara was labeled as sexually promiscuous during her first year at MMS. At that time, she had many close friends and a positive social reputation. In March of her first year in middle school, however, Sara started talking to her ex-boyfriend José, who was in eighth grade. He was dating another Mexican girl, but Sara snuck out of her house at night to go on walks with him. One day in March, Sara decided to skip an entire day of school to be with José. Sara later claimed that she skipped school to "make out" with him and have fun. This contingent event turned out to be pivotal in Sara's involuntary identification as a sexually promiscuous girl. Stories about this event circulated in and out of school, and this strongly influenced Sara's pathway both in school and out.

Sara's mother found out that Sara skipped school with José because one of their neighbors saw Sara walking with him in the neighborhood during school hours. Her mother asked MMS for help, and she scheduled a session with Sara and a guidance counselor. Sara subsequently told us that she was "really embarrassed" because her mother had said "all this stuff" about her and boys in front of the MMS administrator. She claimed that she hated her mom and frequently fought with her, and she called her a "bitch." She also said that since the incident she had felt bad at school because people had been spreading rumors about her having sex and that people—including people who she thought were her friends—were calling her a "slut," a "bitch," and a "prostitute." We did in fact hear stories about Sara from other girls at school. One eighth grader, for example, claimed that Sara "went to bed" with this young woman's ex-boyfriend Luis and that Sara was pregnant. We asked if that story was going around school and all the girls said yes. Another girl said that lots of stories go around about Sara because "she is a slut." A third then added, "and she's only in sixth grade!" This experience was particularly painful for Sara, and she ended up being ostracized by Mexican peers for the rest of her middle school career. Her experience was unusual, however. Educators used her story to confirm the stereotype, but the vast majority of Mexican girls at MMS used the story to distance themselves from Sara and were not themselves sexually active.

Nancy and her friends knew about educators' stereotype about hypersexuality, and they objected to it. They considered Mexican girls cooler and more adventurous than White girls, whom they characterized as "lame," studious, and conservative. But they characterized themselves as more conservative than the Black girls—a group they called "morenas"—whom they identified as "dirty," "poor," "ghetto," and more sexually promiscuous than Mexicans. Nancy said: "Isn't it weird that people think that we're the ones that lose virginity first?

But, I swear to God, man, Black people be losing their virginity first." The girls unfortunately resisted widespread characterizations of them as promiscuous by characterizing Black girls as more promiscuous. Black girls were not the primary people circulating the stereotype about Mexicans, but Mexicans nonetheless repeated widely circulating stereotypes about Black girls as hypersexual. This failed to target the influential people who most often circulated the stereotype about hypersexual Mexican girls—White educators.

Despite this particular kind of mutual stereotyping between Mexican and Black girls, relations between the two groups were often positive. As more and more Mexicans became fluent in English and enrolled in mainstream classes, they interacted regularly with Black and White students. In some cases, this led to dating across groups. When they arrived at Marshall High School in ninth grade, Nancy and her friends reported that there was much more interracial dating than they expected. Nancy told us, "Nowadays, you see Latina girls going out with Black guys, and even having mixed babies. And some Black girls do go out with Mexican guys." One of Nancy's friends described how she had started to be attracted to boys of other racial groups for the first time. She said that in middle school she had only dated Mexicans and thought that she would never date a Black boy. But when she got to high school she found many Black and White boys attractive. In ninth grade she started dating Carter, who was half Black and half White, and that changed her perspective. You cannot maintain negative opinions about a racial group, she said, if you love someone in that group.

The stories about Mexican girls as hypersexual illustrate how networks of contingent resources contributed to the positioning of Mexican migrants. The early Mexican community in Marshall contained many more men than women, and a few of these men did in fact date girls who were still enrolled in school. Educators noticed and told stories about these few cases. By the time we started our work in 2005, the story about Mexican girls being taken advantage of by older men was well entrenched among educators, and we heard it from several people. When Nancy was in middle school, many years later, however, the gender imbalance was mostly gone and the Mexican community was dominated by intact families—with many fewer single young men living on their own and with vigilant parents who tended to monitor their daughters. But school staff continued to tell the stories, and one example like Sara's was taken as confirmation of widespread hypersexuality among Mexican girls. This story drew on larger-scale resources as well. Girls and women of all ethnicities have to navigate accusations of "sluttiness." Black and Hispanic girls are often stereotyped as dropping out of school, becoming teenage mothers, having relationships with gang members, and being hypersexual and exotic (Denner and Guzman, 2006; Lundström, 2006; Rolón-Dow, 2004). But the particular situation faced by Nancy and her friends emerged at a historical moment in the changing Marshall Mexican community. Stories from an earlier era continued to circulate, and they positioned Mexican girls as victims prone to self-destructive early sexual behavior. These stories might not have circulated so densely in a community that had not gone through a phase of young, unattached Mexican men as Marshall did. The story faded somewhat by the time Allie and the next cohort of Mexican girls reached adolescence in Marshall schools. For a student like Sara, however, this story became crucial to her pathway—strongly influencing her choice of friends, her engagement in school, and her relations with family. For students like Nancy, it had some influence but was not as crucial.

Nancy enrolled in the culinary vocational program at Marshall High School and received her diploma. She planned to work in a restaurant or bakery kitchen. Unlike most members of Juan's generation, Nancy graduated from high school, spoke unaccented English, and had the training to pursue a career. But she pursued an educational and career pathway that resembled Juan's—from vocational tech programs to working-class jobs. Nancy did not consider postsecondary education, while Allie received more encouragement from educators to consider it. Nancy's school experiences were also influenced by stories about race, language, and sexuality that were less likely to influence student pathways in Allie's generation. These stories shaped how others treated Nancy and affected her own sense of self, making her feel more stigmatized and less promising than Allie did. Nancy's experience also differed from Juan and his peers in important ways. Members of Nancy's generation mixed much more with non-Mexican students. With this interethnic contact came tensions and stereotypes that constrained how Black and Mexican students could position themselves. During the first decade of the Mexican community, Black and Mexican residents were often wary of each other and had limited contact. By the time Nancy was in middle and high school, Black and Mexican students had significantly more contact. This created events with more explicit conflict and interethnic stereotyping, but it also opened new opportunities for interethnic connection and solidarity.

For Nancy and her friends, contingent historical events ended up becoming important catalysts for solidarity between Black and Mexican youth. They went through the middle years of adolescence at a social moment with increased awareness of racial violence and police racism. The murders of Black youth such as Trayvon Martin in 2012, Mike Brown and Tamir Rice in 2014 received national media attention, and widespread discussion of these events encouraged the girls to think about racism. After Trayvon Martin was killed in 2012, Nancy and several of her friends discussed their horror at this racist act. During a casual lunch at a local restaurant, following the acquittal of Trayvon Martin's killer George Zimmerman, the girls said that the murder of Trayvon was racist and one of her friends said that she was going to "kill Zimmerman." Nancy claimed that if Zimmerman had been African American and Trayvon had been White, then Zimmerman would have been found guilty. Her friend pointed out that the murder of Trayvon was portrayed as racist by news media, but that the media often overlooks racist crimes against Hispanics. She reported hearing a story about twelve Hispanic gang members being shot in a revenge killing at a funeral, and she was mad that no one talked about this event as racist.

At this historical moment, one striking instance of interethnic solidarity took place in Nancy's ninth-grade year. A White school district staff member posted on social media in response to a recent shooting of a police officer in a nearby city, writing that the Black community should be "mortified" by the criminals they "breed," and that they should "pull up their pants" and take off their "hoodies" in order to look less "shady." In response, 100 mostly Black and Mexican high school students, including Nancy and several friends, walked out of school during class, stood outside, and held hands in protest for twenty minutes. Mexican students saw this event as connected to other racialized events across the nation, especially the recent police shootings of Black youth and the Black Lives Matter movement. One told us that "the Black people and Mexican people are getting united." The School Board President condemned the "deplorable thoughts and opinions we can only describe as racist," and the Board voted unanimously to terminate the employee in question. This moment of Black-Mexican solidarity influenced Nancy because she and her friends happened to be together in school at the moment when these racist events happened. A network of contingent resources—increased contact between Black and Mexican youth in Marshall, national publicity surrounding police shootings of Black men, Mexicans' growing awareness of their own marginalization, as well as the employee's racist post—created an opportunity for change, for different stories about Black and Mexican youth and for new pathways that included interethnic connections. Chapter 6 picks up this theme of Black-Mexican solidarity, describing community organizations that brought Black and Mexican youth together in the same spirit.

Allie in Elementary School

Allie's parents Hernán and Mariana came to the United States in the early 2000s, a few years apart. Hernán came first, to work and send money back to his family. A few years later, Mariana joined him. We met them at St. Joseph's Church. Catherine Rhodes and one other member of the research team ended up spending over 200 hours with them across several years—including babysitting, tutoring, and hanging out in their apartment, offering advice and making trips to translate for them at schools and local government offices, as well as a tourist visit to New York City. They developed such a close relationship with Catherine Rhodes that they made her godmother to their two youngest children, they visited her parents when they were traveling to the DC area, and they enlisted her to visit their parents when she traveled to Mexico. They continue to call her, almost a decade later, to update her on the children or when they need advice.

Hernán crossed the border with a coyote who smuggled Mexicans into the United States. He paid $2,000 and walked through the desert all night. Once we watched a movie with him about a group of Mexicans crossing the border, and throughout the film he kept saying how it was "just like that"—people got hurt, were freezing, got left behind, died. Mariana walked across the border in Tijuana. Hernán and Mariana attended closely to reports of raids by migration authorities. Most Mexicans were very attuned to word-of-mouth reports about migration enforcement. As soon as someone heard about a raid or a roadblock, people would text each other. Because of this rapid dissemination of information, few Mexicans were stopped at roadblocks, while other drivers often waited in long lines. Whenever Hernán and Mariana heard reports of a raid, they would stay home for the day and keep Allie home from school as well. When they heard that migration authorities were going to people's houses, they would sometimes leave town for the day and take the family on a sightseeing trip.

By the time Allie began school in the late 2000s, the demographic transition from single men to intact nuclear families with young children was well established. Hernán and Mariana were part of the large group of young Mexican parents who settled in Marshall and began to raise families in the second decade of the migrant community. Like many others, they became more rooted in Marshall when they had children who were born there. There was Allie, her sister Yari, and a brother named Antonio. Because Hernán and Mariana's children were younger than Nancy and her siblings, Allie's family experience was different than Nancy's. Nancy was able to go to school without any expectation that she would work for money, but her brothers had lives more like Juan's. Allie and her siblings were all expected to attend school and build successful lives in the United States, with no expectation that they would leave school to work.

At home Allie spoke Spanish with her parents, who were monolingual Spanish speakers with middle school educations. When Allie started school, she joined a large cohort of other Spanish-speaking children. Like many Mexican peers she was placed in the ESL program, although her English quickly became better than her Spanish. Her parents often worried that Allie was losing Spanish. They said that she forgot words in Spanish, even though she knew them in English, and that she knew more words in English than in Spanish. They also remarked that Allie's sister started learning English words from Allie at a young age—notably, "juice." When members of our research team were around, Allie eagerly switched to English even though the researchers spoke Spanish in the house. In her later elementary school years, she began to use English syntax occasionally when speaking Spanish, and she sometimes said a word in Spanish with an English accent. Allie's parents nonetheless consistently supported her learning English. They encouraged the use of both languages with a rule: outside the house, speak whatever language you want, but inside the house use only Spanish.

Allie began kindergarten at age five at Grant Elementary School. In school Allie was able to use both English and Spanish. Teachers' attitudes toward Mexican students' use of Spanish differed in elementary and secondary schools (Allard et al., 2014). Secondary school teachers tended to take a "subtractive" approach, seeing Spanish as getting in the way of learning English (Valenzuela, 1999). But many elementary teachers in Marshall believed that Spanish-speaking children should maintain their home language, and many claimed that it was beneficial for them to use Spanish in the classroom. One told us:

> I think it's great [that students use Spanish]. Like my kids use it all the time amongst each other, whether it's in the classroom or outside, and I embrace that. I don't want them to lose that. As long as they're trying to learn English, then I'm happy ... I feel like I say it all the time. They are so lucky to be able to speak two languages. I wish I could, and honestly, it's the world we live in now, you know? Like I hope that they will keep speaking Spanish, and I mean, obviously, English, too. I would never want them to lose it—it's part of who they are.

Most of Allie's elementary school teachers felt that Spanish was valuable, as long as students were also learning and using English.

In her second and third years of elementary school, Allie's skill in English was noticed, praised, and encouraged. She quickly became an avid reader. Her second-grade teacher saw her talent and put her on the Reading Olympics team, where she excelled. Allie's love for reading was clear at the school's periodic book fairs. She repeatedly asked her teacher about the dates for the fair, attended to the posters advertising it, and eagerly awaited the day when the book fair arrived. The day before, she would ask her parents for money so that she could buy herself a book. One year we were at her family's home when she returned from school with a new book. She was particularly proud, telling us that the book had only been released a few days before: "I bought it today. And, this is the new one. The new book. The one that just came out, three days ago." She became a connoisseur, attending to release dates and pursuing recently published books. Her parents supported this both financially and emotionally.

Allie's experiences in school and with reading distinguished her from her parents, however. The day that Allie came home with that new book, her father was caring for the children. Catherine Rhodes was explaining to Hernán what she and his wife and children had spent the day doing, before his wife went to her job and he returned to care for the children. Allie chimed in and excitedly told him about her purchase. Catherine Rhodes explained that Allie had already read half the book since she arrived home from school, at which point Allie proceeded to reread parts of it out loud—correcting herself as she went—while Catherine Rhodes and her father talked. Hernán was happy to see his daughter's enthusiasm, and he admired her success in school, but he could not identify with it. While Allie was sitting next to him reading, he described differences between his own schooling and Allie's. He repeatedly said that, if he had only been asked to read as much as Allie when he was in school, his life might have been different:

> Did I like school? Not at all. [laughs] ... The school was nice. But I mostly didn't like going to school. I only went through the end of middle school and two years of high school. Nothing more ... I didn't like it, but I made a little effort. ... I didn't read books over there. They don't read books. Those who study, those who are in ... higher grades, yes, but ones who are her size, no. If only they had pushed us to read that much.

Allie's parents had fundamentally different educational experiences than their daughter was having in Marshall. In Mexico, in the rural schools Hernán attended, younger students were not encouraged to read. He perceived school as a chore. In contrast, Allie enjoyed school and was intrinsically motivated by reading.

In this respect, Allie also differed from Juan and Nancy. Not all Mexican students in Allie's generation loved reading or succeeded in school as she did. But children who entered school as the Mexican community moved into its second

Figure 2.2 Bilingual sign outside of a Marshall elementary school.

decade encountered resources that gave them more options. Juan confronted challenges like limited English skills and economic pressure to work, as well as the difficulty of entering American schools in ninth grade where he struggled with rigorous high school curricula. He did not have the time or the skills to develop a love of reading. Nancy spoke English fluently, but she entered a middle school environment that was still marked by ethnic divisions, where significant time and energy went into positioning oneself with respect to stories about what it meant to be Mexican. It would have been hard for her to imagine herself as an academic star. But Allie was younger and entered an elementary school context with different realities where such a pathway was more available. Events like book fairs and opportunities like the Reading Olympics team became important resources that influenced her pathway.

Allie's parents came to the United States to improve their lives economically. Initially they planned to save money and return to Mexico, and they continue to consider this possibility up to the present day. Their first goal was to save enough money to furnish their two-bedroom house in Querétaro. They had hoped this would take a year or two. They repeatedly pushed back their return date, however, due to new expenses and plans—primarily the arrival of the children. Having three children meant that they would no longer fit into their two-bedroom home in Mexico. They decided that they would not sell the existing house there but would instead keep it as an investment. Through their parents, they bought a piece of land for a new home. This required monthly payments on the land, plus saving for construction of another house. New expenses in the United States arose as well. A larger car was required for the growing family, for example. Allie's parents also realized that remaining in the United States would give their children opportunities unavailable in Mexico. They believed American schooling was high quality, and they saw their children becoming fluent in English. The children were born in a hospital, with the medical expenses covered, and as American citizens they received state-funded health insurance. As Allie and her siblings grew up in the United States, they became more Americanized and they seemed more and more likely to stay here. When we met them in 2010, Hernán and Mariana constantly talked about returning to Mexico, but by 2015 we spent days without the topic arising at all.

In addition to the heterogeneity we have described across Juan, Nancy, and Allie's cohorts, there was also significant heterogeneity within Allie's family. Allie, her parents, and her siblings were in fundamentally different positions. Allie's parents were undocumented migrants who did not speak English and had limited education. Demographically and economically, they resembled many of the migrants who came to the Marshall Mexican community in its first decade. But their position was fundamentally different than the single men who dominated the first decade, because they had an intact family and young children in American schools. Allie, in contrast, had many resources available to her that Hernán and Mariana did not—she spoke fluent English, and she was a strong student and an avid reader. Allie was a resource to her family, able to translate mail and paperwork from school and to communicate with English speakers outside the home. Many of Allie's peers were not US citizens, however, and this limited their futures. They spoke English and many succeeded in school just like Allie. But they did not qualify for government benefits like health insurance for children, and they would not be eligible for in-state tuition rates at public universities. Allie and her siblings, in contrast, had even more opportunities than Allie's undocumented peers.

When Allie started school in Marshall, she was part of a surge in Mexican school enrollment. Many migrant families started settling and having children around 2005, and Allie began school with the first large group of Mexican kindergarteners. Previous generations contained fewer Mexican students, and those students often moved around with their families and thus were in and out of school. By the time Allie entered school, however, Mexicans were a significant presence in Marshall schools. In 2012, Hispanics made up 27 percent of the school district population. By 2016, 37 percent of the district's students were Hispanic, as were the majority of kindergarteners. Allie also began school at a time when the school district served the large numbers of Mexican students more effectively than it had before. The district had hired a bilingual education coordinator, and each school had bilingual support staff and some bilingual teachers. Around 2010 one of the middle schools hired a bilingual vice-principal whose parents were Puerto Rican, and one of the elementary schools hired a Venezuelan principal. These Spanish-speaking administrators advocated for and reached out to Mexican families, although some of them also evaluated Mexicans' rural, working-class Spanish negatively. Allie received ESL support when she needed it, and she belonged to a large and important group of Mexican students in her school. This contrasted with Juan's experience, and to some extent with Nancy's—because in earlier years Marshall educators had been less familiar with Spanish-speaking students. The realities of schooling for Allie were fundamentally different than they had been for Juan in the first decade of the Mexican migrant community, and they were somewhat different than those faced by Nancy only a few years earlier.

Despite her fluency in English and her academic success, Allie often had to figure things out for herself in school. Her parents had limited experience with the Mexican educational system and no experience with American schools. They could not help her with homework or talk to her teachers without an interpreter. Allie benefited from being placed in ESL classes that provided her with extra attention, and early on she was able to take advantage of summer school that provided academic support to Spanish-speaking students. Allie also found mentors at school who got her involved in her school's book club and Reading Olympics team, and she was able to participate in district-wide competitions. Despite their lack of English, Allie's parents encouraged her academic and extracurricular activities, gave her money to purchase books, and attended her school events when they could.

When her younger siblings started school, as we were ending our time in Marshall in 2016, the landscape had changed further as more Mexican students made their way into and through the school system. Yari and Antonio had Allie's experience to help guide them. Allie's sister was doing well in both English and Spanish, but her brother struggled. It was hard to understand him when he spoke. His kindergarten teacher noticed this and had a conference with his parents. The school evaluated him and offered extra support. He was also enrolled in summer school. Since Allie and Yari grew up in the same home, the problem did not originate there. He may have had learning differences or a developmental challenge. Crucially, the school noticed the issue, paid attention, and offered him support. Marshall educators communicated successfully with his parents, and his educational prospects were much better than they could have been.

Allie was English-dominant by the middle of elementary school, and thus she did not fall victim to the stories about Spanish that Nancy experienced—for example, that Spanish is threatening and often used for the purpose of speaking badly about others. Allie was seen by teachers and peers as an excellent student, and her ability to speak Spanish was either not noticed or not held against her. At school she used Spanish rarely, mostly to interpret for her parents when they interacted with school staff. Allie was also "nerdy"—she wore glasses, always had her nose buried in a book, did not wear the latest fashions, stayed close to home, and in middle school was more interested in academics than boys. She was not considered promiscuous like Nancy and other middle school girls who liked to wear stylish jeans and name-brand shirts. She was nonetheless more mature than most children of her age. Like many children in similar situations, Allie was the primary means of communication between her parents and the English-speaking world and she bore significant responsibility for helping to run the household (Orellana, 2009).

Allie was not immune to stereotypes about Mexicans, however. People saw her as passive and nonthreatening, and this fit with the model minority stereotype. Like all Mexicans, she also encountered racism in school and in public spaces. But her case shows how, later in the second decade of the Marshall Mexican community, the story about Mexicans as diligent workers but unpromising students began to lose its influence over some Mexican children. Organizational arrangements that limited Juan and Nancy did not affect Allie. She was not segregated into a separate ESL track, for example, and her academic English was as good as her peers'. In the elementary schools especially, most educators had no difficulty imagining Mexican students like Allie as academically successful children who could represent the school in the Reading Olympics and go on to postsecondary success.

Allie's parents had talked for years about wanting to live in an unattached house with a yard, somewhere outside downtown Marshall. They wanted to move away from the types of people who lived downtown—primarily low-income Black and Mexican residents whom they described as sitting outside drinking alcohol and creating an unsafe environment for their kids. After Allie's first year of middle school, they moved to an unattached home away from downtown. This was a more affluent area, one with many White and fewer Mexican residents. They told us that there were no "paisanos" or fellow Mexicans there. They considered this a good thing, even though they had to drive downtown to find Spanish-speaking businesses and buy Mexican groceries. Their primary concern was escaping their loud, drunk neighbors in downtown Marshall and giving their children what they perceived as a better chance.

Hernán and Mariana had mixed feelings about the Black residents they encountered. Mariana in particular taught her children not to discriminate based on skin color. One day Yari came home from school and said that she did not like "morenos," and her mother immediately told her not to say that. At the same time, the family did not swim in the pool close to their apartment because, Mariana told us, "only Black people swim there." Mariana also told us about racism by African Americans against Mexicans:

> I don't know what the motive is, for why they don't like us. I don't know. There is a lot, a lot of racism. Even on the news I've heard that there are American people who kill Hispanics, African Americans who kill Hispanics, for the same reason, for racism. No, I don't know what the motive is for them having this feeling inside of themselves towards us ... There is a lot of racism, a lot of discrimination, on behalf of many people [of all races].

She immediately went on to add, however, that things were not all bad. In addition to racism, many Americans reached out.

> But, there are also American people ... who are good people, very kind, who help us ... I have encountered American people who don't speak Spanish, but they have tried to help me understand them, so that we understand one another, and this is very beautiful, too.

Living in the United States was challenging for migrants like Hernán and Mariana. They had to deal with homesickness, racism, the language barrier, and economic challenges, in addition to the hard work required to make a living and raise a family. But they nonetheless felt hopeful. They wanted to enact the classic positive American migrant story—working hard, overcoming difficulties, and successfully providing a brighter future for their children. This story vastly oversimplified the heterogeneous resources available to and the divergent pathways traveled by Mexican migrant families and children across cohorts and across individuals. The story sometimes unjustly characterized people who did not accomplish traditional "success" as deficient and to blame for their own difficulties. But it nonetheless guided many Mexican migrants' behavior—both motivating them to work hard and also leading them to distance themselves from those Black and Mexican residents whom they perceived as having diverged from the classic migrant pathway "up and out" of downtown Marshall.

While we should not uncritically accept this story as an accurate description or as the only admirable goal, we also should not condemn the many people who strove to enact it.

When Allie was younger, she helped take care of her younger brother and sister, but her mother was mostly home. With the move to the new house, however, and her uncle's subsequent return to Mexico, Hernán and Mariana had increased expenses. They both worked, Hernán at two jobs. After school and on Saturdays, Allie cared for her younger siblings. This limited her ability to socialize with other children and participate in extracurricular activities. Things would have been different if they had lived in Mexico. There most people rely heavily on family, and they would have had grandparents, cousins, aunts, and uncles to help with money, chores, and child care. But in the United States, Allie's family resembled a more typical nuclear American family. This created burdens and loss. But here too Hernán and Mariana emphasized the positive. They saw something beautiful in building their own family.

> Hernán: Two years ago, we spent New Year's alone, or Christmas alone?
> Mariana: New Year's
> Hernán: New Year's.
> Mariana: Yes.
> Hernán: We were alone, the three of us. It was Allie, her [Mariana], and me, alone, watching TV on New Year's, and … we started thinking, and we started talking, how it was before, in Mexico, we would have been with her parents, with my parents, and, no, it feels bad—but at the same time beautiful, because we are together, that is, as they say, we are made for each other.

Allie's family was not fully living the American Dream of migrants moving "up and out." Her parents were undocumented and spoke limited English, and each family member sometimes encountered hostility and racism. But they told a positive story about their lives, working hard to accomplish upward mobility for their children and believing that they would succeed. Many Mexicans in Marshall aspired to this, but even those children who entered school at the same time as Allie often did not follow a similar pathway. Most students, Mexican and otherwise, were not identified and supported for their academic skills as much as Allie, and some had pathways that were more strongly influenced by lack of documentation, racism, financial pressures, and other important resources.

Diverse Pathways through School

Juan, Nancy, and Allie represent the three most common types of Mexican students who enrolled in Marshall schools across the first two decades of Mexican migration. Over time, more and more Mexican students spoke fluent English, were academically successful, and expected to build lives and careers in the United States. By the end of our time in Marshall in 2016, the schools at all levels had many Mexican students. The large majority spoke English fluently, and most were American citizens. But the experiences and pathways of Mexican students from these different cohorts tended to vary, in part because of the different experiences they had in Marshall schools. The age at which a Mexican child entered school in the United States and the stage of the community's development at their time of entry were important resources that affected most students. The earlier in the development of the community they came, and the older they were on arrival, the more difficult it was to succeed in American schools.

In addition to these differences across cohorts, we also observed heterogeneity within cohorts. Even when they had similar backgrounds, not all Mexican students fared the same. As Allie's case illustrates, even more recently arrived Mexican students continued to face obstacles. Many migrant families struggled economically, and this burdened students like Allie with extra responsibilities involving work and childcare. Those without documents continued to live in fear of deportation, and undocumented students could not access educational benefits like in-state tuition rates at public universities. Many continued to face racism, as Nancy and others did with the "hypersexual Mexican girl" stereotype. Juan, Nancy, Allie, and their peers were in some ways representative of their cohorts, but individual Mexican students' pathways varied—depending on which of the many possibly relevant resources shaped their particular experiences and how these resources came together into networks that facilitated pathways that solidified in one direction or another. Nancy's friend Sara, for example, had her pathway shift and solidify in an atypical and unjust direction because of the stories about hypersexual Mexican girls that circulated widely among educators and the condemnation she received from educators and peers. In a more positive case, Juan graduated from high school at a time when most of his Mexican peers did not, in part because of his brother's support and his admiration for a friend who was succeeding in a particular trade. The diverse pathways individuals traveled were shaped by different networks of contingent resources that facilitated movement in various directions. These networks included oversimplified and often untrue stories—like those about "hypersexual" Mexican girls—but they included many other kinds of resources as well.

In classic stories, schools are crucial institutions for helping migrant students achieve better lives. These stories oversimplify. Marshall schools did provide opportunities to migrant students, and some moved toward academic and professional success. These successes sometimes relied on contingent resources—like the brother who offered to support Juan while he stayed in school or the teacher who noticed and nurtured Allie's love of reading. However, as they do everywhere, Marshall schools also foreclosed opportunities to some students at the same time as they offered opportunities to others. This happened sometimes because of more durable practices like segregated ESL classes and entrenched racist stereotypes about Mexicans' lower academic aptitude and aspirations. Some of Juan's peers, for example, left high school because no one gave them a sense that they could get jobs beyond those that require physical labor. But these more durable stories and practices did not determine individual outcomes. In Juan's case, others' low expectations did not keep him from finishing high school. On the other hand, unexpected, contingent resources sometimes pushed students toward less promising outcomes, as when Sarah decided to skip school that day and go off with her ex-boyfriend. In tracing Mexican migrants' emerging pathways, we must attend to contingent configurations of diverse resources that sometimes facilitate pathways toward familiar outcomes and at other times push individuals in more unusual directions. For ethical reasons, we should deplore and work against some stories and some institutional arrangements. The hypersexual Mexican girls stereotype, for example, was wrong ethically as well as empirically. However, we should not let our political commitments or our allegiance to particular academic theories obscure the empirical complexity of migrant experiences and pathways.

3

Churches: An Emerging Irish-Mexican Community

The last chapter illustrated several important components of our argument. We described individual Mexicans like Juan, Nancy, Allie, and Sara who followed both familiar and unexpected pathways, with divergence among individuals explained by the different configurations of resources that became relevant in each case. We analyzed how individuals' ontogenetic development took place in and was shaped by the development of the Mexican community across its first twenty years, and we also showed the occasional importance of discrete events (like Sara's date), thus illustrating how a complete account must include resources from at least these three scales. We showed how pathways emerge and solidify over time, as when Allie shifted from being an unpromising

Figure 3.1 Church in Marshall.

English-language learner to a promising student—as resources like her own love of reading and hard work, an attentive teacher, her supportive parents, and the Reading Olympics team coalesced. We also introduced oversimplified stories about Mexicans and explained how these combined with other resources to make diverse pathways possible, like stories about Mexicans as diligent but unpromising and stories about hypersexual Mexican girls.

This chapter on churches focuses more directly on stories about and realities of interethnic relations as another set of important resources that shaped Mexicans' diverse pathways. In addition to ontogenetic development over years and community development over decades, we must also consider realities that emerged across decades and centuries as successive migrant groups settled in town and interacted with each other. Mexican migrants entered a setting deeply influenced by previous migrant groups that were following divergent pathways of their own. This chapter begins to provide more detail about these interethnic relations, focusing on Mexicans' emerging connections with Irish Americans in church. We trace the development of an interethnic community across two decades in one church, emphasizing collective pathways. Individual pathways always take shape within, and are often deeply influenced by, the collective pathways being traveled by relevant groups. In order to give a more complete picture of these nested pathways in Marshall, the last chapter introduced divergence in individual Mexicans' pathways and this one describes divergent collective pathways being traveled by two different church communities. Subsequent chapters add descriptions of complex relations among Black, White, and Mexican residents. A full account of migration in Marshall must describe interconnections among pathways at all these scales.

At St. Joseph's parish, interethnic relations developed in a way that is recognizable from familiar positive stories of migration. Some parishioners were more welcoming than others, but a core group of Irish Americans gave Mexican migrants opportunities first for involvement and eventually for leadership in the church. As many Mexicans came to play more central roles, the church and many Irish American parishioners incorporated Mexican elements into their worship and the two groups created emergent, hybrid beliefs and practices. Our analysis shows how—despite the fact that these Irish American and Mexican parishioners traveled a positive, somewhat familiar pathway toward interethnic rapprochement and productive mutual change—this outcome depended in part on contingent, local resources and did not simply unfold according to a predictable script. In contrast to this positive case of interethnic connection and mutual transformation at St. Joseph's, we describe another church where efforts to welcome Mexicans failed because of negative stories about and actions toward migrants. Despite many similarities, these two church communities took different pathways because of different contingent resources that became salient in each case. The descriptions of interethnic relations in this chapter begin to illustrate how the two-decade development of the Mexican community and the two-century development of relations among migrant communities in Marshall intersected in various ways.

In both Mexico and the United States, church plays a central role in many Mexicans' lives, as a site for religious practice and cultural events (Badillo, 2006; Donoso, 2014). For many Mexican migrants in Marshall, church was particularly important. They went to church for emotional support, for spiritual guidance, for the opportunity to speak and hear Spanish in a public space, and for cultural events that reminded them of home. In church Mexican migrants also built relationships with longstanding Marshall residents. This encounter was more complex than one might expect from simple migration stories. Mexicans did not just assimilate to American practices in church, nor did they create their own separate cultural space. St. Joseph's allowed Mexicans to enact some of their own traditions in ways that eventually connected them to longstanding residents, and the connections between the communities caused both groups and the church itself to change significantly in the second decade.

Marshall had been home to churches of various denominations since its founding. Catholic churches had predominated since the late nineteenth century, but several Protestant churches remained and a few evangelical Protestant churches were growing during our time there. These latter churches had been proselytizing to Mexican migrants, as they have been doing throughout the Americas, and some migrants had begun to attend them. But by far the most important church for Mexicans—in the whole region, well beyond Marshall—was St. Joseph's Catholic Church. There were two other Catholic churches in town, which had traditionally served the Polish and Italian communities. But it was the historically Irish Catholic church that welcomed Mexicans. By 2010, St. Joseph's had over 1,000 Mexican families as members. The weekly Spanish-language mass on Sunday at noon often had 400 and occasionally as many as 600 in attendance, with the balcony sometimes overflowing and people standing several deep in the back of the sanctuary.

This chapter describes St. Joseph's and its growing success in engaging Mexican families. In the first decade of the Mexican migrant community, a few Mexicans attended St. Joseph's regularly. However, before 2000 the parish priest did not speak Spanish. In 1995, he invited a Spanish-speaking priest to begin offering one mass on Sundays. Those who attended this mass appreciated it, but the Spanish-speaking priest was in town only for that mass and the Mexican community did not connect deeply with the church. Two contingent things changed the situation at St. Joseph's in the next decade. First, as the Mexican community shifted from single men to intact families, many parents with young children wanted their children to participate in various church ceremonies. Second, Father Kelly was assigned to the parish in 2002. He spoke Spanish well and was particularly successful both in welcoming Mexican migrants and in building connections between Mexican and White parishioners.

In his early years at St. Joseph's, Father Kelly's parish offered a separate but welcoming space for Mexican migrants to participate in Spanish and enact culturally familiar religious practices. Father Kelly and his Mexican parishioners celebrated events that ranged from widely known ones like *las mañanitas a la Virgen de Guadalupe*, the Mexican celebration of the Virgin Mary on December 12, to festivals for patron saints of small villages where particular residents had been raised. Over time, Father Kelly involved White parishioners in many of these Mexican events, and he hosted hybrid events in which White and Mexican parishioners could draw on both English and Spanish and participate together. Almost all White parishioners felt secure in their status as natives and expected that Mexicans would follow the familiar but partly inaccurate story and assimilate, just as they imagined their own immigrant ancestors had. But in practice—as described by Alba and Nee (2003)—the longstanding community was also changed by the participation of Mexicans. Spanish became more familiar, aspects of Mexican Catholicism became more salient, and White parishioners began to participate in events unfamiliar to Irish or other American Catholics. By 2010, there was a robust bicultural community, one that included several hundred families who participated at least occasionally in bilingual masses and celebrations. This was good for the church as well as the migrants, because the large influx of Mexicans revitalized a parish where attendance had been dwindling.

The interethnic connections that developed at St. Joseph's did not include many African Americans. The parish had consistently welcomed a handful of Black parishioners for almost a century, but by the time of Mexicans' arrival there were fewer Black parishioners left. We did not observe any overt exclusion of Blacks, but the church did not reach out to African American residents in the same way that it did to Mexicans. Whatever the causes of their absence, almost no Blacks participated in the rapprochement between White and Mexican residents that took place at St. Joseph's. The contingent fact that relatively few African Americans in Marshall were Catholic—together with the fact that St. Joseph's turned out to be the community space where Mexicans built positive interethnic connections most effectively in Marshall—meant that Black Marshall residents were not in a position to connect with Mexican migrants at church. This contingent fact was unfortunate, because such positive interethnic contact might have provided opportunities to dispel stereotypes on all sides.

The following account of Mexicans' experiences at St. Joseph's comes from hundreds of hours we spent both in church and following members of the congregation into their homes and the broader community. We interviewed Father Kelly during our first year in Marshall, and members of the research team attended mass and other celebrations there throughout our eleven years. Three members of the team spent at least 200 hours in and around the church in 2010 as part of an intensive data gathering effort. In the process, we interviewed several dozen parishioners and spent extensive time in the homes of four families. We also interviewed Father Kelly several times and observed him at dozens of masses and celebrations. We have continued to maintain contact with him, after he was reassigned to another parish and subsequently to an inner-city mission, including a trip that he made to visit us after the end of our data collection in 2016.

The History of St. Joseph's

The emergence of a robust interethnic community at St. Joseph's provides our first extended analysis of collective pathways. St. Joseph's was founded by Irish migrants about twenty years after the incorporation of Marshall. During Father Kelly's tenure, it celebrated its 175th anniversary. Like most other churches in town, at its founding it largely served one ethnic group. Most Irish migrants came to the area to work on the railroads, and many settled in and around Marshall. St. Joseph's offered both Catholic religious services and cultural events that were familiar to Irish migrants. It was, however, a "territorial" church from the beginning. As the first Catholic church in town, throughout its history it has been open to all Catholics in the area. Other Catholic churches were founded as "national" churches to serve specific ethnic communities. Holy Trinity, for instance, was founded around the turn of the twentieth century to serve Italians in particular. It offered masses in Italian, and a parishioner had to be Italian on at least one side of the family to belong. In its heyday, Marshall had five Catholic parishes, but by our time in town there were three. Throughout its history, St. Joseph's was the primary territorial church. Most Catholics nonetheless identified it as the "Irish parish," and there were Irish symbols like shamrocks carved into the building itself. Throughout our eleven years in town, the church continued to celebrate Irish festivals in which parishioners dressed in traditional Irish costumes and held banners naming the counties of Ireland.

According to some parishioners, the Irish history of St. Joseph's facilitated the incorporation of Mexican migrants. Meghan McCarthy, the Director of Faith Formation, told us that the memory of Irish migration made parishioners more welcoming to Mexicans. When Mexican migrants started arriving, she said:

> It was more of a sense of pride of including them ... It wasn't like an overnight, oh my gosh, what are they doing here kind of thing ... I'm sure there may be one or two that we have lost because of the influx of Hispanics to our community, but ... there's a sense of pride at St. Joseph's for being a community that welcomes migrants. And I think a lot of that has to do with the fact that our parishioners don't forget that our church was founded on Irish migrants.

As Meghan mentioned, not every parishioner accepted the arrival of the Mexican migrants. Most Irish migrants to the United States arrived long ago, and many Irish Americans do not have personal memories of their migrant ancestors—although many in Marshall did. Some parishioners were not welcoming, and some circulated racist stereotypes. Nonetheless, both we and Father Kelly were surprised that most of the active Irish American church members embraced the church's efforts to include Mexicans. We never experienced an event in the church where White parishioners were publicly hostile to Mexicans. We did hear some hostile comments outside of church, however, and some former parishioners did stop attending the church after Mexicans' arrival.

It is interesting to contrast Irish and Italian American residents. As documented in the next chapter, Italians and Italian Americans in Marshall were more likely than the Irish to remember their migrant histories. In most cases, Italian migrant ancestors had arrived more recently. Many Italians also saw significant similarities between their ancestors' experiences and Mexican migrants'. The partial mutual intelligibility of the Italian and Spanish languages and some cultural similarities between Mexicans and Italians led many Italian-origin Marshall residents to empathize with Mexican migrants. Many Italians had felt stereotyped and excluded by the Irish when they migrated in the first half of the twentieth century, and the memory of that discrimination continued into the twenty-first century. As a result, some Italian Americans tried not to do the same thing to Mexicans that other residents had done to them. On average, in our experience, Italian Americans in Marshall were more welcoming than Irish American and other White residents. But in church, despite the fact that

Mexicans and Italians were both overwhelmingly Catholic, there was almost no connection between Italian Americans and Mexicans. Mexicans were not allowed to join the Italian church. Many tried, but they were redirected to St. Joseph's. At St. Joseph's, it was mostly people of Irish origin who welcomed the newcomers. This church was an exception to the general rule of Italian Americans being more welcoming to Mexicans in Marshall, for two reasons. First, Father Kelly himself was determined to bring the communities together, and the efforts of this one leader made a difference. Second, St. Joseph's faced a more rapidly dwindling membership than the Italian church, and committed Irish American parishioners seized the opportunity to revitalize their parish.

Black Marshall residents mostly attended African Methodist Episcopal and Baptist churches in town. Ever since the beginning of the Black community, however, there had been a few Black Catholic families that belonged to St. Joseph's. During the Civil Rights Movement, St. Joseph's School was perhaps the most visible space for integration between Black and White residents in town. Starting in the 1960s, each class had several Black students, up until the school closed because of low enrollments in the early 1990s. Molly Trent, a parishioner whose ancestors included an Austrian migrant grandmother, recalled it this way:

> When I went to grade school at St. Joseph's it was a humongous school ... We probably had 45, 50 kids in my class ... It was integrated. I think it was integrated in a time when there wasn't a lot of integration ... There weren't Hispanics, but we had African Americans in our class. People have always said St. Joseph's is a welcoming parish, and I think it is ... The segregation in grade school was boys and girls—boys sat in front and girls sat in back.

In retrospect, at least, the welcome that the church had extended to African Americans foreshadowed its openness to Mexicans. But African American and Mexican migration took place in different eras, and by the time Mexicans began coming to St. Joseph's the school had closed and there were fewer Black parishioners remaining. Despite its history as a progressive site of integration during the Civil Rights Movement, the church was not able to build community between Black and Mexican residents in the way it built connections between White and Mexican residents. Mexicans and African Americans did not have an opportunity to build interethnic relations in church because of the scarcity of Black Catholics and the closing of the parish school before Mexicans arrived.

The church community itself had dwindled dramatically in the 1990s. We heard varying accounts—with some saying fewer than 50 people regularly attended Sunday masses in the late 1990s and others estimating 100–150. The numbers were in any case much lower than they had been in previous decades, and the large sanctuary felt empty with only 100 people in it. Less than ten years later, Spanish-language masses attracted 400–600 people. Father Kelly described this change when speaking to us in 2010:

> The parish started a mass in Spanish about 1995. A different priest would come who spoke Spanish, to take care of their cultural needs and the different feasts and celebrations they had in the Mexican community. And I've been here for eight years and I would say that coming to church we have about 1000 different Mexican families ... We do still have here about 500 English-speaking families. Some are African [American] and others have different backgrounds. We also have a few from Haiti. We still have two masses in English. We also have two masses in Spanish on the weekend ... This past year we had 250 baptisms, and about 248 of them were Mexican, because they are a very young community too.

In 2002, with the arrival of Father Kelly as a full-time bilingual priest, the church became more welcoming and Mexicans started to engage more deeply.

St. Joseph's White parishioners had mostly moved out of Marshall itself and lived in surrounding suburbs. In contrast, the Mexican parishioners almost all lived downtown, relatively close to St. Joseph's. Father Kelly said that his Hispanic families were "95 percent Mexican. We have a few from Costa Rica, a few from El Salvador, a few from Honduras, one or two from Bolivia, Peru, a few Puerto Ricans." Many Mexicans:

> are coming from Querétaro in Mexico. You know, I joke with them, "Is there anyone left in Querétaro?" because everyone here is from Querétaro. Some from Veracruz ... They're coming from the ... more rural areas, and they tend to have minimal education ... A lot of the jobs that the men are doing are landscaping, hotel work, restaurant work, and the women, a lot of them work at the mall.

When we spoke to Father Kelly in 2005, in his third year at the parish, he already described a thriving community and strong interest in church even among second-generation Mexicans.

> The Mexicans identify themselves as Catholic. *US News and World Report* did an article a while back that the second or third generations of Mexicans aren't identifying themselves as readily with the Catholic Church. But nonetheless, around here—I laugh, because now and then someone will say, "They're leaving the Catholic Church in droves." And I'll go up to Sunday Mass and say, "Well where are they going?" ... It's pretty packed! ... All young. It's amazing. The median age is ... more younger than older. Still a lot of single men who come up,

you know, to work. I'm wondering if they're thinking of going back. And some of them do go back—some of them actually do leave their wives and come up here to make money and go back, a lot of back and forth. A lot of young families—like I said, last year there were 160 baptisms.

In 2005, Father Kelly was already seeing the first group of young Mexican families having children in Marshall and bringing them for baptism. The 160 baptisms he reported in 2005, though a healthy number, were significantly fewer than the 250 he reported in 2010—as the number of Mexican couples with young children grew. The transition from single men to families was well underway in 2005 but accelerated over the following five years.

White parishioners like Molly Trent started to notice the contrast between packed Spanish-language masses and sparsely attended English-language ones.

When I started noticing how many were going to the 12 o'clock mass and they were filling the church, that was pretty amazing. Having a separate Spanish mass and having the church filled—you know, it wasn't filled with Anglos.

One year her husband Aaron attended the traditional gathering on December 12 at 4:00 a.m. that begins the celebration for the Virgin of Guadalupe, and he told us that "I felt like I was someplace else. I don't speak Spanish, so I didn't understand what was going on … but it was an experience" to see the church completely full at that hour, with people singing and everyone's vehicles decorated with flashing lights and images of the Virgin. Molly added: "Filling the church at that time of day is pretty amazing, you know, with people of faith who show up."

Figure 3.2 Early morning celebration of the Virgen de Guadalupe.

Molly and her husband illustrated two different responses to the Mexican migration. Molly herself was deeply observant and had been involved in the parish her entire life. She felt connected to the Mexican migrants because of their shared faith, and she was moved by many migrants' devotion to Catholicism and to the parish. She told us more than once about her own (Austrian) migrant grandmother's difficulties learning English, and she empathized with Mexicans' struggles. She also volunteered to host events in her home that brought together Mexican and White parishioners. Her husband was not hostile to the migrants, but his comment that "it was an experience" to see so many Mexicans in church communicated his ambivalence. On one occasion in their kitchen, when we were speaking with the two of them and their son, he commented that "it's not St. Joseph's anymore—it's St. José's." He said this as a joke, but with a trace of bitterness. He continued to attend church with his wife occasionally, and we did not hear him object to the bicultural events hosted in his home, but he did not welcome the newcomers in the same way his wife did. We heard occasional stories about former parishioners with similar negative feelings about Mexicans who often drifted away from St. Joseph's.

Mexicans became more and more visible as members of the church in the mid-2000s. By the late 2000s, Mexicans themselves felt as if they had a significant place in the church, as if they were not just guests but central members. Julio Cervantes was born in Mexico. After migrating to Marshall, he served as an altar boy. He told us how participation in a church event one day made him realize how important Mexicans had become to the parish. "We are growing, we are growing as a community … In the parade at St. Joseph's—I think it was last year—they had people dressed in their different cultural dresses, and that made me realize we [Mexicans] are really all over the place now." Because of Father Kelly's efforts to include them, because of their growing numbers and involvement, and because the church provided a space to hear Mexican Spanish and participate in culturally familiar events, St. Joseph's became one of the first places in Marshall where Mexican migrants felt as if they belonged and had some ownership of the institution. This was not a simple story of assimilation by migrants, however, because Mexicans changed St. Joseph's at the same time as it changed them.

Growing Mexican Involvement

Mexican migrants came to St. Joseph's for various reasons. Almost every Mexican parishioner we spoke with cited Father Kelly and his consistent efforts to serve their community as a crucial factor drawing them to this particular church. Almost all loved the opportunity to hear and use Spanish. Most appreciated the Mexican cultural themes and celebrations they found at St. Joseph's, and many attended church events in order to feel more connected to Mexico. Some went to mass for religious reasons, to feel close to God and to obey church teachings. Some went in order to connect to American culture and to practice English, hoping to learn more about their new home and become "better Americans." Some appreciated the meetings with town officials whom Father Kelly invited to share information with Mexican parishioners. Whatever their motivations, almost all Mexican parishioners felt more welcomed and appreciated in the church than in almost any other space in town.

Hernán and Mariana, for example, were not devout people or regular church attendees, but they considered themselves part of the St. Joseph's community and felt comfortable in the church. They originally began to attend St. Joseph's because they had grown up with the Catholic church. As Mariana said, "many Mexicans in Marshall feel a connection to the church" because it was a central part of their lives in Mexico. They wanted to maintain those religious and cultural traditions in the United States, for themselves and for their children. On their first visit to the church, Mariana was struck by "how beautiful the building was, ... very different from Mexico." She went to church:

> to give thanks because we are here and we are alive ... [God] is giving the motivation, and he's giving us work, to eat, and to help ourselves and to tend to our families. Perhaps that's our motive, the motivation of many to go to church and give thanks ... I went to church to give thanks to God for my being here, because many people cannot come here.

Many of the Mexican migrants had experienced trauma and dislocation in coming to America. Mariana and Hernán were happy to be together with their nuclear family in the United States, but they needed to process both the traumatic experiences they had while migrating and the unfamiliarity of life in America. The church gave them a space to do this, together with others who were sharing similar experiences. Like many migrants, they were also lonely. As Mariana told us, "here we feel alone, without family; many people are here alone without children or parents." Most rural Mexicans live near extended family and are used to having many relatives around, and living with only a nuclear family was difficult for many of them. The church provided a community that helped ameliorate this loneliness by offering comforting events in Spanish.

Raúl Ortega migrated to Marshall before Father Kelly arrived in 2002. He was devout, and he had attended St. Joseph's since his arrival in town. But he became much more involved over time. Early in his tenure, Father Kelly invited Raúl's wife Carmen to start a prayer group based on Mexican religious practices, and he encouraged her to lead discussions of Mexican culture and religious tradition. She welcomed the invitation and responded by becoming more involved, and Raúl came to church along with her for these events. He found a growing, supportive, like-minded community at St. Joseph's.

> All of us Latinos, together and united. It is very nice that the community, that we understand one another in this way, and it's the reason why St. Joseph's has been growing so much … Thanks to all of the people that it has, people of Catholic faith, and thanks as well to the opportunities offered by the church, the outreach. They … have given us the opportunity to continue our traditions … So we, the whole community, are very grateful … Father Kelly began to give me more opportunity, because one day I saw that he is alone, he didn't have another "párrafo" [server] to help him to give the masses, so it was then that I learned how to light the candles.

As more Mexicans found a welcoming environment and began coming to church regularly, Father Kelly would invite them to take on leadership roles. Some, like Raúl and Carmen, were energized by the opportunities and became even more involved. In turn, their energy and involvement enriched the church.

Most spaces in town were dominated by English speakers, who were at best alien and at worst overtly hostile. In contrast, Father Kelly spoke Spanish and treated them with respect and trust. Raúl described how important this was.

> Simply having the respect of the priest who had given me the opportunity—he gave me his trust, and had talks with me and things. I wanted … to be able to help the church more. It is because of how the priest trusted us, that we feel very content in the church. The whole community there, the American people as well.

Life was stressful for Mexican migrants in Marshall. They mostly worked for bosses who appreciated their labor but did not speak their language and were not interested in them as human beings. Outside of the nuclear family and a few Mexican-owned businesses, they had few places where they could feel comfortable, and fewer where they could experience a sense of ownership and respect. Father Kelly created such a space at St. Joseph's. The environment was not perfect. Some White parishioners, although they did not complain directly to the priest, were not comfortable interacting with Mexicans, and some circulated false and hurtful racial stereotypes. Furthermore, the majority of Mexicans in Marshall did not attend this church. But for the core group of about one hundred Mexican families who attended regularly, St. Joseph's was a crucial space. For another several hundred Mexican families who attended occasionally, it provided an opportunity to connect to their traditions, to each other and to the approximately one hundred White families who also participated regularly in church.

Sister Carmela was a nun employed full-time at St. Joseph's. Her perspective on Mexicans helps us see how the migrant community did not simply experience acceptance and assimilation at St. Joseph's. Originally from Argentina, she had served for many years in other parts of the United States, but she had been hoping to work at a church with a burgeoning Hispanic population. The diocesan leaders had sent Father Kelly to serve the growing Mexican community in Marshall, and after a few years they supported his efforts by assigning Sister Carmela there as well. She encouraged Mexican families to embrace both their home culture and American culture they found in Marshall. She saw the church as a place for intercultural connection.

> I think that for the Latino community, it is important that they get to know the culture of the host country … to love and take in the good that's here … not simply to say, well I'm Mexican and I just want to work. The fact that you're in this country, you have to take in the good of both cultures. It's not completely Mexican, in my case Argentine, or completely from the US, because you already have another culture in you. It's about accepting who you are, and take in the new, and do something different … The host community must learn also—both sides.

In order to be a good community member and a good person, Sister Carmela counseled migrants that they needed to expand beyond their own Mexican culture. They should remain connected to their Mexican heritage and its strengths, but they should also connect to positive aspects of American culture. She pushed them to move beyond treating the church as a refuge for exclusively Mexican experiences, but she did not advocate assimilation either. She saw that the migrants and longstanding residents influenced each other, such that the larger church community became something new.

Her comments begin to move beyond oversimplified stories about migrants assimilating to allegedly stable host cultures. Neither Mexican nor American culture was stable. Instead of imagining assimilation, or a simple combination of two stable cultures, it would be more accurate to imagine two heterogeneous sets of beliefs and practices—both of which were developing—intersecting with and changing each other. St. Joseph's itself was changing as a community before Mexicans arrived—with membership dwindling and regular churchgoers becoming older, with the memory of migrant roots fading, and with the loss of a local parish community that used to live nearby. The migrants transformed the parish, bringing youth and energy as well as Mexican traditions. Father Kelly embraced this, creating more spaces where Mexican and White parishioners could interact with and learn about each other. He held bilingual masses with mixed congregations. He presided over Mexican cultural traditions like *las posadas* that sometimes took place in White families' homes, where Mexican guitarists traveled from home to home and ate American food while singing Christmas carols alternately in Spanish and English. The parish became a new space—not one in which Mexicans assimilated to American culture, nor one that combined two stable cultures, but instead one that saw the development of new practices and identities. At St. Joseph's, as elsewhere in Marshall, individuals, institutions, and communities changed across the two decades of Mexican migration, and the resulting pathways cannot be reduced to simple stories of assimilation, combination, or resistance.

Father Kelly was a key resource that made possible the more welcoming reception Mexicans received at St. Joseph's. The contingent fact of his assignment to the parish, at the same historical moment that young Mexican families were beginning to settle in larger numbers, was key both to Mexicans' deeper, more rewarding involvement at church and to the emergence of productive interethnic relations between Irish Americans and Mexican migrants. He combined the two existing Parish Councils—which had met separately, one in Spanish and one in English—and he ran bilingual Council meetings. He created English classes for Mexican parishioners and recruited White parishioners to teach them. He also followed the suggestion of one Mexican volunteer and created Spanish classes for White parishioners, which were taught by Mexican parishioners. He presided over Mexican cultural events—not just big ones like the celebration of the *Virgen de Guadalupe*, but also feasts for patron saints of small villages, and ceremonies where forty-day-old babies are blessed.

The emerging, positive interethnic connections at St. Joseph's contrasted with a neighboring Protestant church, Good Hope, that also tried to attract Mexican migrants. Like St. Joseph's, this church had seen its membership dwindle—from almost 1,000 families in the 1970s to less than half of that when we first spoke with the pastor in 2005. This church brought in a Spanish-speaking minister to offer services and invited Mexican migrants to join them. Good Hope and St. Joseph's had some important differences, however. The bilingual minister did not replace the regular pastor, but simply came once a week to offer services in Spanish. This did not foster interethnic connections. St. Joseph's had a similar situation until Father Kelly's arrival in 2002. Neither church succeeded in building community with part-time Spanish-speaking clergy. A small group of devout Mexicans continued to attend each church during these periods, but the group remained small and a robust Mexican church community did not develop in either place.

The other crucial difference between the churches was the leaders' different attitudes. The full-time pastor at Good Hope, who asked us to call him "Pastor Dave," expressed negative, racist views about Mexicans. This probably discouraged some migrants from joining his parish. In our first interview with him, we were taken aback when he began by talking about how, with Mexicans' arrival in Marshall,

> you're gonna being seeing a lot of STD's and one of the STD's is going to be AIDS and no Mexican male is going to admit to it or get treatment because AIDS is not a macho thing. "It's only maricóns [male homosexuals] that have AIDS," that's one of the things. A lot of them are also becoming trapped in American materialism. I don't know how this is going to work, but they come up here to help feed their families and all of a sudden you see them driving around in SUV's and I don't know what's happening with their families. Uh, you know about cristo paganism? [Interviewer: no] OK, when the Spanish first came there was an established religious system, and the Spanish insisted on conversions, and the Indians were just clever enough to put a veneer over what they already had so that the Spanish thought they'd already succeeded. There are many stories about how that worked ... They may call themselves Catholic and have no sign in their life of anything related to God, alright? I had a funeral not too long ago and there were a couple of gravestones that had Spanish names on them. They also had roosters, you know little plastic roosters and other things on the gravestones. I didn't know what they were. I didn't want to ask, but my suspicion is that they were a very different kind of symbol than the crosses that were engraved in the stone.

Early in our conversation, within a few minutes of meeting two members of the research team—and sitting in his office at the church surrounded by Christian symbols—Pastor Dave told us a remarkable series of false stories about alleged disease, promiscuity, machismo, materialism, and paganism among Mexicans. He did not interact regularly with Mexicans, and he did not speak Spanish, but he seemed confident in his false, racializing claims about Mexicans' beliefs and actions.

In the next three sections, we provide more detail about church practices that created a more welcoming community at St. Joseph's, and we contrast these with the lack of success at Pastor Dave's church. First, we discuss the use of Spanish and bilingual activities in church, contrasting St. Joseph's efforts to have both

Spanish-language and bilingual activities with the segregated Spanish masses at Good Hope. Second, we discuss the integration of Mexican celebrations into church life at St. Joseph's a few years into Father Kelly's tenure, something which did not happen at Good Hope. Third, we describe the joint participation of some White and Mexican parishioners in new, hybrid activities at St. Joseph's, which happened toward the end of Father Kelly's time there. Our descriptions of these two churches show how divergent collective pathways emerged among subgroups of Mexican and White residents. We trace the different sets of contingent resources that facilitated these divergent pathways.

Spanish at Church

Father Kelly's earliest innovations centered around Spanish-language events for Mexican parishioners. His own bilingualism was crucial to his success at St. Joseph's. Elsewhere in Marshall, Spanish-dominant Mexicans felt uncomfortable and had to worry both about failures of communication and about the stereotypes often applied to people who do not speak English well—that they are unintelligent, that they are rude, that they do not care enough about America to bother learning English. At St. Joseph's, in contrast, the leader of the church valued Spanish, spoke it well, and worked hard to master the dialect that most Mexicans in his parish spoke. Many migrants told us that within six months of his arrival he spoke Spanish like a Mexican—despite the fact that he had learned the language in Puerto Rico—and several said that he was the first White person they had met who spoke Spanish fluently.

Rosa, the church secretary, described the situation when she first arrived at St. Joseph's, a few years before Father Kelly.

> At the beginning it was Americans and mostly elderly. The church had little community. Then, since there was a Father Keating who spoke Spanish, they started coming, the Hispanics. There was only one mass in Spanish, one time on Sundays. They started to come, to look for the Father. They started to come and each time it grew and many children were born, which makes them come to church even more to baptize the babies … There were changes in the church, like increasing masses in Spanish … Recently the new Father has added another mass in Spanish at 8 AM on Sundays.

Father Keating was sought after by Mexican parishioners, but he was only occasionally in Marshall and could not serve many of their needs. Hiring a Mexican woman who did not live in the town as church secretary was an important early step. Before Rosa's arrival, she said "there were Hispanics who came to the church and they knocked a lot on his door in the rectory and the person who was there at the time was an American woman. Since she couldn't speak Spanish, she would tell them that there was no Spanish, so they would leave." Whenever parishioners wanted to schedule blessings for their children, or baptisms, or weddings, they had to go through the church secretary, and before Rosa arrived that was difficult. Rosa was also able to prepare bilingual materials for masses, and a bilingual newsletter, and she scheduled visits at local hospitals. After her arrival, Mexicans felt more comfortable approaching the church and the church served their needs better.

Once more Mexicans started attending St. Joseph's, the diocese brought Father Kelly back from his position in Puerto Rico to serve in Marshall. Rosa and the Mexican parishioners were grateful to have a full-time Spanish-speaking priest. They also appreciated Father Kelly's energy, character, and charisma. As Rosa told us:

> We got along really well. I always tried to help him. He was always a beautiful boss. I was very happy. Father Kelly, they tell me he was their favorite Father … He was the one who made this church grow … Father Kelly's Spanish was very good, but six months after he arrived he was speaking like a Mexican. And then imagine it, if Father Kelly is speaking like a Mexican, it attracted so many people. A lot of people. Very charismatic. Very affectionate. Very excellent father. He picked the right profession.

Father Kelly's Spanish was a crucial asset, and he also brought a full-time, supportive presence as leader of the parish. He deeply cared for the Mexican migrants, as individuals and as a community, and the care was palpable to anyone who observed him.

One of Father Kelly's first projects was to convince parishioners that Spanish was a valid language for church business. In 2005, he told us:

> That was another switch that we made. We try to do as much as we can in English and Spanish—one, because the [Mexicans] are here and two, it's just good for even the Anglos to realize that we are a mixed community. Even our parish bulletin, it used to be just in English and then a gentleman from the Spanish community would make up a hundred flyers that he would slip in for the Spanish Mass. Now the whole bulletin is bilingual. Again, very well received by the parish. You know, there's no complaints. Actually, we have a seminarian staying with us this summer, from Chile. And so someone asked me if he would teach Spanish class, so that the Anglos could at least pick up some basic Spanish to be able to have a little bit of a conversation … So there's like 20 people. It's not

a humungous class, but that's decent ... And again, it's just that spirit of wanting to reach out that I've been very happy to see.

Making the church bulletin fully bilingual was a small act, but it represented a larger shift. Father Kelly envisioned a community where Mexicans and their language had equal status. The church offered English classes for Mexicans, but it also offered Spanish classes for English speakers. After the seminarian left, Mexican parishioners volunteered to continue teaching Spanish. Father Kelly also created sessions in which English-speaking parishioners helped Mexican parents understand their children's homework. These initiatives began to create connections between new and longstanding parishioners, encouraging them to communicate and participate together in church activities.

Father Kelly told us that he was not sure what to expect when he began using Spanish in church. In an earlier placement, at a church not that far from Marshall, he had had a very different experience.

> When I did a bilingual mass for Holy Thursday ... people knew [we were going to use Spanish]—we talked about it forever. But when Holy Thursday came and we started the mass, the first time I used the Spanish language, a group got up and left ... I just felt more resistance there, especially because Mex- not Mexicans but Hispanics had been there for like 15 years, 20 years by the time I was there ... When we did this [in Marshall], we were surprised by the results because they were more positive than we thought ... We didn't get a lot of people who thought like, the Mexicans are taking away our jobs. It was mostly positive.

Father Kelly's story about his experience using Spanish at the earlier church was wrenching. It must have been horrible for Hispanic parishioners to hear Spanish for the first time at a mass, with the priest trying to acknowledge and welcome them into joint worship, and have some Anglo parishioners get up and leave because of their xenophobia and racial biases. Because of this bad experience, the priest was surprised by the largely positive response at St. Joseph's to his use of Spanish and his welcoming of Mexican migrants. White, non-Hispanic parishioners' unexpectedly positive responses to his use of Spanish helped his innovations work. We do not know why many White parishioners in Marshall were more tolerant of Spanish. It could be that they recognized the importance of Mexicans for revitalizing and ultimately saving their parish. In addition to providing large numbers of new church members, Mexicans spearheaded funding drives that allowed upgrades to the physical plant. Marshall was also more welcoming than many similar towns because the regular arrival of migrants was an unusually salient part of the town's history, across two centuries, such that longstanding residents were more familiar with migrants' struggles.

The town was not as welcoming to Spanish-speaking migrants in other spaces, however. Beyond St. Joseph's, Mexicans faced discrimination or ridicule for not speaking English. Hernán and Mariana described how speaking in public was stressful for them.

> Mariana: I've heard [it said that] "this is America, this is the US, this is my country, and English is spoken here." At times I say that's racist, but I thought about it and there's some truth, because it's his country and English is spoken here. If it were my country, we'd speak Spanish.
> Hernán: I don't speak English because I'm afraid they won't understand me, that I won't be able to explain.
> Mariana: What happens is that we speak it, but perhaps we don't speak it with the accent of a White person. Suddenly, we say a word incorrectly and then they laugh. Perhaps they laugh because it sounds funny, but for us it gives us fear and insecurity for the next time we speak, so we stay quiet.

Competence in English varied among Mexicans. But most, like Mariana and Hernán, were anxious about having to speak in public.

At St. Joseph's, however, all Mexicans felt comfortable using Spanish. This contrasted with other churches. Hernán told us: "Here there are almost no Catholic churches where they speak Spanish. This is the only one I know." Because St. Joseph's offered mass and activities in Spanish, the church became a crucial space where many of them felt safe, connected, and confident. As Hernán said, "I feel good in the church … In this moment we don't miss our country." Mariana agreed:

> Yes, in the church, apart from the fact that he speaks to us in Spanish, the people who go there speak Spanish. The events that they do, we speak Spanish, the food is Mexican. Also, in the church they celebrate Cinco de Mayo, they celebrate Mexican independence, they celebrate the Virgin of Guadalupe, Mexico's virgin, the 12th of December. I feel like that church [on the day of the virgin] is like being back in our country because they celebrate things that we celebrate and the Father gives us that liberty to go and live our culture.

Because Spanish was spoken there and the congregation engaged in familiar Mexican cultural traditions, St. Joseph's made many migrants feel comfortable. The hard work of Mexican parishioners, encouraged by the priest, created an environment where many Mexicans felt, if only briefly, as if they were at home.

In contrast to St. Joseph's, Pastor Dave's church did not create a welcoming space for Mexican migrants who attended. Throughout our time in Marshall, they had a Spanish-speaking minister come to town and offer one weekly service, while day-to-day church business was run by Pastor Dave. The Spanish-speaking minister had been working at the church for two or three years when we first met Pastor Dave in 2005. Before his arrival, there had been no Hispanic members of the church. Pastor Dave told us that this visiting minister "pulled together a congregation which has been relatively stable but not growing" over his first two years. The church had no bilingual staff or Spanish-language materials. It felt as if there were two separate churches using the same building—the primary, English-speaking congregation and then Mexicans who came for services once a week when the Spanish-speaking minister was there.

Pastor Dave described what happened when they tried to hold bilingual services at one point.

> Dave: We've been doing joint services. The Anglos go nuts. Two hours.
> Interviewer: Joint services with whom?
> D: With the Latinos, with the Mexicans. I mean, they have two-hour services … When they're having- you know, there's no problem when it's an afternoon Latino service, but when it's a morning service jointly or when it's an afternoon service jointly and it goes two hours. We had a second anniversary service in June. It was a hot day.
> I: It was the second anniversary of what?
> D: Of the Latino ministry.
> I: OK
> D: It was a hot day. The service lasted two and a half hours. It had to be ninety in there. People left and I was grateful for the- you know, my congregation, the Anglo congregation, I'm one of the youngsters, OK? A lot of them are over seventy. And older. And when they left it was a relief because I didn't want to have to carry them out.
> I: So the two- is it the two congregations are fairly separate, the Anglo group and the Latino group?
> D: Most of the time. The Latino pastor keeps expecting the Anglos to learn Spanish. I mean, you're talking about people that are seventy years old. And they keep hoping he'll learn English, but in two and a half years he hasn't.

At Good Hope church, they tried some of the same strategies used at St. Joseph's—a Spanish-speaking minister, bilingual services, Spanish classes for White parishioners. But the Mexican community did not flourish. The core group of Mexican congregants who felt loyal to that denomination continued to attend the Spanish-language masses, but the community did not grow and fewer connections were established between Mexican and White members of the church. This happened in part because the Spanish-speaking minster was available for only a couple of hours a week, and in part because Pastor Dave did not understand or respect the Mexican congregants. At St. Joseph's, Father Kelly was present all the time and he consistently respected Mexicans. He brought both excellent Spanish and a determination to include Mexicans as equal partners in his church, and many Mexican parishioners accepted his invitation and worked hard to create a robust Spanish-speaking community. In 2002, St. Joseph's and Good Hope both struggled to retain Mexican parishioners, but in the first few years of Father Kelly's tenure their pathways diverged. St. Joseph's became a more welcoming interethnic community—with one of the key resources behind this change being the dispositions and actions of the particular priest who had been assigned there.

Mexican Celebrations in Church

In addition to encouraging the use of Spanish in church, Father Kelly also welcomed Mexican celebrations. This started relatively early in his tenure. The church had traditionally hosted various culturally themed celebrations, especially Irish festivals. We attended several events with the flags of the thirty-two counties of Ireland held proudly by men in kilts, together with lots of parishioners wearing green. As Mexican migrants became more involved, many of them asked if the church would host Mexican celebrations too. Individuals took responsibility for organizing, they educated Father Kelly about the relevant saints and customs, and the church began to hold many Mexican events. Raúl Ortega praised Father Kelly for his welcoming attitude toward Mexican parishioners and Mexican celebrations, telling us that the priest welcomed "whatever people want to do ... He is very open to all of this ... He has never said 'no, I can't.'" Mexican parishioners created prayer groups, led open discussions of Mexican culture and its place in the United States, and organized celebrations of patron saints from their home villages as well as larger festivals like the December 12 celebration of the *Virgen de Guadalupe* and Mexican Independence Day on September 16. The church hosted information sessions where local officials from the police, local government, the Mexican consulate, and elsewhere shared information with parishioners. The increase in young Mexican families also created demand for more lifecycle ceremonies, like the blessing of the child at forty days and at three years, baptisms, *quinceañeras*, and weddings.

Victor was a parishioner known in the Mexican community for taking leadership in organizing Mexican celebrations at church and in his home. He was grateful that "Father Kelly has given us good support. He's extended his hand to us. He's a good person who understands us, and he wants to continue our tradition since we are in a country that is not our own." Like many Mexicans who came to the United States as adults, he felt strongly about his cultural traditions and wanted to pass them on to his children.

> My children weren't born over there [in Mexico], so I tell them about the traditions of our town … I try to explain to them what the feelings from over there are like. If they want to continue the tradition, that will be their choice, right? I have a tradition, I have something from my parents, they inculcated in me the practice of going to church, and now I try to teach my children.

Victor saw the church as a place to keep Mexican traditions alive. In early December every year, for example, he organized a gathering in honor of "La Purísima," a celebration for Mary traditionally held in his home village. Dozens of people came to his house, starting at 6:00 a.m., to prepare food and a life-sized statue of the saint that they carried to mass. At dawn one year we arrived to find half a dozen relatives already cooking food both in his kitchen and on portable burners spread throughout the house. His wife circulated, stirring the contents of the large pots in different locations. Several of Victor's male friends arrived shortly thereafter. They dug a pit in the back yard, built a fire, and barbecued a dozen slabs of beef ribs, covering the pit with agave leaves. After they returned from mass and the subsequent reception in the church, family and friends gathered to enjoy the barbecue back at Victor's house. Celebrations like this among expatriates provided an opportunity to reconnect with valued traditions, and St. Joseph's was an important catalyst.

In addition to the important functions that Mexican celebrations served for the migrants, over time they began to provide an opportunity for White parishioners to participate in and learn about Mexican culture. After establishing some Spanish-language Mexican events in church, Father Kelly began to invite White and Mexican parishioners to the same events and made the events bilingual to facilitate joint participation.

> We started, after I got here, several bilingual celebrations. 40 hours, which is a Catholic tradition of the blessed sacrament … We thought that since … we are the body of Christ we would do that together to form unity. And that worked out very well. And … we had a celebration of the hundredth anniversary of the church building—again bilingually, with a little reception downstairs afterwards with some Mexican food and some American food and whatnot. And there has been a very positive, very positive response.

Simple migration stories expect migrants to learn English and "American culture"—as if that is a monolithic thing—while Americans just wait for them to assimilate so that "they" can participate in "our" activities. All Mexicans in Marshall did learn about and adopt some American traditions, usually out of a desire to connect better to their new home. But Mexican celebrations in church allowed this to happen in both directions—with some White parishioners also learning about Mexico and participating in Spanish-language events. Some White residents participated more like tourists, coming for the display of an alien culture. But others came to appreciate and more deeply participate in Mexican celebrations. These celebrations then became more complex—no longer just Mexican events, but Mexican-inspired events with bilingual components and opportunities for intercultural connections where White and Mexican parishioners enjoyed food, singing, and celebration together.

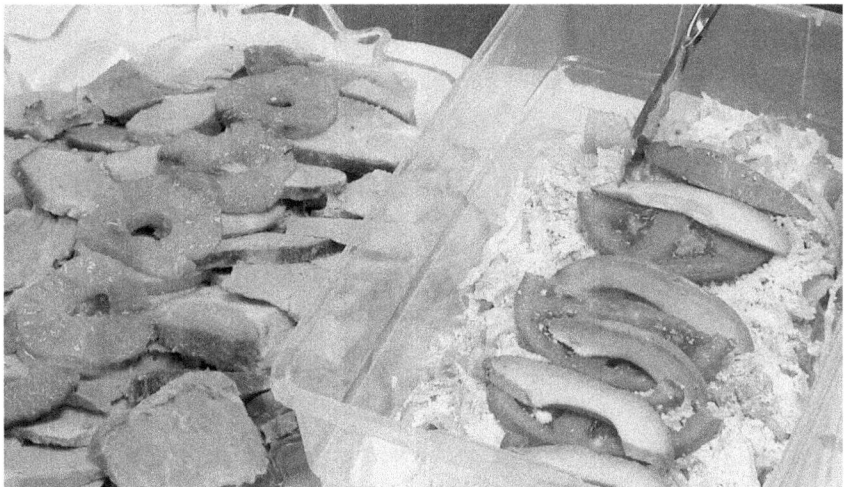

Figure 3.3 Mexican and Irish food, side by side, at a St. Joseph's celebration.

Meghan McCarthy, for example, really enjoyed the Mexican celebrations she was able to learn about and participate in.

> Some of the things that I wasn't aware of ... was first of all the *quinceañeras*. It's the sweet 15, not the sweet 16. It's a 15-year-old party for the girls. Their coming out party. It has a secular and a religious aspect to it. I had no idea what it was about. The feast of our Lady of Guadalupe. Of course I knew about Guadalupe but I never knew about the *mañanitas* and waking up the blessed Mary at four o'clock in the morning and all of the wonderful mariachi bands and the devotion. She's right up there with God as far as the Hispanics go. A wonderful

> patron of the Americas. And the *Posadas*. I love the *Posadas*. That's the journey that Mary and Joseph took through Jerusalem before she gave birth, traveling to all the different houses nine days before Christmas. It's been a great, great experience and I keep trying to get more people involved in it because for them not to experience that at least once, they're missing out on something great. And just the welcoming into their homes and the singing, the carols—most of all it's the introduction to all of their foods: the sweetbreads, the arroz con leche, the flautas and all of the things they bring to all of their celebrations.

This enthusiastic response by some White parishioners was only one small step toward more genuine intercultural connection. Mexican culture is of course more than food and celebrations. But the involvement of White residents in Mexican events at church started to change the institution. Most White parishioners felt that they were being charitable by welcoming Mexicans at church, often in a patronizing way. But their church was also changing as it incorporated Mexican traditions. The traditionally Irish Catholic community was starting to become something new. The resources that made this possible included Father Kelly himself, a core group of longstanding parishioners who welcomed Mexicans and participated in bilingual events, Mexican migrants who spent time and energy sharing their traditions, and the vulnerable situation of the church at this historical moment—as well as contingent facts like Holy Trinity's refusal to include Mexicans and the failure of other churches like Good Hope to offer an attractive alternative.

Creating Interethnic Connections

In 2005 Father Kelly described how there had been some resistance but, overall, he was optimistic about the emerging interethnic connections in Marshall. He told us some positive stories about Mexicans that circulated among Irish American and other longstanding residents—oversimplified but powerful stories that provided one resource that helped St. Joseph's incorporate some Mexican traditions.

> It's wonderful. You can walk around Marshall and see the shops or just the people walking through the neighborhood, and a lot of them are Mexican … I've been here three years and my experience has generally been positive in that those who are long time parishioners—many of whom do not technically live within our boundaries anymore, but still come because … they have an affiliation with the parish … They're all—I shouldn't say all—there are probably some that aren't. For the most part they are very positive about the fact that the Mexicans are here.

> They identify with them as Catholic. They see them as very pious Catholics. They always talk about them as very hardworking people. They're thrilled about the large numbers. They've even said it reminds them of years gone by when their Mass would be that crowded, so it's nice to see that vitality in the community. Every now and then there has been a comment about, you know, "Well, maybe Father is here for the Spanish and so he's going to forget about the English-speaking people." But you try your best to prove that that's not the case.

Some older longstanding parishioners were skeptical about the incorporation of Mexicans into their church, especially early in Father Kelly's tenure. Some of these people stopped attending St. Joseph's. And some who remained needed to be reassured in oversimplified terms about "them" being like "us." But the priest worked hard to continue meeting the needs of the Anglo community, at the same time as he worked to integrate Mexicans into his church.

> The Catholic Church, whatever language you speak, Catholics come to the church looking for the same things: the Mass, the sacraments ... The biggest challenge has been dealing with different language and culture in trying to be welcoming, along with staying sensitive to those who've been in the parish for years ... Here the English-speaking community has been very open and welcoming. They see that the parish has a future with this vibrant community. It has been a little harder to get the Mexican community involved with the regular activities of the parish for a number of reasons. One is that they work many jobs and don't have a lot of time. Two is that there is a little bit of intimidation because they know they don't speak English and feel that they might not be as well received by the English-speaking community. It might even be that they think the English-speaking community is perhaps more educated and better off financially. You will always find people who say "why don't they speak English," but by and large people have been very welcoming of the Spanish community and want the communities to come together to work as one parish.

Over the first five years of Father Kelly's tenure, most of the events were in either English or Spanish, and only a small group of Anglo parishioners interacted with Mexicans. But by the late 2000s, growing numbers of Anglos participated in bilingual events alongside migrants.

Some longstanding parishioners who had been skeptical came to participate in Mexican celebrations over time. At the end of 2010, Molly Trent told us:

> The one thing I have noticed over the years is that there always seem to be the locals, the old St. Joseph's people, and this Hispanic group, and they didn't used to blend together. But this year in particular [is better] ... This is the year of the coming together of the Hispanic community and the old community.

Molly and her husband Aaron described the change in attitudes at the church, across Father Kelly's time there. Aaron described how some of the older parishioners felt uncomfortable with the change and how Father Kelly worked to overcome this. Molly told us:

> It's not like I'm hearing a lot of that, but I think there are some people who are unsettled by it, as you would find in a community where people are thinking … "learn English, abide by our rules and traditions." I think Father Kelly has done a good job of communicating that all migrant populations come in and go through this. I remember we had the Irish Festival mass, Our Lady of Knock mass, and there are all these middle-aged people … like the ancient order of Hibernians, who wear the kilt and they maintain the traditions of Ireland. And he tied his sermon into migrant populations and justice for migrants. You could feel people saying, my people went through this, and that's what these people are going through now … If they start to relate to it and think, my grandfather was a migrant from Ireland, they start to understand a little bit differently.

Over time, bilingual masses and joint participation in celebrations helped to overcome some longstanding parishioners' discomfort with the changes in their parish. They came to participate in hybrid practices similar to those found in many other settings with cultural contact and changing traditions over historical time (Hall, 2002; Lukose, 2009).

The story that Father Kelly, Molly, and others told was the familiar one introduced at the beginning of the first chapter: our ancestors came as migrants, worked hard, and joined the American mainstream, and we should welcome Mexicans who are going through the same thing now. This story oversimplified the actual situation. As longstanding groups moved into and then out of downtown Marshall, in the cycle of migrants from English to Irish, Italian, Black, and Mexican, descendants of the earlier groups changed. Their economic interests and their stories about themselves shifted, such that they were different than their migrant ancestors had been. Longstanding residents typically imagined that it was exclusively hard work that explained their ancestors' success and their own situations—without acknowledging the fundamentally different positions African Americans are in, for example, and without recognizing how migration enforcement had shifted in ways that made life more difficult for Mexicans. The oversimplified stories comparing Irish migrant ancestors and contemporary Mexican migrants nonetheless helped some Mexican and White residents create intercultural connections. Some cross-cultural contact and sympathy occurred because people idealized their own ancestors' experiences and told stories that compared Mexican and earlier migrants.

Rosa the church secretary described how celebrations for the *Virgen de Guadalupe* had been held early in her time at the church, but she emphasized they were nothing like the celebrations they had in the late 2000s.

> It was done but it was a small celebration, not like now. Now it's a huge event, where it can last from 4 AM ... until 8 or 9 PM ... It's so beautiful because the two, Mexicans and Americans together, celebrating ... And we have ... their Irish festival ... and the Mexicans, not all, but some, do come to those events.

We witnessed many events in which Anglos and Mexicans were emotionally engaged while participating together in familiar activities. The songs "Noche de Paz" and "Silent Night" are generally sung with the same melody. When Father Kelly led an ethnically mixed group of parishioners in singing this song in a White parishioner's home—alternately in Spanish and English—members of both groups felt involved in the song and hummed along with verses in the language they did not understand. During home visits for *las posadas*, a group of about two dozen, mostly Mexican parishioners would arrive in a neighborhood with guitars, singing traditional Mexican songs. When they arrived and were admitted to the house of a White family, they found familiar things: a buffet, Father Kelly and Sister Carmela, guitars, and group singing. The Mexican children were not accustomed to eating chips-and-dip and Christmas cookies at celebrations of *las posadas*, but they nonetheless seemed at ease during the visit. Molly Trent told us about a pot-luck brunch in which everyone brought a dish.

> I remember early on where we would have just one [Mexican] family show up and I would urge them to take food and make them feel welcome. Now it has flipped so that the majority of people who come to the brunch are Hispanic. There are still plenty of Anglos who show up for this, and I think this is a really good social event.

Events like this had warmth and emotional resonance. They allowed people who could not easily speak with each other to feel connected. As Sister Carmela told us after participating in one event, "I was very happy that there was the opportunity. What an opportunity to feel loved ... Not all of us have that experience."

Even Molly's mother-in-law participated in events with Mexicans. She did not live in town and "is not exposed to immigrants too much," Molly said. At one event Molly hosted, her mother-in-law:

> was sitting in the living room and this little kid slides over to her and the next thing you know he climbs up on her lap. And we thought, oh my, there's a little Hispanic kid on mom's lap. And when that was over and it was time to

get refreshments, the kid got off my mother-in-law and we had to clean her up because the kid had wet her pants. We were surprised she was not more upset.

If community relations had involved more distrust and suspicion, perhaps Molly's mother-in-law and other White parishioners might have taken the opportunity to complain about Mexicans and parrot racial stereotypes. But everyone took it in stride, and Aaron's mother returned to future intercultural celebrations despite what Molly euphemistically called her "discomfort with strangers." In intercultural events like these, some Anglo and Mexican parishioners connected to each other, recognizing common faith and common experiences despite their differences.

Stories and Complex Realities

Sister Carmela compared the experience of migration to religious conversion. When she worked as a missionary, converts would transform their lives and choose new pathways for themselves. She participated in "the transformation of the people ... When we're done with the process, their faith has grown. Something has changed in them." She told us that migration involved a similar sort of struggle and rebirth. When you arrive as a migrant, "either you grow in terms of faith or the contrary." Mexicans who came to Marshall needed to have faith that they and their families would survive and eventually flourish in an unfamiliar place. They had to find support where they could, as they worked to create better lives. Many Mexican migrants found support at St. Joseph's from fellow Mexicans, from the priest, and from the church community. As Sister Carmela described it, "when you feel accepted, and the fact of celebrating, having the opportunity to celebrate your devotions—that makes you feel 'they accept me, they love me.'"

Sister Carmela's view of migration as struggle and ultimate success captured some migrant experiences, but certainly not all. Mexican migrants did not simply find welcome in the church and begin assimilating to American culture. As we have described, they also began to produce new combinations of Mexican and American resources that had not existed before. In the first years after Mexicans' arrival, St. Joseph's did not provide much community—only a Spanish-language mass with an itinerant priest. Then Father Kelly came and began to welcome Mexican celebrations, as a separate set of church events. Over time, longstanding residents and Mexican parishioners worked together to create joint events. Despite the fact that some Anglos felt pity for Mexicans and perhaps congratulated themselves too much for welcoming the newcomers, over time Mexicans' participation changed the church. It became a place where elements of Mexican traditions mingled with traditional Irish festivals, where the church became partly Hispanic as both migrants and longstanding residents changed.

Father Kelly often said that the ethnically diverse community at St. Joseph's allowed them to be closer to God's design for human society.

> You know as a Catholic that the church is supposed to be open and welcoming to the migrant, but when you're in a parish that has to do it, it becomes more real. One thing that has become more clear is God's call to unity. I always tell the parishioners that we are quite blessed because it is a challenge to bring people of different cultures and languages together, and this is a little foretaste of what the Kingdom of God will be like, with people of all backgrounds and colors together.

Father Kelly spoke about the "Kingdom of God" in part to convince longstanding parishioners to welcome Mexican migrants—reminding them that their religious tradition demands love for all people regardless of their backgrounds. But he also drew on the tradition to articulate a simple but powerful vision of how different ethnic groups should relate. His appeal worked for some longstanding residents, who embraced the migrants, though not for others. As Mexicans became part of the community, their presence helped Irish American and other parishioners to experience a diverse, more ideal community in the present. This was inspirational for many. Their belief in a diverse Kingdom of God, a heterogeneous ideal community, inspired some longstanding residents to welcome Mexicans to the church and helped Mexicans to build positive relationships with those longstanding residents. This religious ideal was also sometimes exemplified and reinvigorated by the presence of the migrants. Mexicans had diverse experiences at St. Joseph's and in Marshall, but the overly simple story of them revitalizing the church did capture one important dimension of what happened. And this story influenced some parishioners' behavior, despite its oversimplifications and inaccuracies.

The actual situation was more complicated, and there were some reasons for concern. Meghan McCarthy, for example, described how the presence of Mexicans deepened her own faith and participation in the church.

> My faith is more of a ... get back to the basics Christianity. It's not the pomp and circumstance ... It's back to what would Jesus do and how best to feed his people and how best to spiritually feed these people. And [Mexicans] have helped me keep it real ... For the most part [their faith] is so simple and so sincere and so

genuine that you can't help but absorb that ... It's a genuine love for their faith. Their faith is their life ... It's not just something they do on Sunday. You go into any of their homes, they always have shrines. There's always a prayer area, an area of reverence and respect to *La Virgen* or to Jesus himself. It's beautiful ... Immigration is near and dear to my heart. I dare people to find a harder working, more sincere group of people than the people I come into contact with at St. Joseph's ... There is no pretension at all. All they want to do is make a living. They want to provide for their family and they want to love God.

Meghan found the openness, the alleged simplicity, and the lack of pretension in Mexicans' faith to be inspiring. She herself changed from having negative views of Mexican migrants to being very positive about them. She told us that many of her friends continued to have negative views of migrants. Her story clearly included condescension toward Mexicans, however—as she imagined them to be simple, wholesome, and childlike. On ethical grounds, Megan's position was better than the xenophobic perspectives of her friends, and it was heartfelt, but it did not treat Mexicans as equals.

Longstanding parishioners welcomed Mexicans for various reasons—not only because the newcomers revitalized a dying parish, because they identified with the struggles of migrants, and because they cared for them as fellow human beings, but also because they were curious to learn about another culture and because they felt good being the benefactors of others whom they could position as less fortunate. We were struck by one bleary-eyed Irish American parishioner attending the early morning celebration of the *Virgen de Guadalupe*, walking up to the front of the sanctuary with his video camera, wandering right in between the altar and the congregation and filming in both directions, apparently unaware that he might have been disturbing people. White and Mexican residents had varied reasons for participation, and only some of these had the potential to create productive connection and belonging.

Mexican and longstanding parishioners thus did not simply enact familiar stories of welcome or assimilation. As we have shown, changing migrant and longstanding communities intersected with and influenced each other. During Father Kelly's tenure, the parish brought together a combination of resources that were in some ways specific to this location. For example, Marshall was more open to newcomers than many other towns, in large part because of its own migrant history. Over two centuries, several groups of migrants had begun their time in America there—because of its proximity to transportation and various jobs, because of dense, relatively inexpensive rental housing, and because it did not suffer from the ills of nearby cities—and the descendants of these migrants were more likely to remember their ancestors' struggles and empathize with Mexican migrants than residents of some other New Latino Diaspora towns. St. Joseph's was more open to migrants than other churches in town and elsewhere because of its history of serving migrants, because of the church's recent decline and need for parishioners, because of the character and charisma of the priest who was assigned there, and because of the efforts made by a core group of Mexican parishioners. Father Kelly's arrival happened to coincide with the transition in the Mexican community from single men to families, and this coincidence was important as well. Mexicans were more settled and likely to attend church as the Mexican community entered its second decade, and they were having children whom they wanted to baptize and involve in various church activities. Longstanding residents also told oversimplified but powerful stories about their own immigrant pasts and Mexicans' allegedly similar trajectories, as well as about Mexican revitalization of the town. The intersection of the historical pathway of the parish, the developing Mexican community, widely circulating stories about migration and assimilation, and the town's own migrant history—together with a committed, charismatic priest—made possible the emerging pathway followed at St. Joseph's. If some of these realities had been different, the parish could have followed a different pathway. Mexicans' experiences at St. Joseph's were contingent on this configuration of various resources, on intersections among emergent processes involving the church, the town, the migrant community, and various individuals. Good Hope, as we have seen, followed a different pathway, constituted by a somewhat different set of resources.

Just as individual pathways can emerge and solidify in divergent directions, as we saw in the last chapter, collective pathways like those of the two church communities can also diverge. Individual and collective pathways also influence each other. Any individual migrant is positioned as various resources facilitate his or her pathway, and some of these resources come from particular institutional or community contexts that are themselves developing. In order to understand how an individual ends up following the pathway that he or she does, we must understand not only the various resources relevant to that case, but also the institutional pathways that they intersect with. A Mexican newcomer who attended Good Hope had different experiences than one who went to St. Joseph's, and someone who attended St. Joseph's in 1995 had different experiences than someone who attended there in 2005. Furthermore, newcomers who spent lots of time at church had different experiences than those who devoted themselves to particular community organizations or to starting a business. Both individual and institutional pathways are contingent, emerging and solidifying as individual ontogeny intersects with collective developments and as sometimes-unexpected configurations of resources become relevant.

The future of St. Joseph's parish changed when Father Kelly was reassigned in 2011. Parishioners heard of the transition relatively late, only two weeks before it took effect. As Raúl Ortega said, "They are going to change our priest to another church. And when he told us, about the news, things became very sad." Molly Trent spoke with us right before his last Sunday at St. Joseph's.

> I think it will be emotional to have the final Mass with him. I think it will be tough for everybody. I was emotional on Sunday. He announced to everybody that he was going, at 10 o'clock mass. Word had gotten around to everybody, but it was still very emotional. People were very sad. I thought that this is a special time we will never have any more. It sounds obnoxious and goofy because, he's only the pastor, but he has made a big difference. He really tried to build a bridge between the two communities.

The farewell mass was in fact very emotional. Both longstanding and Mexican parishioners packed the sanctuary, standing in the back and the aisles. Members of our research team arrived half an hour early and almost all seats were already taken. Father Kelly used lots of Holy Water, walking around the entire sanctuary, making sure to look at each individual and blessing everyone by sprinkling them. It seemed that he focused particularly on ethnographers, as far as the sprinkling went, and we left the event quite damp. There were many tears in response to his farewell, and a long line to say goodbye to him in person after the mass.

To the delight of the Italian American community in town, the new priest at St. Joseph's was one of them—a descendant of Italian migrants who grew up in Marshall and was the first non-Irish or Irish American priest ever assigned to the parish. He spoke Spanish and reached out to Mexicans as soon as he arrived, but it was not clear how the church community would be affected. He did not seem to have the same determination and charisma as Father Kelly. But Father Kelly himself was optimistic.

> Who's to say that in 10 or 15 years there's not going to be an influx of some other migrant community? And the church will respond to them and find a priest who speaks their language to welcome them to this country to help them maintain their faith, and will meet them as individuals, recognizing their dignity as they try to make their way in the country.

Whatever the future of St. Joseph's turns out to be, it will come from the intersection of emergent, interconnected individual, institutional, and

Figure 3.4 Parishoners entering St. Joseph's carrying the Mexican and American flags.

community pathways. Migrants and longstanding residents together created a complex, emerging reality at St. Joseph's that continues to change.

Stories about and realities of interethnic relations played a central role in the development of church communities at St. Joseph's and Good Hope, with very different outcomes in the two cases. Relations between Mexicans and African Americans were even more complex, and we turn to these in the next two chapters.

4

Neighborhoods: Diverging Stories of Decline

Chapters 2 and 3 have illustrated the core elements of our approach to understanding migrants' diverse pathways. We have shown how migrants sometimes follow pathways that fit with simple stories of migrant success and sometimes do not. Allie seemed to be following a pathway "up and out," for example, but Nancy's friend Sara did not. We have shown how both familiar and unfamiliar pathways are contingent, solidifying only as a set of relevant resources establishes their direction. The development of an interethnic community at St. Joseph's fit a relatively familiar, positive migration story, for example, but this only happened because a particular priest was assigned at an opportune time in the migrant community's development, in a town that still remembered its own migrant past. We have shown that processes from at least four scales—the centuries-long cycles of migration to Marshall, the decades-long development of the Mexican migrant community and the town institutions that served it, the years-long ontogenetic development of individuals, and the hours-long emergence of pivotal events—all provided essential resources that shaped migrant pathways in Marshall. We have also shown how relations among ethnic groups were important resources that influenced migrant pathways. For many Mexicans who attended St. Joseph's, for example, relations between Mexicans and Irish Americans became important. And we have shown how oversimplified stories can become crucial resources in determining individual and community pathways. Some Irish Americans at St. Joseph's built an interethnic community with Mexicans, for example, in part because they embraced oversimplified stories about their ancestors traveling the stereotypical migrant pathway from struggle to success.

Now that we have illustrated these elements of our central argument, in the next two chapters we turn to a more complex phenomenon that incorporated them all: the complex, triangular relationship among Black, Mexican, and White residents of Marshall in residential neighborhoods and other public spaces.

Interactions among these groups, and stories about their interactions, were crucial to the pathways many Mexican migrants traveled. By the time Mexicans arrived in large numbers, some African Americans had accumulated wealth, power, and status in town, but many had not. African Americans' aspirations were often thwarted by more intense racial stereotyping and exclusion than that faced by earlier migrants. Mexicans had to engage with this important group of longstanding residents, but their relations with African Americans were more complex than the positive or negative receptions described in simple migration stories and more complex than their relations with Irish and Italian Americans. This complexity made the pathway of the Mexican community in Marshall unusual in some respects.

In this chapter and the next, we describe how relationships between Black and Mexican residents in some ways followed patterns common in earlier migrant cycles—with African Americans unhappy about being crowded out of traditionally Black neighborhoods, for example, and working to preserve their recently developed political power against encroachment by Mexican newcomers. But many Black residents had not moved "up and out" in the same way as other migrants. Some African Americans did not have the means to leave downtown Marshall. Many Black residents also chose to move "up and in" instead of "up and out," staying in a community they valued even once they had sufficient money to move elsewhere. In addition, African Americans were often misrepresented by White and Mexican Marshall residents, who told stories that systematically ignored their successes. It is important to see that White residents played an important role in the phenomenon of "Black-Mexican relations"—because many stories included White characters and were told by White narrators, and because socioeconomic interactions with Whites were crucial to the pathways traveled by both Black and Mexican residents.

The complex position occupied by African Americans in Marshall helped open up divergent pathways for Mexicans as they engaged with stories about and realities of their relations with Black residents. In some ways, in both residential and public spaces, the Mexican community developed according to the classic positive story. In the first decade, Mexicans were stereotyped and also often experienced life as economically struggling, transient laborers at the bottom of the status hierarchy. By the end of the second decade, however, many Mexicans had become upwardly mobile business owners and successful students. This classic story was too simple, though. Many individual Mexicans continued to struggle even in the second decade, and they faced pressure from racist stereotypes, lack of documentation, and economic hardship. Centrally, the presence of the Black community, and the question of how Mexicans would be positioned with respect to them, was an important resource that helped shape many Mexicans' pathways.

The complex relations between and stories about Blacks and Mexicans made available diverse resources, and individual Mexicans' pathways diverged, depending on which of these resources became salient in particular cases. This chapter spends more time on the first decade of the Mexican migrant community, describing residential neighborhoods and the divergent stories told by Black, White, and Mexican residents about when Marshall began its decline. We emphasize the systematically inaccurate stories told about African Americans by White narrators, as well as Black residents' partly inaccurate stories about Mexicans. The next chapter spends more time on the second decade, describing public spaces and the growth of Mexican businesses, as well as political struggles between Black and Mexican residents. Together, these chapters show how the pathways of successive migrant groups in Marshall did not follow the simple "up and out" pattern, at least when it came to African Americans, and how Mexicans encountered various possibilities for positioning themselves with respect to longstanding Black residents.

Housing and neighborhoods are central to people's everyday lives. The physical and social situations of home and neighborhood shape experiences—ranging from how difficult it is to get groceries, to whether one feels safe, to the kinds of people on the street and the character of interactions one has with them, to the urgency of needed repairs, to the degree of crowding and the consequences for noise, parking, and other daily activities (Jencks & Mayer, 1990; Sampson, Morenoff, & Gannon-Rowley, 2002; Small & Newman, 2001). Just as important as the actual situation of one's home is the central role neighborhoods play in imagined social geography. People tell evaluative stories about themselves and others partly by characterizing their neighborhoods. Imagining one's own and others' residential lives is a central way of judging them (Casey, 1996; Dixon & Durrheim, 2004; Proshansky, Fabian, & Kaminoff, 1983).

This chapter explores Marshall residents' experiences in and stories about the residential neighborhoods that Mexicans moved into during the first two decades of the migrant community. Housing was one of the first places where Mexican migrants became visible in town, especially to Black residents who lived in the same areas. Suddenly there were many unfamiliar faces parking their cars, sitting on the stoop, and having family gatherings in neighborhoods that longstanding residents remembered as home to Black and—in an earlier era—Italian people. Many townspeople characterized these neighborhoods and their residents in stories that contained evaluative stereotypes. For example, early in our fieldwork several longstanding residents told us that Mexican people ate chicken on the stoop and threw the bones on the sidewalk, endangering dogs that sometimes choked on them. We found little evidence of Mexican-induced dog injuries, but some longstanding residents nonetheless told this story and circulated an image of careless people who ate in inappropriate places and threw dangerous objects into public space. Many such stories about the "other"—some positive and some negative—were created, repeated, and modified as Mexican migrants and longstanding residents encountered each other in residential neighborhoods in downtown Marshall.

This chapter moves chronologically through the first two decades of the Mexican community, although we spend more time on the first decade. We start with stories about residential life in Marshall before Mexicans arrived, then we describe stories of the decline in residential neighborhoods that happened toward the end of the twentieth century, and finally we introduce stories of revitalization that became more prevalent in the twenty-first century. We show how these oversimplified stories influenced the lives of both migrants and longstanding residents. In this chapter, we focus particularly on the contrast between the stories told by Black residents, of invasion and decline, and the stories told by White residents, of decline and revitalization. Because Mexicans did not directly experience the era narrated in stories of the town's decline, we focus on Black and White residents' voices in much of this chapter. We continue our analysis of the divergence between Black and White stories in the next chapter, where we describe stories about and struggles over commerce, politics, and other public spaces, and there we are able to include more Mexican voices.

Starting in the 1970s, Marshall experienced "White flight" as Irish and Italian American residents left the town for wealthier suburbs (Quillian, 2002; Seligman, 2005). Many White residents were unable or unwilling to sell their homes, which became rental properties that attracted African American and later Mexican tenants. With the arrival of Mexicans in the 1990s, these rental properties became the site of three migrant archetypes that appeared widely in stories that circulated in town: the *soltero* or "unattached male Mexican worker," the "absent White slumlord," and the "naïve Mexican victim." This chapter describes the important role these stereotypical characters played as residents from all ethnic groups imagined residential spaces and the types of people who lived in them. People's stories about glory days, decline, and revitalization oversimplified the situation, but they also influenced residents' ideas and actions. Black residents told stories about the history of decline that often positioned Mexican migrants as invaders.

On the other hand, by the second decade of Mexican migration White narrators most often positioned Mexicans as revitalizers. This divergence helped to propel historical change. Black residents' stories helped encourage African American migration away from downtown (Nichols & Wortham, 2018). White residents' stories imagined Mexicans jumping over Black residents and following the Italians "up and out," and this created opportunities for some Mexicans. A new configuration of stories and other resources emerged and solidified, as formerly Black areas became symbols of revitalization for White and Mexican residents. This characterization of Mexicans as revitalizers has appeared in many New Latino Diaspora towns (Gordon, 2015, 2016; Grey & Woodrick, 2005; Jordan, 2012; Sulzberger, 2011; Zúñiga & Hernández-León, 2005). This more positive characterization of Mexican migrants is not available in all migrant locations, however (Hamann & Harklau, 2010; Hamann, Wortham, & Murillo, 2002; Millard, Chapa, & Crane, 2004; Wortham, Mortimer, & Allard, 2009; Wortham, Murillo, & Hamann, 2002). Contingent realities about the large Black population in Marshall and the town's recent history of economic decline allowed some Mexicans to follow a pathway different than Mexican migrants in some similar towns.

Members of the research team spent hundreds of hours speaking with White, Black, and Mexican residents specifically about Marshall's history, its residential neighborhoods, and public spaces. Briana Nichols and several other members of the research team spoke extensively with two dozen current or former Black residents about these topics. Across the thousands of hours we spent in town, we interviewed more than fifty White and Mexican residents specifically about

Figure 4.1 For rent sign in Marshall's East end.

the history of the town, its housing patterns, commercial areas, and politics. We conducted interviews across generations, focusing on those who grew up in Marshall at the time Mexican migration began. We also conducted several projects in which we used similar interview protocols to ask about town history, about early Mexican residents, and about street crime and law enforcement.

Nostalgia and Decline

In the last three decades of the twentieth century, Marshall suffered economic decline that involved decreasing household incomes, loss of jobs, declining population, and lower rates of home ownership. This historical trend is connected to larger patterns of deindustrialization and suburbanization in the United States at that time (Bluestone & Harrison, 1982). The decline in Marshall resulted from the construction of nearby malls, the steady elimination of industrial jobs that once sustained the town's middle class, and the closure of a nearby state hospital that was a large employer, among other factors. As jobs disappeared, residents had less disposable income to spend in the stores along Main Street, and their shopping increasingly took place at the mall. As a result, the once-thriving commercial area of downtown Marshall declined. Residential areas became less well tended, property values went down, and many single-family homes were converted into rental units. Marshall's economic decline paralleled those of "inner ring suburbs" in many metropolitan areas (Short, Hanlon, & Vicino, 2007).

This economic decline happened to coincide with the latest iteration of the historical cycle in which one ethnic group was replaced by another—as migrants moved into the least expensive downtown housing and longstanding groups moved out to more affluent areas. As one White resident described,

> When [the Irish] moved up and out, then the Italians moved in. A lot of them moved into the houses of the Irish. And then they moved out—a lot of them— and the African Americans live in there now, in the areas where the Italians lived. And now they're being moved [as Mexicans arrive].

In the nineteenth century, the Irish moved into formerly Protestant areas. In the first half of the twentieth century, Italians and African Americans moved into formerly Irish areas, and in the 1960s and 1970s a second wave of African Americans from large cities moved into formerly Italian areas. In the 1960s and 1970s, however—unlike in most earlier eras—the cyclical turnover of ethnic groups in downtown residential neighborhoods co-occurred with substantial economic decline. White residents' stories of "decline" late in the twentieth century were intensified by the serious economic challenges the town faced, the lack of jobs, the increase in rental units, and the deteriorating conditions of many residential properties. Black residents did not cause the decline, but many Whites nonetheless associated them with it.

White and Black Marshall residents tended to offer divergent stories about this historical period. Both recalled glory days and then a decline, but the two groups dated the beginning of the decline differently: for White residents, it began with White flight in the 1970s, while for African Americans it began with the arrival of Mexicans in the 1990s. Neither group's story accurately captured the actual situation. White residents' stories oversimplified by erasing Black residents' successes. Despite the fact that many African Americans worked hard and accumulated both money and status, as other migrant groups had, White narrators characterized Black residents as unsuccessful. In our conversations with hundreds of White residents over eleven years in Marshall, we cannot recall hearing one story about Black upward mobility. Black residents' stories oversimplified by emphasizing Mexican culpability. Many African Americans felt as if their neighborhoods had been invaded by Mexicans, causing Black residents to move out, but in fact the forces that led to a decline in Marshall predated Mexicans' arrival by two decades. Despite the oversimplifications in these stories, they nonetheless influenced residents' perceptions of each other, their decisions about where to live, and how they treated members of other groups.

White Stories

How Marshall residents imagined the economic and social history of the town, and the roles they assigned to different groups within these stories, varied based on ethnicity and generation. As we have described, the White community in Marshall was heterogeneous—English, Irish, Italian, and other groups had distinct histories and tended to occupy different positions. There were also generational divides between White residents who were closer or further away from family migration experiences. Nonetheless, when discussing transformations in Marshall's residential spaces, there were many similarities in the ways White residents of varying backgrounds narrated the history of the town, its likely future pathway, and the roles they assigned to themselves and other residents.

White adults usually described Marshall's distant past nostalgically. They portrayed town spaces in ways that expressed a sense of community and connectedness that characterized Marshall "before." For these interlocutors, "before" meant before the economic decline that began in the 1960s and 1970s, when the malls were built and the town began to experience White flight. Rebecca, for example, grew up in Marshall and emphasized "the culture and the fabric of the community" before the decline.

> Everybody knew everybody. I married my childhood sweetheart, and ... he lived around the corner. Marshall means everything. It means pride. It means culture. It's secure. It means security. It means safety to me. It feels very natural to be here. The most memorable things that people think of, if they're from Marshall ... they think of Main Street. They think of Woolworth's. They think of the P&W. They think of the bustling streets, Mike's bargain store, Sweeny's ... And they think of the sidewalks being full of people. And when you see it now, you know, it's pretty empty during the day. Aside from the theaters there really isn't anything going on there ... [Before,] everybody in the house was employed, went somewhere in the morning, had some sort of specific career ... There was a clear sense that you had to get up every day and go to a job.

Rebecca focused on the stores and amenities, the family connections and sense of community, the economic and social ambition that made Marshall vibrant. Stories like this, filled with nostalgia, were common among White residents regardless of their ethnic background—and, as we will illustrate below, among Black residents as well. As one teacher described Marshall's past: "It used to be a great place to live, with quiet streets, with families, and it was clean and safe." A taxi driver told us that "Marshall used to be a place where there was no crime, no drugs, the nicest neighborhoods you'd ever want." Another resident explained how the town began with Italian, Irish, and some Polish families who were "the kind of people who scrubbed their front steps" and had street fairs. Carlo, whom we met in Chapter 1, said that in the old days "people cared about people. And my buddies ..., we would meet at somebody's house. We would sit on the front porch and listen to the radio." These densely circulating stories characterized both the community and the types of people who allegedly used to live there—hardworking, clean, proud, law abiding, supportive, and family oriented.

Particularly striking in White narrators' stories of Marshall "before" was the consistent erasure of the Black community, which in fact started in the early 1900s. African Americans rarely appeared in White stories of Marshall's past, until the arrival of poorer African Americans from nearby cities began around 1970. This erasure shaped White residents' explanations for the town's decline. In their stories, the people who made Marshall "clean and safe" were Irish, Polish, and Italian—not Black. The Black residents who appeared in their narratives came later and contributed to decline, despite the fact that thousands of Black residents had in fact arrived before 1970 with aspirations and in many cases pathways similar to their Irish, Polish, and Italian American neighbors. The dominant White narrative of residential space before the decline oversimplified by erasing the presence of thousands of ambitious, upwardly mobile Black residents who had lived in Marshall neighborhoods since early in the twentieth century.

This erasure fit with another aspect of the stories often told by Italian residents in particular. Italians and Italian Americans described struggles against racism that they and their families faced as migrants in the first half of the twentieth century, when they were not yet seen as White. Leo Ciccone, the former "Ambassador of Marshall" and child of Italian immigrants, for example, described an experience making funeral arrangements for his grandfather. In the 1940s, Leo was a police officer. His parents had migrated as adults and were not comfortable speaking English, so when his grandfather died he was sent to St. Joseph's to arrange for the burial. Despite the presence of several Catholic churches, there was only one Catholic cemetery in town, and that was controlled by St. Joseph's. The Irish American priest took Leo to the cemetery to select a plot, and they drove right by the broad, open front area—despite the fact that it had many available spaces. The priest took him to the back, where the plots were smaller and crowded together. Leo asked if his grandfather could have a larger plot up front, but the priest refused. When one goes to the cemetery today, most of the names in the still-crowded rear of the only Catholic cemetery in town are Italian. The front has mostly Irish, German, and Polish names, although some more recently deceased Italians now rest there.

Some long-term Anglo residents confirmed the existence of discrimination against Italians as well as African Americans. A local minister told us:

> There was another whole class of folk in town: the bankers, the doctors, the lawyers. And this [West] end of town from Center over was developed as an area that did not have to deal with Blacks and Italians. Kind of a gentleman's agreement, such as the Jews had to deal with in the '20s and '30s. One of the members of this church who was Italian managed to buy a piece of land for a house here in this end, and he was never fully accepted. When the color line broke in the '50s, you have White flight like you wouldn't believe.

Some of our Italian interlocutors even claimed that they were treated as badly as African Americans. Marco, a long time Italian resident in his seventies, described his grandfather's experiences, and those of early Italian residents generally, by (inaccurately) comparing the treatment of Italian migrants to the treatment of Black slaves:

> Right now the Black people say "ohh, they used to treat us as slaves." The Italian people were the same thing. They didn't treat them right at all. I remember my grandfather used to say every time he used to come into Marshall to go to the stores to buy stuff they used to stone him, and they throw stones at him and everything else.

Marco went on to explain that this situation had changed by the 1950s. Italians were no longer treated as badly, and they became upwardly mobile. They "started joining the police force and the mayor's office" and had "control over half of Marshall."

We were unable to substantiate Marco's claims about stoning, and his comparing the mistreatment of Italians with African American slavery was both false and jarring. His claim minimized the extraordinary dehumanization and far-reaching socioeconomic disadvantage that continues to affect descendants of African slaves in America. But Italians were in fact racialized as non-White in the first half of the twentieth century (LaGumina, 1999), and their descendants' stories about this mistreatment continued to circulate in Marshall. These stories contained a recognizable character: hardworking Italian migrants who were able to succeed despite having to struggle against racism and economic disadvantage.

Many Italian American residents' stories also contrasted Italians and Blacks, who allegedly were not able to progress in the same way. As Marco told us:

> Nobody lives in Marshall anymore ... It used to be a very nice place and then a lot of people come from the South. And when one somebody buy a house, colored people used to buy a house. The next year you sell the house. The Black people coming in, the Italian people they go out.

Another narrator described White flight similarly: many of the "original" families moved out in the 1970s and 1980s, when they "noticed the influx ... That's when the complexion of the town really changed." In fact, as we have seen, there were many successful Black professionals and businesspeople in Marshall across decades—including by 2010 the majority of the City Council, several members of the School Board, high-ranking police officers, and school district administrators. Furthermore, many Italian and Black residents had lived together in the same neighborhoods in the East end for decades, in an era when they were both treated as undesirable by Irish and White Protestant communities. But some Italian American narrators nonetheless positioned Black residents as the undesirable "other" responsible for community decline.

Italian Americans' stories about White flight were not completely false, but they oversimplified the complexities of residential life across the twentieth century in Marshall. Many Italians and Italian Americans did in fact move out as more African Americans arrived in the 1970s and 1980s, but for decades before that they had lived side by side with Blacks in the same neighborhoods. Mexican migrants did resemble Italians in some ways, and their pathways may in some cases be similar, but many Black migrants also had ambitions and worked hard, and some moved "up and out" just as Irish and Italian migrants had. The African American community in Marshall, like other migrant communities, was heterogeneous, with arrivals in different historical eras and varying pathways with respect to housing, work, and employment. The dominant story told by White residents about Marshall's decline erased this fact and focused on working-class Black residents who had moved out from nearby cities starting around 1970 and had not yet achieved upward mobility—thus inaccurately characterizing all African Americans as recent arrivals who caused the decline of downtown residential neighborhoods. In fact, many Blacks were successful and the economic decline was caused by factors that had nothing to do with African American residents.

According to many White residents, the demographic shift co-occurred with an increase in "Section 8"—government subsidies given to poor tenants to allow them to afford rental housing—and with the emergence of slumlords. As one White educator noted:

> Somewhere along the line in the 1960s or '70s landlords began to buy up houses. They were allowed to subdivide them and rent them out. They're looking to make money instead of selling them to families. Five to six men in town started buying up property and making a lot of money off of section 8 housing.

Another White resident echoed this:

> Housing values have dropped ... People tend to inherit their homes or pay off the mortgage and then not do any improvements ... so property values are dropping. There are these guys who say "we pay cash for houses" and they buy them up and these landlords tend to cut up the houses. This tends to happen in African American neighborhoods.

Marshall in this period of decline was also frequently described as the "dumping ground" of the county, where the poor came because of cheap rental units. One community leader told us that there were "drugs and prostitution ... it has the highest proportion of Section 8 housing ... it has a high proportion of homeless, alcoholic, lots of street people." Another White educator summarized: Marshall is "going to hell in a handbasket."

In fact, as attested by James Smith and others, many Black families throughout the twentieth century in Marshall had the same aspirations as other residents. Many worked hard, bought a house, raised children, and enjoyed community life. But White residents' stories about the economic and social trajectory of Marshall oversimplified the changes in neighborhood makeup as good-to-bad, owner-occupied-to-section 8, White-to-Black. As many Black residents themselves acknowledged, the arrival of poorer African Americans from inner cities starting around 1970 did coincide with and may have contributed to problems in some residential neighborhoods. But the typical White narrative ignored the longstanding Black middle class, as well as the community-oriented working-class Blacks who moved from cities to Marshall for a better life, and it failed to appreciate the solidarity that existed in the Black residential community well into the 1990s.

Black Stories

African American narrators did not erase the history of the many Black migrants who worked hard to achieve upward mobility, and they described their ancestors' hard work in ways that resembled stories from other ethnic groups. But many Black narratives about residential space were nonetheless similar in other ways to those told by White residents. Like White residents, most African Americans highlighted the sense of family and community they felt in Marshall's neighborhoods "before." They also focused on the importance of home ownership and residential stability. Unlike White residents' stories, they described the Black community as hard working and family oriented. In the passages from James Smith presented in Chapter 1, for example, he compared the work ethic of Black Marshall residents to that of early Italians. "There wasn't a lot of rentals back then. It was home ownership. And everybody was interested in buying. That was the dream [for Blacks too], to own your home." Many Black residents in James' generation described a Marshall in which families worked together in order to achieve upward mobility—as his father and uncle worked and saved to buy a house together, then worked and saved to buy a second house so each family could have its own. For African Americans as well as White residents, home ownership was an important distinguishing feature between Marshall "before" and Marshall "after" the decline, when rental units predominated. In these stories, the financial and material conditions of residential neighborhoods were also connected to ideological constructions of success and worthiness. Prototypical residents before the decline were characterized as hardworking and upwardly mobile, while those after were often portrayed as lazy and irresponsible.

As described in Chapter 1, James accurately narrated how Italian and Black residents lived together on the East side of town for several decades. He noted that both groups had pride in their heritage and worked hard to start new lives in Marshall. Younger African Americans who grew up in Marshall told stories that were similar in some crucial respects. Keon was a Black law school student in his thirties whose mother grew up in Marshall and who volunteered in a program to build connections between Black and Mexican youth in town—a program we describe in Chapter 6. He told us about the Marshall he remembered in the 1980s, when it still had many Italian residents.

> Marshall ... was an Italian dominated community. They're very proud, and they let you know they're very proud, good and bad. But I'm shocked to this day at what Marshall looks like today. Not necessarily a bad thing, but it's just totally, completely different than what I remember as a kid.

Keon was thirty years younger than James, but he too described a time when African Americans and Italians lived together and shared core values. He did not position Italians as distant social others. This was different from most White residents' stories, in which Black community members were inaccurately characterized as unfamiliar new arrivals who had fundamentally altered the town.

Jamar and Darrell were African American community organizers and educators in their thirties. Both grew up in Marshall, left to attend college, and then returned to work in the community. Although their stories about Marshall described different eras than those narrated by James Smith and Doreena, their stories were similar. Jamar explained how he lived in a quiet neighborhood on the West side of town.

> When I moved here I was 8 or 9, from [a nearby city]. Moved into the West end, a quiet neighborhood. 8AM all the kids came out on the block, and we played around in the parking lot, the church parking lot all day. Come and get something to eat, go back out and play ... Marshall had basketball courts everywhere ... and then when I met Darrell I used to hang out on his block with him ... We used to sit in my friend's garage all day and mess around with bikes, and ride bikes all night.

Darrell described a similar feeling of community:

Growing up, in my opinion, it was a small-town feel. All the families were connected. You know, you had your East end, you had your West end, but it was still a small town ... Things changed a lot today. [Back then] it did seem a little bit more prosperous, a lot more families, a lot more working families, a lot more two parent households, even recreation and education opportunities were out there.

These younger Black men described a historical moment in the 1980s and 1990s, before Mexican migrants began coming in large numbers. At that time, there were still working-class White residents living in the West end of Marshall, although most White residents had moved out. As Harrison said: "The closer you got to [the Western suburbs] the more Caucasian it got. In the middle of Marshall, though, there was nobody except African Americans ... [The East end] was all Black, and then on the West end ... you had different ethnic groups."

Darrell, Harrison, and Jamar described connected families, a sense of community, relative prosperity, and a "small town feel" in Marshall "before"—just as Leo Ciccone and other White residents did. But the time period they were describing—their childhoods in Marshall during the 1980s and early 1990s—was an era when White residents claimed that the decline had already taken place. Many White residents told us that they had been "afraid to drive through Marshall" in the 1980s and 1990s. Both White and Black residents narrated a positive time "before," but they were talking about different historical moments. Narrators from both groups also talked about subsequent decline, but in White residents' narratives that decline started decades earlier. Each story was accurate in some ways and inaccurate in others. White flight did in fact start in the 1960s, but there were still some White residents until the 1990s. Crime did increase in the 1970s and 1980s, at the same time as working-class African Americans moved in from inner cities, but the town's decline had more to do with deindustrialization, suburbanization, and corruption among White politicians.

Despite the challenges faced by the town in the 1980s and 1990s, many Black residents in downtown neighborhoods felt safe and experienced a sense of community. During this era, many Black residents chose to move "up and in," not "up and out." That is, they achieved financial success and could have moved to more affluent surrounding towns, as Irish and Italian American residents had done. But two factors kept these Black residents in Marshall. First, despite laws against housing discrimination, African Americans were unjustly steered away from many surrounding towns and often feared that they would not feel welcome. Second, despite the changing economic situation in Marshall, Black residents valued the sense of community there. "Up and out" was thus not an inevitable or unilinear pathway for all migrant groups. Many African Americans had the resources to move out of town, but they did not perceive such a move as desirable. They chose to stay in or near downtown Marshall, while nonetheless also moving "up" as they developed economic and social capital. In most cases, it was these Black residents' children, like Keon, Darrell, Harrison, and Jamar, who left for college and subsequently settled in surrounding areas.

White residents attributed the town's economic and social decline to Black migration into Marshall and the resulting White flight. Black community members did not present either Black migration or White flight as the cause of economic decline. The town still felt moderately prosperous and communal to many Black residents during the period of White flight, as long as there were homeowners who cared for their properties. But White flight did open up housing stock that turned from owner-occupied to rental. Starting in the mid-1990s, many Mexicans moved into those rentals. For most Black narrators, this was a crucial symbol of the town's decline. White flight contributed to a critical transition in Marshall from an ownership community to a rental community. Home ownership meant prosperity, success, and stability for the town, while rental properties promoted transience and damaged the sense of community that Black residents felt "before" (Nichols & Wortham, 2018). The new rentals also opened up a significant amount of inexpensive housing stock. Initially these rentals were occupied mostly by African Americans moving out from cities, but most Black narrators did not describe this as a sharp decline. In their stories, the decline began when Mexican migrants moved in.

Joyce was Doreena's daughter-in-law, a Black woman who grew up and still lived in Marshall in 2016. She described her experience of this transition:

> It's just when you have a lot of transient population coming in, it becomes hard. Like I said, I don't know whether that's Mexicans, or whether it's just transient. Or maybe I'm just seeing a lot of people who aren't taking care of their properties, because they're poor people ... My house, I mean it's, it's gone down in value from when I first moved into it.

Michelle, Joyce's neighbor, had similar concerns and directly connected White flight with Mexican arrivals:

> I'd say that there were a lot of Whites moving out. More Mexicans moving in, and it's unfortunate too because I feel like with the Mexicans moving in a lot of them probably were not supposed to be here so that gave landlords more of an opportunity to take full advantage of their living situations.

Despite the fact that White flight began in the 1970s and few Mexicans arrived before the 1990s, both Joyce and Michelle saw them as linked. They remembered an era of Black property ownership and robust community, during White flight but before the Mexicans' arrival. Many Black homeowners like Joyce complained about their falling property values and attributed this to the arrival of Mexicans. Beyond the economic impact, long-term Black residents lamented how once-stable neighborhoods began to feel unfamiliar and unsafe as people ceased to care about the community.

White and Black residents, then, told similar stories about the history of downtown Marshall residential neighborhoods. It used to be a good place to live, but that changed when economic conditions deteriorated and a new group moved to town. A similar story had also been told in the first half of the twentieth century, when longstanding Irish and White Protestant residents complained that the town had deteriorated with the arrival of Italians and African Americans. In contemporary iterations of the story, however, White and Black residents diverged in their accounts of who caused the decline and when it occurred. According to White narrators, African Americans caused the problem. According to Black narrators, Mexicans caused it. Each group ignored some facts. White residents' stories typically erased the many successful African Americans who migrated from the South before 1970. Many Black narrators ignored lower-class Black residents who migrated from urban areas and occupied rental housing, and many also ignored the economic decline that was underway well before Mexicans arrived. The groups consequently imagined Mexicans very differently—as a source of revitalization after the decline, or as a primary cause of the decline. These divergent, partially inaccurate stories of Mexicans were crucial resources shaping the pathways of many residents. We will describe in the next chapter both how White residents' stories about Mexican revitalization led them to offer some Mexicans opportunities that were unavailable to Blacks and how African Americans sometimes resisted Mexican bids for increased influence in town.

The First Decade: *Solteros*, Slumlords and Victims

When Mexicans began arriving in large numbers in the mid-1990s, longstanding residents adjusted their stories about the history of the town to include this new group. We summarize these stories, as they circulated during the first decade of the Mexican community, with three archetypes that appeared in many narratives: *solteros*, slumlords, and victims. *Soltero* means "bachelor" in Spanish. Stories that included these characters were often inaccurate, but the familiar character types nonetheless influenced residents' perceptions and actions. When the Mexican migrant population began to increase dramatically in the 1990s, most of the new arrivals were single men who came to work—although many of them were married and supported a wife and children back in Mexico. Most sent money back to family in Mexico and hoped to return once they had saved enough for a better life there. They often lived in Marshall with a brother, an uncle, or a cousin, occasionally with a sister or a niece. Some families came together, but intact nuclear families were not typical during this period. There were already some established Mexican families in town, like Juana Faccone and several of her siblings. But Mexicans arriving after the mid-1990s were different. They tended to come from other parts of Mexico—more from Querétaro and the center of Mexico, fewer from the coasts—and they had less social and economic capital.

These new migrants initially settled in the near West side of downtown Marshall, which was almost entirely African American at the time. Mexican men tended to live many to an apartment in the surrounding neighborhood, to save money on rent. Some landlords charged rent by the person, which allowed them to make more money from a given apartment. The first Mexican store opened in that area in the mid-1990s. It was owned by Juana Faccone's cousin, who also opened the first Mexican restaurant next door a few years later. A bilingual Spanish-English social service agency that had originally served Puerto Ricans was located on the main shopping street in this area, right across from the first Mexican store. This agency had been reinvigorated by the arrival of Mexican migrants and provided important services.

The young male Mexican workers who moved into this neighborhood were said to work hard, but many longstanding residents believed that they lived in dirty, crowded conditions and spent their non-working hours with alcohol and prostitutes. White, Black, and Mexican residents all told stories about how these *solteros* were victimized by unscrupulous absentee "slumlords" who divided substandard properties into small rental units and made money renting to fearful, allegedly compliant undocumented migrants. In these widely circulating stories, the Mexicans were victims, fleeced by landlords and sometimes robbed by Black criminals. These three recognizable characters—the *soltero*, the slumlord, and the victim—recurred in stories told about Mexicans and other residents during and about the first decade of the Mexican migrant community. There were some differences between narrators from different ethnic backgrounds, but all three characters appeared in stories from each of the groups.

These characters accurately represented the first decade of the migrant community in some respects but not others. There were many young Mexican men in town, and they often did live together in crowded apartments. But there were also Mexican families, including some that had lived in Marshall for almost two decades, and not every Mexican lived in crowded conditions. Some landlords were unscrupulous, but many respected the migrants and treated them fairly. Not all Mexicans were passive victims. Many feared drawing attention to themselves and endured exploitation by landlords and bosses, but most took control of their lives and cared for their families, many fought back against unfair treatment from landlords and others, and some opened businesses of their own. The inaccurate stereotype of Mexicans as passive and victimized erases the agency that they showed in difficult conditions (DeGenova & Ramos-Zayas, 2003).

In this section, we analyze how these stories were told by Black, White, and Hispanic narrators. Taken together, stories about *solteros*, slumlords, and victims represent some important aspects of the residential situation in Marshall in the first decade of the Mexican community. The divergence across narrators from different ethnic groups also shows how residents struggled to account for the broken cyclical pattern in the historical pathways of migrant groups. African Americans as a group were not moving "up and out" as consistently as earlier groups had, according to White narrators, and Marshall residents had divergent beliefs about how and why that happened. In order to make sense of Mexicans' pathways in Marshall, we must engage with the realities of and stories about Black residents—because the juxtaposition between Black and Mexican residents was one important resource that shaped how White, Black, and Mexican residents felt about the migrants' prospects.

Black Stories about *Solteros* and Slumlords

Black residents often felt overwhelmed by the new residential patterns. They described uncomfortable crowding and how they felt excluded, like in this conversation between Doreena, Joyce, and Tiffany—a mother, daughter, and granddaughter:

> Doreena: If you get a couple of them in the house and then you look up you have fifteen to twenty people in the house ... That's what maybe make the people move too.
> Joyce: Because nobody wants to live next to-
> Tiffany: I guess overwhelmed is like the feeling, is a good way to describe it.
> Doreena: Right, right because they have twenty-five people live in one house, and you can't have that many people in the house. My sister say they sleep in shifts.

Joyce: They sleep in shifts. [laughing]
Doreena: That's what they do, they bring a truckload of people, and then they empty a truckload, and then … they all stay in the one house.
Tiffany: Well, I'm sure that's … a cultural thing, the family kinda stays together … and it's probably alien to us, just as anything to people outside of us is alien to them, like that we do, like "I can't believe those …, " you know what I mean? That they do that, but, I don't know, just overwhelmed is the, is the [right word to describe it].

We know of no cases with twenty-five men in one apartment, but there was high occupancy in small spaces. Black community members felt "overwhelmed" by the crowding they felt Mexicans brought to neighborhoods that African Americans had lived in for decades. The men who arrived in large numbers in the first decade, and who often slept many people to an apartment, felt like an invasion to many Black residents.

The perceived crowding caused problems with parking. A local clergyman told us:

> You have 10 or 15 single men living in one apartment in a side street and each of them has a car, and all the neighbors need to park too. I heard that from some of the Black folk in the area. They … say "we used to live big in houses but back then we didn't each have a car." … It doesn't take much to fill up a street.

Black residents did in fact complain about overcrowding on downtown streets. A reporter for the local newspaper listened to recordings on the town's hotline for

Figure 4.2 Parked cars along a downtown residential street.

neighbor complaints, and he told us that it was mostly African Americans who complained about overcrowding. This makes sense, since African Americans were the ones living downtown in close proximity to new Mexican residents.

Michelle, another longtime African American resident, provided a similar story about the Mexican "invasion" and the resulting unsafe conditions.

> I think people have this perception that Mexicans are not the cleanest and there's a lot of crime that happens, like drunk driving, let's say, accidents, being uninsured … the cleanliness, the just being irresponsible … I lived next to a Mexican family when I rented a house in [downtown] Marshall on Fox Street and it was, I'd say, about 3 different families in the house … And they had this thing where, from the bathroom—because there was a baby—they had a sheet tied from the tree to somewhere on the roof and they would throw dirty diapers on the sheet. And they had like pots of food out on the back porch. It was kind of disturbing. I actually broke my lease to get out of there because it just wasn't a good environment.

Like some other Black residents, Michelle characterized Mexicans as unclean and blamed them for the decline in housing conditions. But African Americans also often blamed the slumlords who exploited allegedly undocumented Mexicans. Michelle went on to say:

> There were a lot of Whites moving out. More Mexicans moving in, and it's unfortunate too because … a lot of them probably were not supposed to be here so that gave landlords more of an opportunity to take full advantage of them … There are a lot of Mexicans that live in town and they're paying way above what they should be for apartments and houses and that's why … a lot of them live together, to try and afford their rents. So, it's unfortunate … [It] seems like the owner doesn't care as long as they're getting the money off of the renters.

Michelle was disturbed by her new Mexican neighbors, by the crowding and allegedly unsanitary conditions. But she also blamed the slumlords.

Despite their concerns, Black residents often tried to understand Mexicans' point of view. In the passage above, Tiffany empathized with the new residents and imagined how they might be similar to her. She observed that, while Mexican practices are "alien to us," the practices of her community are probably "alien to them." Another resident told us that her grandparents were the first Black family to move onto their block and "there wasn't a big welcome wagon outside their door." She noted that Mexicans were facing similar discrimination. Black residents often characterized Mexicans as "other" while simultaneously describing their own similarities with them. African Americans' attitudes toward Mexicans were thus complex. Individual Black residents differed in their views—with younger people often being more empathic than older residents— and many Black residents described both how they had been displaced by Mexicans and how they were similar to Mexicans because members of both groups were often poor and suffered racial discrimination.

In another interview, Joyce compared histories of African Americans and Mexicans in Marshall:

> We're used to having a lot of families, but not quite like they would have a lot of families in their houses. And it just seemed like they were running down the houses. And that's just because they're probably poor people coming in to- Even though we were poor, we still, we had a little bit of money. It's like, you just didn't have enough money to move out of that neighborhood, but you had enough money that you weren't *poor* poor.

Here Joyce noted similarities between her family's experience and the Mexicans'. But she also distanced herself from them, claiming that Mexicans had even fewer resources than earlier Black residents.

As described above, Italian and Italian American residents also sometimes empathized with Mexicans and compared their families' migrant histories to the pathways being taken by the new migrants. But White and Black stories diverged in important ways. Italians imagined Mexicans following in their own footsteps "up and out." They also celebrated Mexicans as the primary cause of revitalization after the decline that had been substantially caused, in their view, by African Americans. Black residents did not view the Mexicans as a revitalizing force in Marshall. Despite some empathy, many Black residents considered Mexicans an "overwhelming" presence that pushed them out of town, and they described the arrival of Mexicans as pivotal to the town's decline. While telling this story of decline, Black narrators circulated the stereotype of single Mexican men who lived many people to a house and did not care about the condition of the house or the well-being of the community—even though most African Americans also saw the Mexicans as victims of slumlords and other unjust circumstances.

White Stories about *Solteros* and Slumlords

Many White residents also told stories about *solteros* and the White slumlords who victimized them. These stories often contained some sympathy for Mexicans. They emphasized slumlords' culpability in taking advantage of migrants, and narrators generally empathized with Mexicans' plight. But White narrators also positioned *solteros* as participating in the decline of Marshall. As we have seen, most White residents believed the decline had started decades earlier. Mexicans were not responsible for starting the decline, in the typical White resident's story, since they arrived relatively late in the process. But *solteros* rented the decaying properties, and they packed many people into each apartment. This generated crowding, trash, and noise. In the first decade of the community, most Mexicans also focused on work and sending money home. This led many White residents to conclude that Mexicans did not care about the physical condition of their residences or the downtown area and that they would run Marshall down even further before moving back home.

One White woman told us: "I always tell people [Marshall] is like a little inner-city ghetto." She told a story about how, one day near her house in the far East end, there was an eighteen-year-old pointing a gun at his girlfriend. "The dichotomy of the town has totally changed." It used to be Black people and White people. She offered an inaccurate folk geography: "there was a horseshoe," she said—the East end was the bad neighborhood and there were White people in the rest. But now there were no more good areas of town, she claimed, only "worse" ones. Marshall had become one quarter Black, White, and Asian, she told us (incorrectly), and all the rest were Mexican. She added that around the time Mexicans started coming, crime started going up. "I don't want to sound prejudiced, 'cause I'm certainly not," she said (unconvincingly). She had Mexican neighbors down the street, and they were great. But other Mexicans lived twenty men to a house. She concluded by telling us that "it's the landlords' fault; they don't take care of the houses." This contradictory stance toward Mexicans—sympathetic at times, but also providing extensive misinformation and blaming the migrants for the latest phase in the decline—occurred in many White residents' stories about Mexicans during the first decade of the migrant community.

Like African Americans, White residents told stories about Mexicans living in crowded, dirty, unsafe conditions. Anastasia told us that "some of them live like sardines." Others described "hot-racking," the practice of renting beds by the hour and by the head to people who had nowhere else to sleep. Anastasia claimed that landlords didn't object to overcrowding, but instead took advantage of it: "if you have the three bedrooms apartment and you're taking, you know, a friend of friend and friend of a friend and then when the landlord see that there is more people ... he wants per head a hundred dollars a week." She went on to describe how Mexican migrants have been abused by landlords, telling us the story of one family she knew.

> All three children have lead poison and the pregnant woman and little unborn child ... You have a person who knows the law who rents this apartment ... He owns many apartments. But for this quick buck, he will do something like this. He will damage the life of the whole family sometimes ... I can tell you about an "efficiency" [apartment], this was created not long ago. It was a bathroom ... So, you have this huge bathroom and I know this house ... you have a bathroom with a toilet with a curtain with a teeny, tiny stall and a place to put maybe a single bed and this [is an] efficiency apartment. Costs five hundred fifty dollars.

Both White and Black residents told stories about greedy slumlords who cared nothing for the health and well-being of their tenants, nor about the condition of their buildings. The narrators described how, because they did not speak English and may have been undocumented, Mexicans were easily victimized. Across Black and White narrators, the familiar characters of the *soltero*, the White slumlord, and the Mexican victim recurred.

Hispanic Stories

Mexican migrants did not typically tell stories about how their arrival changed the town, because they had not experienced Marshall before their arrival. But a few residents from other Latin American countries worked in Marshall and interacted with Mexican migrants in schools, churches, social service agencies, and government offices. These were largely Puerto Ricans, with a few from South America—typically people whose parents had migrated to nearby areas and who themselves grew up in the United States. Many of these Hispanic residents also told stories about Mexican migrants that included *solteros*, slumlords, and victims. A Puerto Rican staff member at the Marshall police department, for example, told us that there was a "lifestyle clash here in Marshall. There can be 10-11-12 Mexicans in one house." This created tension between neighbors. She rushed to clarify that she was not using stereotypes about Mexicans. The young male Mexicans "are louder, they drink, there are prostitutes—because they are men," not because they are Mexican. That behavior made them undesirable neighbors. On Friday, Saturday, and Sunday, she said, they drank and everything escalated. There was tension with whoever was living next door.

Don Miguel, the Puerto Rican director of the main Spanish-speaking social service agency in town, confirmed that Mexicans often came to live with aunts, uncles, grandparents, or other family members. Mexican men came to Marshall to get jobs and to buy a car—often the first car ever in their families. They sometimes drove without a license or insurance. Rent was expensive in Marshall: in 2005, he told us it cost $800 for a small two-bedroom apartment. So two families often lived in one space. "Slum landlords abound," he said, and the living conditions could be quite bad. He said that some of the community resentment resulted from petty issues such as senior citizens not being able to find parking because a large group of Mexicans next door had taken up all the spaces. He counseled Mexicans to "park a few streets away or in nearby lots" to avoid this problem. In his view, Mexicans paid their rent on time, were clean and hardworking, and had improved the condition of the town by fixing up their apartments.

Another Puerto Rican professional blamed Mexicans to some extent for the decline in housing. "These guys, there's like 20 of them living in an apartment. They're the ones that are destroying the area. They're not speaking the language and, quite frankly, it's hostile because they are the ones living right on top of each other." But he immediately added that they were victims of racism as well. "You know, we live in a country where the color of your skin absolutely matters." He also described the Mexican migrants as victims of horrible slumlords.

> Unfortunately for me, I had the experience of going on some home inspections ... and I wanted to vomit. It was ... power cords, hanging from a window, with wires coming to it across the way. And ... take this room and we'll divide it in two with plywood in the middle. Do the landlords put it there? It's one of those don't ask, don't see, don't know. And some landlords, I imagine when they have a heads-up, they go first and take things down before the inspector gets there, ask people to leave while the inspector is there.

This Puerto Rican man offered a telling eyewitness account of the substandard housing occupied by Mexicans, and he mostly blamed the slumlords. Mexicans were victims of unscrupulous landlords who crammed extra renters into a unit—even going so far as to nail up flimsy plywood dividers so that they could charge for extra rooms. The landlords also played cat and mouse with city inspectors, hiding unsafe conditions and asking tenants to stay away from the property during likely inspection times in order to obscure the number of people occupying the property.

Juan Castro, the young Mexican man described in Chapter 2, told us about an experience he had with an unscrupulous landlord. He consulted with us in 2007 when his landlord filed an unjustified claim against him for failure to pay $100 rent. After discussing the situation, we agreed that the landlord summoned him not because he planned to follow through with a lawsuit but because he thought it would scare Juan into paying. Juan took a day off and went to contest the claim, and members of our team went with him. The landlord did not appear in court, despite the fact that he filed the claim. "Why else would they file for $100 and not show up," Juan mused, "unless they were trying to scare me?" He told us that Mexican tenants are often afraid to go to court, afraid that they might be asked for documents or worried that they did not speak English well enough. So instead of going to court, they will "go ahead and pay. People do it all the time."

All of our interlocutors—Black, White, and Hispanic residents—told similar stories about Mexican housing in the first decade after the migrant community began to grow. They agreed that Mexicans were victimized by unscrupulous landlords, and they agreed that *solteros* and Mexican families packed into apartments in ways that generated crowded and perhaps unsafe conditions. Black residents were often upset by the invasion of what they considered their neighborhoods, but they also often empathized with Mexicans' plight. White residents were less emotional about the "invasion," because few lived in those neighborhoods, and their empathy more often felt like pity than solidarity. Puerto Ricans and other Latin Americans tended to blame the slumlords, but they acknowledged the concerns caused by overcrowding.

These stories captured something real about many Mexicans' lives in Marshall during the first decade of the migrant community. There were abusive landlords who took advantage of Mexicans, and the early migrants often lived many to an apartment. But the three archetypes of *solteros*, slumlords, and victims foregrounded only one kind of Mexican experience in Marshall while obscuring others. Many Mexican residents told us, for example, that they refused to be victimized—describing how they came together to protect each other and how they fought back against landlords, employers, and bullies. Despite their inaccuracies, these stories nonetheless influenced many Mexicans' perceptions of themselves, making them feel like outsiders who were not welcome in the community. The stories also shaped White and Black residents' reactions to Mexicans, leading them to position Mexicans as pitiful or as threats. Stereotypes about *solteros*, slumlords, and victims were one important resource that influenced migrant pathways.

But these archetypal characters were also tied to a historical era—the first decade of the migrant community—and things changed as the community developed. Many White residents' stories shifted in the second decade, toward characterizations of Mexicans as revitalizers who saved the town. At the same time, many Black residents' stories about Mexicans continued to focus on decline.

The pathway being followed by the Mexican migrant community changed around 2005, as more young families settled and there were fewer *solteros*. Stereotypes from the earlier era continued to circulate and did influence some migrants even during the second decade, but new characterizations of Mexican migrants as revitalizers also emerged as potential resources. Another central resource that continued to Mexicans' pathways as they moved into the second decade was their relationship with African Americans—both the realities of their diverse relationships and the oversimplified perceptions of those relationships that circulated in stories.

The Housing Ordinance

Before describing how stories and realities changed in the second decade of the Mexican migrant community, we briefly discuss a town ordinance that was directed at *solteros* and slumlords primarily because of Black residents' concerns about a decline in downtown neighborhoods. In 2004, a local newspaper article reported:

> In recent years, Council members and community leaders have launched accusations that unscrupulous landlords have rented homes to significantly more than allowed under the law. Those accusations, though, had gone largely ignored, in part because code enforcement was unable to prove units were overcrowded ... Council voted to implement inspections at night.

Night inspections failed to catch the unscrupulous landlords, however. In response, in 2005 the City Council created a housing ordinance that targeted both landlords and Mexican tenants. According to the newspaper:

> The new rules tie the number of people permitted to live in a dwelling to its size. One-person bedrooms must be a minimum of 70 square feet; bedrooms for more than one person must be a minimum of 50 square feet per person ... Members of Council claim the rules are targeted to improve quality of life.

The ordinance contained other restrictions that seemed unreasonable—for instance, requiring that some apartments have dining rooms.

> A living room shall not be mandated if there are only one or two occupants per dwelling or apartment. If there are three to six occupants in a dwelling or an apartment there must be at least 130 square feet allocated for a living room. If there are six or more occupants in a dwelling at least 160 square feet must be allocated for a living room ... A dining room shall not be required if there is only one or two occupants per dwelling or apartment. If there are three to

five occupants in a dwelling or apartment there must be at least 90 square feet allocated for a dining room. If there are six or more occupants at least 100 square feet must be allocated for a dining room.

Needless to say, similar restrictions were not in place for dwellings typically occupied by non-Mexicans. Newspaper reporters told us that the ordinance was sparked by Black residents' complaints about overcrowding in downtown residential neighborhoods.

The Council justified the ordinance this way:

> Council has recognized that overcrowding is often a concern in rental properties and in small single-family dwellings. It can create serious problems; for example, disease spreads with ease, privacy is lost, mental health is impacted and buildings are subject to more abuse and wear. Overcrowding can have a damaging effect on a whole neighborhood if it takes place in multiple houses on the same block or in multiple units in the same apartment building.

The ordinance itself did not say whether Mexican migrants were perpetrators or victims of the threats created by overcrowding. But it was clearly Mexicans' apartments that were imagined by the Council. This was confirmed by minutes from the Council deliberation, in which the African American Council president said: "no one on this council would discriminate against anyone. Council is obligated to uphold public safety. We are aware of the significant contributions by the Latino and Spanish community in Marshall." She mentioned several Mexican businesses and stated how great they were. She also claimed that real estate values had gone up, not down, and that "Marshall is really looking good." Whatever the motivations of Council members and the residents they represented, however, this ordinance presupposed the soltero, slumlord, and victim stereotypes—Mexicans who lived with many people crammed into apartments, causing health and safety concerns, and landlords who victimized them and profited from overcrowding.

The ordinance appears designed to reduce the high density of Mexican residents in downtown neighborhoods and perhaps to punish the White slumlords who were profiting from overcrowding. The ordinance may have reduced crowding, but for several reasons it did not reduce the number of Mexican residents. First, it was not enforced consistently. Politically connected landlords did not want to lose rental income, and they were often able to avoid the ordinance. Second, Mexicans moved to other areas of town, especially the East end, in larger numbers. The migrants spread out, reducing density but increasing their presence across town. Third, the Mexican community was changing by the time this ordinance was passed. The days of single men living together were waning, and more families were settling. Many Mexicans were becoming established, saving money, and opening businesses. Many had enough money that they no longer had to share apartments, and some were willing to spend money that earlier migrants would have sent back to Mexico.

Narrators from all groups portrayed *solteros*, slumlords, and Mexican victims as central characters in Marshall from 1995 to 2005. Some longstanding residents from every ethnic group told stories about Mexicans living in crowded, unsanitary conditions downtown. At that historical moment, the Mexican migrant community could have moved in various directions—in its material conditions, its self-image, and its reputation among longstanding residents. Mexicans could have stayed downtown, living in the low-rent neighborhoods alongside working-class African Americans. They could have done so as allies of Black residents, or they could have maintained their own separate community. Mexican migrants or their children could have moved "up and out," following Italians toward business and home ownership. They could have moved "up and in," as some African Americans had, accumulating resources but staying to build a Mexican community in downtown Marshall. In fact, some Mexicans followed each of these pathways, as well as others. In the rest of this chapter, we introduce the divergent stories told about Mexicans' future during the second decade of the migrant community, together with some contrasting realities in Marshall during that decade. Black residents often continued to characterize the Mexicans as problematic, as invaders responsible for decline, although some also worked to become allies. White residents tended to change their stories, seeing many Mexicans in the second decade as revitalizing the town. As more and more intact Mexican families with young children settled in the 2000s, White, Mexican, and other Hispanic residents more often characterized them positively.

Revitalization, Conflict, and Reconciliation

Starting in the 2000s, fewer migrants arrived directly from Mexico. The most common type of Mexican resident in town changed. In the first decade, it had been a single man hoping to return to Mexico. In the second decade, it was an intact nuclear family with small children who were likely to remain in the United States. This transition happened partly because of increased enforcement at the Mexican border. As Durand and Massey (2004) show, increased border policing had the unintended effect of disrupting habits of periodic return to Mexico. Mexicans with families in the United States risked one last trip north across the border. Those already across did not risk returning to Mexico. The new US policy was intended to lock undocumented migrants out, but instead it locked them in. This contributed to a demographic change: before the early 2000s, the US Hispanic population increased primarily because of migration; afterwards, it increased primarily through births (Pew Hispanic Center, 2011). The Mexican economy also improved, and many Mexicans decided that they would stay in Mexico instead of trying to cross the border for uncertain job prospects in the United States. The resulting transition from *solteros* to families was accompanied by a shift in many White residents' stories, from narratives of decline to narratives of revitalization.

From *Solteros* to Families

Beginning in the mid-2000s, most Mexicans already in Marshall chose to stay in the United States. Some migrants with connections to family in town continued to arrive, either directly from Mexico or from other parts of the United States, but by the end of the decade the rate of new arrivals slowed substantially. A local police officer characterized the transition in the Mexican community for us: "the second generation is just beginning," he said, and Marshall was changing from a community of mostly first-generation migrants. He said that the Mexicans used to be largely male, living fifteen or twenty people to a house, and "getting ripped off by White no good bastard landlords." They would work and send money back to Mexico. But "the Latino population is starting to change now big time." As second-generation migrants entered the school system, many intact families were intent on giving their children a better life here. Parents were getting better jobs or starting businesses. Their children spoke English and would have educational and employment opportunities in the United States, he told us.

In the early 2000s, young Mexican families started to have more children born in the United States. These children, and their siblings who came from Mexico at young ages, were often more comfortable speaking English than Spanish. Despite parents' ties to Mexico, it became more difficult for them to imagine moving their families back. Many Mexican families also invested in new businesses. Julie Ortiz, a Puerto Rican woman who commuted to her administrative job at the police department, described the consequences this way:

> I had heard ... that this was a transient town, and people don't understand that. People think Mexicans are going to leave. Everyone else left. The Dominicans, the Puerto Ricans, the Nigerians. They all left. But the Mexicans are not leaving, because they have businesses.

According to Julie, White and Black residents thought that Mexicans would move out of Marshall, either back to Mexico or on to more desirable towns. But this did not happen. Many Irish, Italian, and African American migrants had either stayed in town or maintained ties through businesses, properties, and institutions like churches. Mexicans also chose to stay in large numbers, and this changed the town's historical pathway. Across the United States, the New Latino Diaspora became something different during this period, as described by Hamann, Wortham, and Murillo (2015). As Mexican families settled, opened businesses, and sent their American-born children to school, the situations faced by migrants and longstanding residents in communities like Marshall shifted. The second decade differed significantly from the first.

It is important to recognize the contingency of the ethnic landscape in Marshall. The town had received groups of migrants from various places across its history. Over the previous several decades, there had been Dominicans, Puerto Ricans, Nigerians, and Koreans, and further back there had been Poles, Swedes, Slovaks, Germans, Dutch, and others. But the Irish, Italians, African Americans, and Mexicans came in larger numbers and many stayed, while the other groups mostly moved on. This particular history of migration had consequences for how groups were positioned. Irish and Italian Americans who remembered their migrant roots were more positively disposed toward Mexicans than longstanding residents in other towns, and thus Marshall was more welcoming than many similar places (Flores, 2014; Jones, 2012; Wortham, Mortimer, & Allard, 2009). African Americans and Mexicans lived together in close proximity, in ways not found in some other New Latino Diaspora towns across the country (Hamann, Wortham, & Murillo, 2015), and this confronted Mexicans with a more complex ethnic landscape. Interethnic relationships and the varying ethnic configurations that occur in particular towns play an important role in shaping the future of migrant communities, and migrant prospects vary depending on the local realities they happen to encounter (Hamann & Reeves 2012; López-Sanders, 2009; Millard, Chapa, & Burillo 2004; Rodríguez, 2012).

White residents typically interpreted the transition to settled Mexican families as the beginning of town revitalization. As one area educator described it:

> One thing is, it is revitalizing the areas because families are moving in ... You have some unaccompanied minors who get into groups of men, and this and that, and you do have groups of men living together and there are sociological problems with that. But a lot of it is families coming and bringing stability and revitalizing the neighborhoods.

In the second decade, White residents more often characterized Mexicans as a revitalizing force. We will document this more extensively when describing the growth of Mexican businesses in the next chapter.

Italian Americans in particular compared Mexicans favorably to earlier Italian migrants. In a conversation with an Italian American staff member in her shared office at school, one longstanding resident told us that "old Marshall residents" think the Mexican migration is bad. "Property values are going down." She pointed out that many of these "old Marshall residents" are Black, and that the same thing happened when African Americans moved in. She said that the near East side had for a long time been a Black neighborhood. Now Mexicans have moved to the East side as well as the West. At this point, another staff member piped in from across the room: "I see 'em all over." The first staff member continued, claiming that "the Mexicans who come here work," that they're not "sitting on a stoop drinking beer with a Cadillac in the driveway." We asked her who she meant, and she said, "take a ride through Marshall and look around. It's the Blacks." They sit there while they're "collecting welfare checks." In contrast, the Mexicans "send money home." Family is important to them. Because of the Mexicans, she said, Marshall has "come up a lot."

This story was inaccurate, and it also circulated pernicious racial stereotypes that continue to disadvantage African Americans. It erased Black successes, ignoring the many middle-class Black residents who had accumulated financial resources and held high status positions in Marshall. It also circulated longstanding racist stereotypes about allegedly lazy, parasitic African Americans. This kind of story nonetheless contrasted Mexicans and African Americans in consequential ways. It positioned Mexicans as a "model minority" (Lee, 1994; Wortham, Mortimer, & Allard, 2009), claiming that they were diligent and unproblematic while Black residents were allegedly lazy and undeserving. As the Mexican migrant community moved into its second decade, White residents talked less about *solteros* and more about families, less about Mexican-inspired problems and more about how Mexicans' hard work was improving the town. This positioned Mexicans as the next group likely to follow the positive migration story and move "up and out."

These stories also positioned African Americans as failing to act like earlier waves of successful migrants. Characterizations of Mexicans as revitalizers often accompanied inaccurate stereotypes of Black residents as unmotivated and unsuccessful. African Americans struggled against this account. Many Black residents saw themselves as having succeeded and having then chosen to stay in

Marshall because of its sense of community. They told stories about successful middle-class Black residents who had risen to important positions. The density of these conflicting stories about Mexican and Black residents' relative positions shows the importance of this issue in residents' oversimplified, imagined visions of their town. Relations among Black and Mexican residents in fact involved more struggle and indeterminacy than captured in any of these stories. Mexicans encountered a Black community that sometimes reacted to them just as earlier groups had. African Americans were unhappy to have Mexicans competing for space in town, just as earlier migrant groups had been at analogous moments. But because the African American community was internally heterogeneous—with some still struggling, some having moved "up and in," and others having moved "up and out"—Mexicans' position with respect to Black residents was complex and ambiguous.

Black Flight

Relatively few White residents lived in the neighborhoods where Mexicans settled starting in 1995. Many Black residents experienced Mexicans' arrival more directly. Several of our African American interlocutors described Marshall as not having "a lot of African Americans anymore" because the "Spanish people have moved in" and "Black people moved out." This Black outmigration was not evident in the 2010 census numbers, which showed a small increase in Black residents, although the rate of increase had slowed from a decade earlier. But the outmigration of longstanding Black residents was accelerating. We have called this "Black flight" (Nichols & Wortham, 2018). Doreena, who herself moved out of Marshall in the early 2010s, told us in 2015 that there were "not many Black people there no more on the East end" and explained that she moved because of the way her neighborhood was changing.

Darrell described how he and his friends used to frequent Black-owned stores in town, and how this had changed.

> We had a store that we loved, where we hung. There was about 30 of us ... at least on any given day, any given night. It looked bad, of course, but it wasn't. We was out there having fun. We was in and out of the store all day. It was Black owned. We had like water ice shops, Black owned, we had Jamaican stores, Black owned, we had so many things that were Black owned. And now you go to the street and you can't read the sign ... 'cause it's owned by Latinos ... I think the biggest thing honestly was the whole moving in of the Latinos, which is, honestly—they my brothers and sisters too, so I don't care about that. But I think a lot of us, African Americans, we

actually moved out ... I go through here, and I see a lot of people I just don't know. 15 years ago I could drive through here and probably name almost anybody.

Many Black residents like Darrell felt as if they had lost their neighborhoods over a short period of time. They used to know everyone, and they used to have Black-owned businesses that welcomed them. But few of those acquaintances lived in the community anymore.

As we have mentioned, this transition sparked by the arrival of Mexican migrants was preceded and accompanied by another demographic change in the Black community. Before 1970, most African Americans who settled in Marshall were migrants from the South. Most were upwardly mobile and many became middle class in their incomes and residential properties. After 1970, more Black residents moved to town from urban areas to escape difficult conditions (Berry & Dahmann, 1977; Massey & Denton, 1998). Some of these later arrivals had similar values and expectations for upward mobility as earlier African American migrants. But as time went on, the Black middle class began to move out and more poor African Americans moved in. Darrell described this change:

> Black middle class, you know, I guess they, they didn't agree with the changes and they found a better fit somewhere else. So, but we were getting a lot of influx from the cities too ... You knew every family, you know all the last names, you're connected that way, and then you do start to see a lot of folks from the cities ... Opportunities kind of dwindled a little bit, you know, mentalities changed.

Within the Black population there were different groups, and Darrell attributed the decline partly to these changes. But Black residents of different ages and socioeconomic positions nonetheless reported feeling displaced by the arrival of the Mexican migrants. They felt as if they did not know their town anymore. In fact, the alienation of middle-class African Americans from Marshall involved the arrival of working-class Black residents from the cities as well as the arrival of Mexicans. Black residents did not often speak about class differences among African Americans, however. Their stories typically portrayed Mexicans as the primary cause of their displacement.

Doreena was one resident whose pathway was influenced by these stories. As we have said, she was an African American of about seventy years who lived her entire life in Marshall, until 2014. Various resources contributed to her decision to move out of town. We have described the decline of downtown neighborhoods and several socioeconomic factors which precipitated that. Changes in the Black community also contributed, with a breakdown in community ties as longstanding residents moved out. But the story commonly told by Black narrators about the ongoing decline in traditionally African American neighborhoods and their sense of alienation also played a role in her decision. We will see in Chapter 6 how her pathway contrasted with several younger African American residents, who came back to Marshall after college in order to build Black-Mexican solidarity through community organizations that they founded. These residents told different stories—not about being pushed out by Mexicans, but instead about shared struggles.

Interethnic Conflict

Both White and Mexican residents noticed many Black residents' negative reactions to Mexican migrants. They often described the situation as "Black-Mexican conflict." One White resident described the demographic changes in the community this way: "I think one [Mexican] just comes and then they call home and others come, friends, family, and they just all end up in the same place ... The housing is relatively cheap even though it's all in bad condition, but it must be better than what they're used to." She said that Marshall used to be mostly Italian families, and then Black people came, and then one thing she had heard was that people were worried that the Mexicans were "taking over" the Black community. Her comment about the conditions Mexicans are "used to" revealed her ignorance about their actual situations, but her story about Mexicans "taking over" Black territory was common. Another White educator described the transition from Black to Mexican residents similarly: "People on the street corners aren't the same people they used to be. Now they're Mexicans, but they used to be Blacks." The all-night laundromat that used to be Black became "Mexican territory." The Mexicans "are a unified community," he said, unlike the African Americans. He went on to describe interethnic conflict. "There are candy stores owned by Mexicans who won't let Black kids in there," and Black residents complain about being excluded.

This White resident's use of terms like "corners" and "territory" inaccurately anticipated an incipient gang war of the kind one hears about in stories of race relations in big cities. He explicitly spoke of potential for "gang activity" among the Mexicans but told us that it "hasn't happened yet." A local police officer told a similar story, telling us that there was "a lot of racial tension ... in Marshall ... It's a gang war waiting to happen." In fact, senior police officers assured us that real gang activity was rare in Marshall. Occasionally, someone associated with a violent national gang would move to Marshall and cause trouble. But Black and

Mexican youth were at worst "gangster wannabees," with a few wearing scarves and flashing hand signs in attempts to look tough. There were occasional fights at the high school between Black and Mexican boys along ethnic lines, which other students attended as spectators, but these did not have anything to do with violent street gangs.

Many Mexicans reported tension between themselves and Black residents, however. Juan Castro told us that "Blacks don't like Mexicans." He told a couple of stories to illustrate this. He reported that once Black criminals stole the car of one of his relatives and broke the windows of another one's truck. Another time, he was outside washing his car and two little Black kids came around and wanted to help him, but he was almost done so he said no. They hung around because they wanted to play and they wouldn't leave him alone. Then their mothers called out and told the kids to "be careful because I was going to hit" them. And then they called the police, and "all I was doing was standing there washing my car." So, he told us, he got out of there and was gone by the time the police showed up. Juan also said that Black residents sit on Mexican neighbors' stoops, throw trash, drink, and smoke. You can't go out at night because of them, he said. "It's too dangerous." Furthermore, black women hit people with bats, he told us—although we did not hear this detail from anyone else. From his perspective, there were "big problems" between Black and Mexican residents.

A group of Mexican mothers told us similar stories. One described her dangerous neighborhood. There were shootings, lots of breaking into cars and stealing stereos, and vandalism. She didn't know why Black people acted that way—racism, maybe, or drugs, she speculated. But she added that crime also happened to some of her neighbors who were African American. They were nice people and it happened to them. It happened to everyone. Another woman then told a longer story about Black-Mexican conflict.

> When there was a lot of snow a few weeks ago, her husband shoveled out their side of the road for half the block. She was parked there, didn't leave a chair or anything to mark her spot, and she left and then came back and parked in her same spot. When she did this an African American woman who lives across the street started swearing at her saying she couldn't park there. She didn't know how to verbally defend herself in English, so she said some words in Spanish. When she was upstairs in her apartment, the woman kept yelling at her and told her to come back down. She did not go back down.

These mothers also had many stories about people breaking into their homes and stealing things. They said the criminals were always African American. But they also said they had some Black friends, neighbors who helped shovel snow, or people they knew from work. "They're not all bad," one said. These Mexican stories from Juan and the Mexican mothers contain some familiar, pernicious stereotypes and many inaccuracies. But their wide circulation among Mexican narrators provides evidence of the ways that many Mexicans characterized their Black neighbors.

Black residents tended to be less dramatic and less prone to expect Black-Mexican conflict than White and Mexican residents were. Many, like Darrell, described the transition from Black neighborhoods to Mexican ones as part of the natural cycle of ethnic turnover:

> The same thing like when Black people came in and White people were like "what are you doing here?" Same thing with the Mexicans. We kinda lookin' at them being like, "well, what are you doing here?" … When it changes, a lot of people don't change with it, they don't want to change, they don't accept it, and they just like, "you know what, whatever, I'm leaving, I'm moving, I'm out because I can't take all these Mexicans here anymore, all these stores are Mexican, everything is Mexican. I'm leaving." And it's that frustration, and it's like, I'm done, they took over everything.

Darrell described this as a natural cycle of new migrants displacing old ones. One just had to be realistic about it.

Joyce similarly described feeling pushed out by "the Spanish people. The Spanish people feel just like the White people probably felt like when the Black people came in. I think we're feeling that same experience." Jamar told a similar story:

> It's funny because, you talking about in the '60s and '70s most of Marshall was Caucasian, and then you know, '80s, '90s, that's when more African Americans came and the Caucasians started moving out to [nearby suburbs], and there was more of us than anything. And now the Latinos came and the African Americans are moving out and it's more of them.

Longstanding Black residents felt as if the Mexicans were alien to some extent, and they were hurt by the loss of their neighborhoods to this unfamiliar group. But their reactions to being pushed out were less intense and more resigned than White and Hispanic interlocutors suggested. They saw the "natural," "human" cycle of a new group displacing the previous one, and they adjusted with a sense of resignation.

Many White and Mexican residents, however, did not agree that Mexicans were following Black residents in the same cycle that had allegedly been traveled by previous ethnic groups. White residents' stories about the changes in Marshall's neighborhoods almost always ignored the distinction between longstanding middle-class and recently arrived poor African Americans, as well as distinctions among more and less successful Black residents. White narrators typically acted as if the African American community was homogeneous, thus erasing the significant group of middle-class Black residents in Marshall who had moved "up and out" or "up and in." White narrators' erasure of successful African Americans contributed to a feeling of exclusion and lack of opportunity for many Black residents. White residents' complementary characterization of Mexicans as revitalizers also provided greater opportunity for some Mexicans to follow the Irish and Italians along more stereotypical migrant pathways. These stories about Mexicans as revitalizers and Black residents as less successful migrants were one important resource that facilitated and constrained migrant pathways. In the next chapter, we pick up the story about Mexicans revitalizing the town, describing many migrants who started businesses and one who ran for political office. It took a configuration of resources to make these pathways possible—including economic capital and hard work, among others—but the stories helped some Mexicans as well as other residents to imagine Mexicans moving up. At the same time as many White residents' stories helped to open opportunities for some Mexican migrants, some Black residents also used their power in town to keep migrants from pushing them out. The next chapter describes how this happened in the political campaign of the first Mexican to run for political office.

In this chapter, we have sketched the complex landscape of residential life in Marshall, the network of material and ideological resources that accompanied the shift in the Mexican community from *solteros* and alleged victims to more established families. In some ways, Mexicans' experiences followed a familiar pattern. According to almost all residents, Mexicans started out as either a symptom or cause of decline in the town. They were allegedly poor and easily victimized, and either their habits or their poverty led to overcrowding and threats to public health. Stories about and many realities of migrant life followed the familiar pathway from nostalgia to despair about Marshall's prospects. As the Mexican community changed from *solteros* to families, however, stories diverged. Many White residents narrated a familiar, stereotypical transition to hope and revitalization. Mexicans were not in fact restoring Marshall to its glory days, because the town was itself changing. Something new was emerging, not something old. But White residents' oversimplified stories of revitalization did accurately capture the energy as well as the educational and economic successes of many Mexican families. Black residents acknowledged Mexicans' "hustle," but their stories more often characterized Mexicans as an important factor in the town's decline. These stories about residential life were one important resource contributing to the pathway taken by the Mexican community as it moved in both familiar and unfamiliar directions. The next chapter describes how these stories combined with other resources to facilitate heterogeneous, divergent pathways for both Black and Mexican residents in public spaces.

5

Public Spaces: Victims, Revitalizers, and Competition

This chapter continues our account of how Black-Mexican relations—including White residents' central roles in construing and creating these—were important resources that influenced Mexicans' emerging pathways across the two decades. We have described some ways in which oversimplified stories about race, decline, and revitalization influenced Mexicans' pathways despite the stories' inaccuracies. Our account of the contradictory stories told by White and Black residents about Mexicans' role in Marshall's decline has begun to provide a more adequate description of the complex relations between Blacks and Mexicans. African Americans sometimes resisted Mexicans in the same way as earlier migrant groups had—with resentment and competition for space and resources. But African Americans were positioned differently than Irish and Italian Americans. Many had not moved "up and out" in the same way as earlier migrants—because of economic hardships that accelerated toward the end of the twentieth century, because of more intense racism than earlier groups had faced, because Black successes were systematically erased in other groups' stories, and because many Blacks chose to move "up and in," staying in Marshall despite economic success. African Americans in America have been positioned at the bottom of the group hierarchy, as an "other," in ways that have restricted their opportunities more than other groups' (Jaynes, 2004; Parisi, Lichter, & Taquino, 2011; Trouillot, 1991), and this kind of othering occurred in Marshall as well. This chapter describes different areas of public space in which Mexicans were positioned as struggling against, moving past, or following after Black residents. We show how Mexicans' encounters with street crime and migration enforcement, their commercial successes, and their political struggles took shape as diverse, contingent resources—centrally including but not limited to their real and imagined relations with African Americans—constituted Mexican migrants' divergent pathways through public spaces.

This chapter also incorporates the ontogenetic timescale back into our analysis. In our accounts of Juan, Nancy, and Allie in Chapter 2, we showed how individual migrant pathways diverged in part because of their different positions within decades-long changes in the migrant community. In Chapters 3 and 4, we foregrounded interethnic relations and intersections between ongoing cycles of group migration and the emerging Mexican community. In this chapter, we describe how resources from years-long ontogenetic, decades-long community, and centuries-long group migration timescales interconnected to facilitate Mexican pathways in public spaces. We do this by focusing on the pathways taken by Juana's siblings in the Martínez family and the political experiences of her nephew Edwin when he ran for office against an incumbent Black politician. This family's pathway solidified only as resources from all three timescales came together. The family's businesses mostly followed a typical story of migrant struggle and success, but Edwin's political career was derailed because of the complex relations among Black, White, and Mexican residents.

The rapid growth of the migrant community quickly became visible in public spaces. As Mexicans appeared on downtown streets, both migrants and longstanding residents began telling stories about what Mexicans were doing there and what kinds of relationships they were developing with members of other groups. When new businesses serving Mexicans opened in commercial areas, longstanding residents began to experience some neighborhoods as foreign. Some described these shifts in terms of revitalization and growth, while others described decline and alienation. Mexicans and other residents in fact had diverse experiences in public spaces, and various resources contributed to Mexican migrants' experiences in public life. But residents' stories about Mexicans in public spaces oversimplified the migrants, their supporters, and their antagonists. In this chapter, we describe how diverse residents told varied stories about these changes and how these stories combined with the more complex, emerging realities of public life in Marshall to facilitate divergent pathways for Mexicans and other residents.

We discuss four aspects of public and commercial space: street crime, local businesses, relations with law enforcement, and local politics. In the first decade, stories about Black criminals mugging Mexicans on town streets became common, and migrants were often seen as victims. These "payday mugging narratives" circulated robustly throughout the 2000s—even though the crimes themselves had become less common before our arrival in 2005—because the central characters of Black criminals and Mexican victims conformed with popular stereotypes about these groups. A different type of Mexican character became more common in the second decade: industrious Mexican business owners who were often praised for revitalizing downtown areas. A few Mexican businesses had opened in the 1990s, but by 2010 there were about two dozen Mexican stores and restaurants in town. As Mexican businesses became more numerous and more visible, many residents credited the migrants with revitalizing Marshall. Fewer Mexican migrants were characterized as transient victims, and many were seen as settled revitalizers.

In the second decade, Mexicans were often described as "model minorities"— as hardworking, family oriented, upwardly mobile, and uncomplaining (Wortham, Mortimer, & Allard, 2009). Many residents cited Mexicans' hard work when explaining the economic and social revitalization of downtown Marshall. This narrative was not unequivocally positive, however, as Mexicans were often characterized as hardworking but not talented enough to succeed on their own. We sometimes heard that Mexicans were not as capable or ambitious as previous migrants. The revitalization narrative was also contested by some White and Black residents who characterized the Mexicans as "illegal," unwelcome, and insular. Instead of always being positioned as a revitalizing force, even in the second decade, then, sometimes Mexicans were blamed for community fragmentation and continued decline. This story was most common among African Americans, but some White residents told it as well.

The stories about and the experiences of Mexicans in public space varied, and residents described them using narratives of revitalization, exclusion, exploitation, and invasion. The preponderance of these various stories changed across the first two decades. At first, there was both fear and sympathy on the part of many White residents and wariness on the part of most Black residents— during the era of *solteros* and the robust circulation of stories about street crime with Mexican victims. Once Mexican businesses started to open in larger numbers in the 2000s, narratives of revitalization and exclusion began to circulate more widely. For some White residents, the history of the Mexican community was an oversimplified, familiar migration narrative—a shift from alien and transient victims to settled revitalizers who were becoming more like "us." Many Mexicans told this story as well, imagining themselves following in the footsteps of earlier Irish and Italian immigrant groups. In some ways, then, the Mexican community developed across its first twenty years in line with the classic, simple story of upward migrant mobility. This upward mobility was partly imagined, especially by Whites in the stories they told about revitalization. But it was also experienced and embraced by many Mexicans. As we have been describing, when Mexicans did travel this classic pathway, they did so because of a contingent configuration of resources that included factors like the large presence of Irish and Italian Americans who remembered their own ancestors' pasts.

The classic migration story was too simple to capture the Marshall Mexican community's pathway, however. Stories of exclusion and invasion persisted in town, told by many Blacks and Whites, with Mexicans continuing to be seen as victims or being positioned as aliens who did not belong. Furthermore, the institutional fact of undocumented status and ongoing deportations denied many Mexicans an opportunity to become revitalizers. The negative characterizations of Black residents in many White and Mexican stories about revitalization also exacerbated interethnic tensions, and this helped motivate African Americans to defend their turf. In the first two sections of this chapter, we describe how the Mexican community appeared in some ways to be following the "up and out" narrative—starting with struggling *solteros*, then moving to successful business owners. But we will go on to describe complexities that made this story too simple and created unexpected pathways for many individual Mexicans.

Classic migration stories about struggle and then success do not recognize ethnic heterogeneity and tensions in the host community, nor do they attend to the ambivalence of longstanding residents who welcome migrants as revitalizers but also sometimes disparage them as weak or alien. The final two sections of the chapter explore this complexity in more depth. First, following national trends in migration enforcement, around 2010 Mexicans in Marshall became more frequent targets of federal Immigration and Customs Enforcement (ICE) raids. Both migrants and longstanding residents began to characterize migrants as victims—although some cast the raids as justified while others characterized them as moral violations. This government immigration enforcement reinforced Mexicans' status as outsiders and victims. Second, the Black community began to push back politically. African Americans had just begun to acquire political power in the 1990s. When Juana Faccone's nephew Edwin became the first Mexican to run for city council in 2012, Black residents mobilized against his candidacy and characterized him as an outsider. His campaign against incumbent Black politicians represented an important step into the public arena for the Mexican migrant community, but it also brought interethnic tensions to the surface and showed the limits of Mexicans' power. Edwin's individual pathway was embedded within emerging tensions between Black and Mexican residents, and these tensions helped block his access to political power.

Data in this chapter come from hundreds of hours of observation across the entire eleven years of the project. We noticed payday mugging narratives in our earliest trips to Marshall. Members of the research team subsequently compiled a corpus of such narratives. We reviewed all recorded interviews and events from the first four years of the project and identified all payday mugging narratives, and we also asked explicitly about payday muggings in dozens of interviews. For our accounts of Martínez family businesses, we visited the locations, interviewed all family members, and attended dozens of family gatherings. We did an in-depth study of one brother's restaurant, spending about fifty hours across three years there and recording many events. Members of the research team ate in the restaurant dozens of times, and they catered many events for us over the years. Stanton Wortham's son also did a month-long internship in this business, as part of a school project requiring on-the-job experience. For our work on migration enforcement, we interviewed police, service providers, and families of deported Mexicans. We also conducted an in-depth investigation of the political campaign described at the end of the chapter, spending over fifty hours attending events and interviewing candidates as well as campaign staff, longstanding politicians, and activists.

Payday Mugging Narratives

Many Marshall residents told stories about "payday muggings." These stories have appeared across the United States for decades. A payday mugging narrative describes a Mexican victim who carries cash because he is presumed to be undocumented, as well as Black criminals who mug the Mexican. Here are three examples we recorded:

> For a long while Latinos couldn't set up savings accounts, because they were sure that that would get them shipped out, so they carry cash. And as soon as the Blacks realized that, they relieved a lot of Mexicans of their cash. (A White clergyman)

> A lot of Blacks are robbing Mexicans because they figure they carry money. You see, Mexicans don't believe in going to the bank. They carry big lumps of money on them. They do have good lumps of money … It's young people, crack heads. … They need money to get dope. … They robbing you, me, the church, anybody. They don't care. They doing their business. (A Black parishioner)

> They assault … the older guys when they've just received their check and all that. Like for example, one of my friends who lives in my house the other day they almost cut off his ear. Why? Because they wanted to assault him and … okay, we already know that when they see us on the street, if it's one or two of us they are going to grab us, you understand me? So we have to walk around carrying something like knives, guns or something like that to defend ourselves, you know? It's not good because then they take guns and everything. (A Mexican high school student)

Police and community leaders claimed that muggings had declined in the early 2000s because banks began to accept alternate forms of identification, making it possible for undocumented migrants to open bank accounts, and because migrants became more careful about carrying cash. We nonetheless commonly heard payday mugging stories from White and Mexican residents throughout the 2000s. We collected payday mugging narratives from police reports, media, and individual storytelling, as they were told by Mexican, White, and Black narrators. The content of these stories characterized one aspect of life in Marshall in the first decade of the Mexican community. The stories also disseminated divergent evaluations of Black and Mexican residents.

Payday mugging narratives were not limited to Marshall. Media reports from that era described payday muggings across the country. Cebreros (2007), for example, wrote about such muggings in Oakland, California, where some African Americans referred to the events as "amigo checking." Police reported that young African Americans tended to be the perpetrators, although Hispanics sometimes committed the crimes as well. Londoño and Vargas (2007) reported that young criminals in Washington, D.C., used the term "amigo shopping" for similar crimes. As in Oakland, most of the perpetrators were Black, but police also charged Hispanics and Whites with some crimes. Matza (2009) reported similar muggings in Philadelphia, describing Mexican migrants as "easy prey" and "vulnerable" because of their presumed undocumented status. In this section, we describe typical White, Black, and Mexican versions of payday mugging narratives that we collected in Marshall. These stories convey a common characterization of Mexicans that circulated widely in the first decade of the Mexican migrant community, and they describe another way in which Black, White, and Mexican residents told divergent stories about life in Marshall.

White Narratives

Many White residents told payday mugging stories. Father Kelly, for example, told us: "They haven't been able to get a bank account because of lack of papers. They were getting their paychecks cashed and they were getting mugged. Some of the people in the neighborhood figured out that it was payday." Another White resident described her own experience with a Mexican man who was stabbed downtown. She called 911. The man didn't want the ambulance to come and didn't want to report anything, but another bystander, a Black woman, told the police what happened. Four Black men had gotten out of a car and threatened the man, demanding his money. He wouldn't give it to them, so they stabbed him. The narrator added that there was a check-cashing place across the street and people knew that Mexicans couldn't have bank accounts, so they carried cash. In this story, a White woman explained the motive for the mugging by describing how undocumented Mexicans could not have bank accounts and thus carried lots of cash on payday. This detail about presumed documentation and access to bank accounts appeared in most payday mugging stories told by White and Black residents, but it never appeared in stories told by Mexicans. It emphasized some Mexicans' undocumented status, characterizing them as alien. Note also that this narrator said the Mexican victim did not want to report the crime. She implied that he preferred to stay anonymous and just be a victim without pursuing the perpetrators, because he feared involvement with authorities. This characterized Mexicans as passive and victimized, which was common in narratives told by White residents.

The police confirmed that payday muggings did regularly occur. One police officer told us that there was a lot of Black crime against Mexicans. Mexicans don't have social security cards, he said, so they can't get bank accounts. "They know you're out there with money." It's "like lions on lambs. Four to five African Americans on one Mexican." He said that the crimes often turned violent. Like many other White and Mexican narrators, this police officer characterized the perpetrators as violent and predatory. Two-thirds of all narrators in our corpus mentioned that the perpetrators of payday muggings were Black, and many White and Mexican narrators described these perpetrators as violent. In contrast to the Black criminals, the officer characterized Mexican victims as passive and outnumbered—like "lambs" being attacked by "lions."

Another White resident told us that Mexicans

> get taken advantage of quite a bit. They get mugged or whatever and they won't go to the police. We had a case recently where they had to put a Spanish person in jail just to keep them until they caught the person that did it and get him to court so he would testify. He was afraid to testify. He was afraid something would happen to him. But in the end they caught him and he was put away, and now this guy can go along and live a normal life.

Both White and Black narrators described how limited access to bank accounts made Mexicans vulnerable to payday muggings and reticent to report crimes. They described Mexicans as passive victims who were "taken advantage of" and did not want to involve the police because they were "afraid something would happen" to them.

This echoed the stereotypes of Mexicans reported by DeGenova and Ramos-Zayas (2003), who describe how Mexicans are often inaccurately characterized as gullible, submissive, and easily victimized. Similarly, Hill (1995) describes widespread ideologies about Mexicans as allegedly hapless, unintelligent, and childlike. The payday mugging stories circulated by White residents in Marshall thus often carried a stereotype of Mexicans drawn from the larger national context, one that fit with local characterizations of *solteros* as transient, fearful, and unlikely to defend themselves. White residents' stories often combined these inaccurate, patronizing characterizations of Mexicans with racial stereotypes about African Americans as members of an "underclass" prone to violence, poverty, and illiteracy (Jaynes, 2004). In the first decade of the Mexican migrant community, through these narratives and in other ways, White residents circulated images of Mexicans as alien, vulnerable, and pitiful. These stereotypes were inaccurate, but they nonetheless became an important resource that influenced some Mexicans' pathways in public spaces and elsewhere.

The payday mugging stories told by many White residents oversimplified the reality in Marshall. White narrators who told these stories were correct that payday muggings occurred often in the first decade and that the perpetrators were almost always Black. They were also correct in characterizing many Mexicans as afraid of both the criminals and the authorities. But not all Mexicans were passive victims. Many teamed up with fellow migrants to defend themselves by traveling in groups. Others went to the police and local officials, and local banks and the Mexican consulate arranged for migrants to open accounts using Mexican identification papers around the year 2000. Many migrants subsequently deposited paychecks into banks instead of carrying cash. Payday mugging stories continued to circulate robustly, however. We were told these stories by many White residents who had never spoken to a Mexican person. White residents' embrace of these stories probably came from the narratives' ability to reinforce powerful evaluative stereotypes about African Americans as allegedly violent and Mexicans as allegedly passive. These stories also capture the historical moment early in the development of the Mexican community, in which Mexicans were positioned and often experienced life in Marshall as struggling victims.

Black Narratives

African Americans rarely told payday mugging stories to us spontaneously. But most Black residents did know about these muggings, and some would tell stories when prompted. James Smith described the situation this way:

Well, at one time, because of the fact that a lot of these guys were laborers, they got paid under the table with cash. And quite a few were getting robbed and mugged, because some ... would go to the local pub and they'll be, you know, flashing their money, getting robbed, drinking and they're easy prey, you know. Or when they leave out of there, guys notice they just got paid, and they would prey on them, you know. Take the money, take whatever else they have on 'em. [Interviewer: Is that situation continuing? Has it changed?] I think it's changing now because ... the Latinos have wised up. They've started being together in groups, three, four of them together. They'll go to work, usually a group of 'em. They get off work, they are usually together. And you know some of them have opened up bank accounts ... and they don't carry large sums on them like they used to.

By 2005, James told us, payday muggings were substantially less common than they had been. Because he was a senior police officer, he likely had access to reliable data.

Black residents' payday mugging stories characterized perpetrators and victims differently than White and Mexican narrators did. James, for example, placed some of the blame on Mexicans themselves—for flashing their money and getting drunk. The three following excerpts come from interviews done after church between a Black interviewer and longstanding members of the Black community. The first parishioner described the muggings this way:

EG: And uh, it's always the first of the month every week. Wait for all the people to go in the bank, get money, come out, they rob them. There's a lot of that.
I: Oh, okay. And who was doing that?
EG: Well, everybody. Blacks, Mexicans, Whites, you know, whoever needs the money ... they're all doing it.
I: So they're mugging each other? So the Blacks mugging-
EG: Mugging each other. The Mexicans taking their money. The Whites, you know, I guess they figured, well, you take my money, I'm going to take his.

This elderly Black resident repeated the familiar claim that payday was the stimulus for such muggings, but he described the perpetrators as coming from all ethnic groups. He also explicitly described the perpetrators' motivation as financial and not due to violent tendencies or racial animosity. In his version of the story, victims were not necessarily Mexican, and being a victim had nothing to do with ethnicity or migration status.

Another Black narrator claimed that most perpetrators were drug addicts.

BA: A lot of Blacks are robbing Mexicans because they figure they carry [money]. You see, Mexicans don't believe in going to the bank. They carry big lumps of money on them ... But there ain't really been no real big conflict, not yet. I think sooner or later it might.

I: Okay, so do you think that it's young people that's doing the, that are robbing the-

BA: Of course it's young people, young people, crack heads. ... They need money to get dope. They ... robbing you, me the church, anybody. They don't care. They doing their business ...

I: So when you think, like you say, that they'll rob the Mexicans, that that's just trying to get what they think what the Mexicans are taking away from them?

BA: No, it ain't that. It's for dope.

This narrator claimed that drug addicted criminals did not single out Mexicans, arguing that they would take money from anyone. Like most other African American narrators, he identified most of the criminals as Black, but he also claimed that the victims were not always Mexican and that interethnic relations were not the issue. He rejected the interviewer's suggestion that the crimes reflected racial tension or resentment. The criminals just "need[ed] money to get dope." The third example comes from an interview with an older Black female narrator, an executive at a social service agency whose family had been in Marshall for several generations.

FE: Well I know among the young people, they [Blacks and Mexicans] probably fight. Well, they do fight. Every once in a while somebody will rob one of them.

I: Rob one of the young people?

FE: Rob one of the Mexicans.

I: Oh, okay.

FE: Because they don't, I don't know. They sometimes carry large amounts of money.

I: So who is "somebody," though? Who?

FE: Young Black people. They live in our community. See, that's the thing, they allow them over here, they give them all the privileges, and they dump them in our community.

I: Umm hmm. And so that's how, so young Blacks are robbing them?

FE: Sometimes. Not a- it goes on. I mean they rob their own, so why wouldn't they rob them?

I: Okay. And so that's causing conflict?

FE: No.

I: No?

FE: What's causing conflict is they're overcrowding our neighborhoods.

Like most other Black narrators, this woman acknowledged Black-on-Mexican payday muggings, although she claimed that they happened only "every once in a while." She also offered the familiar explanation that Mexicans "carry large amounts of money." But she observed, accurately, that the Black perpetrators also robbed "their own"—that is, other Black residents—thus emphasizing that Blacks were often victims also. Because the criminals robbed African Americans too, she argued, Black criminals were not singling out Mexicans. She also denied that payday muggings were a sign of racial tension. She argued that ethnic tension occurred because "they"—that is, White policymakers—"dump" Mexicans in Black neighborhoods, which become overcrowded. Like James, she also assigned some blame to Mexicans themselves, for crowding into apartments. Both Mexicans themselves and White policymakers, she thus argued, deserved some of the blame that payday mugging narratives inappropriately placed entirely on Black perpetrators. In this and other stories told by Black narrators, it is clear that Black residents understood and disagreed with White and Mexican narrators' characterizations of African Americans as allegedly predatory and Mexicans as passive victims. Payday mugging stories were nonetheless widely told by White and Mexican residents, so these inaccurate stereotypes circulated robustly outside the Black community in Marshall.

Mexican Narratives

Mexicans readily told payday mugging stories to us and to each other. In narrating how his father was robbed of 3,000 dollars by two Black men, for example, Juan Castro emphasized the danger from violent perpetrators of payday muggings.

> Well for me Marshall isn't the best place to live. It's dangerous- I think that for me it's dangerous because they've assaulted my father. The same with me. They took my wallet, my cell phone one time, they put a gun to my head and they told me to give them money. Yeah, they put a gun to his head too. They beat him, they sure beat him. They took 3,000 dollars that was to pay his workers.

Juana Faccone's sister Blanca told similar stories. She told us that her store had been broken into three times. She was scared to go to work, but she needed the income. She also told us a story about a woman who had 1,000 dollars stolen from her which she had tucked in her cleavage, and she was horrified that the criminal reached in there and grabbed it. As in the payday mugging stories told by White residents, many Mexicans emphasized the violence of the criminals and the helplessness of the victims.

Female Mexican narrators tended to emphasize danger and fear of Blacks. As one woman told us: "as Hispanics, all of us fear going out in the street because we run into some of these people and they rob or attack us." Payday mugging narratives sometimes turned into stories about unpredictable muggings that were not motivated by the desire for money but by unpredictable animosity. As one Mexican woman told us:

MG: Lots of violence, um, they assault us in the street, whether it's verbally or physically. Sometimes for an insignificant reason, sometimes without a motive. I've heard stories like that.
I: But what do you mean "without a motive," not for money?
MG: No, I feel it's simply for being who you are or because they don't like us, perhaps.

Many Mexicans cited tensions between Black and Mexican residents as an explanation for unprovoked assaults. One mother claimed that the "*morenos*" (literally, "brown people," the most common Spanish term that Mexicans used to refer to African Americans) were bad to them, "muy groseros" ("very rude"). She claimed that she knew one Mexican man who was killed by Black people. They tried to rob him but he didn't have any money so they allegedly killed him. Another mother told us about being in a laundromat when some young Black girls came in and started saying bad things to her, like "get out, leave, you're just Mexicans, get out of here." The following story from a mother and daughter was similar.

DF: Like if a Mexican person walks in the street, maybe they assault him, take his money, hit him.
MF: Oh yes, they hit him, for example, ah, a brother-in-law that I have here, he was walking on Main Street. They were little kids, little boys, twelve or thirteen years old.
DF: He was just out walking.
MF: And suddenly they began to hit him, for no reason.
I: For money?
MF: No, no, no
DF: No, not at all, because he was Mexican.
MF: When he tried to react, to defend himself, they began to run away.
I: And that happens frequent-
MF: frequently. I've heard that it often happens to others too.

This mother and daughter described allegedly unprovoked and sudden violence on the part of muggers, who were understood to be Black because the two were talking about relations between Black and Mexican residents immediately prior to this excerpt. They characterized the Black criminals as violent and unpredictable despite their young age.

Mexican women we spoke with offered various explanations for why African Americans assaulted Mexicans, including resentment, misunderstanding, and racism. "Blacks are more racist ... they don't like Mexicans because they see us as really low." In this way, Mexican narrators sometimes characterized African American criminals differently than White and Black narrators—who consistently cited money as the motive. Many Mexican versions of payday mugging stories, especially those told by women, also followed White narrators in characterizing Mexicans as helpless victims. Some Mexican men, however, described themselves as fighting back against racially motivated violence from African Americans. They rejected the characterization of Mexicans as passive victims and positioned themselves as competent, intelligent, and aggressive when necessary.

We believe that many payday mugging stories told by White, Black, and Mexican narrators described actual events—because of the credibility of many narrators, corroboration from other witnesses we met, and confirmation from police investigations of the events. Some of these stories exaggerated, and some were undoubtedly fictional, but many were at least partly true. Nonetheless, almost all payday mugging stories oversimplified interethnic relations in town. Stories told by White, Black, and Mexican narrators carried varied evaluations of Mexican migrants, of African Americans who robbed them, and of the relations between the two groups, and each of these evaluations presupposed a partly or completely inaccurate stereotype. White and Mexican residents cast Black perpetrators as violent and unpredictable. White and some Mexican residents cast Mexican victims as passive, although many Mexican men disputed this. African Americans accurately pointed out that only a few members of the Black community committed such crimes, and they denied the implication in White and Mexican narratives that many Black residents disliked Mexicans. White and Mexican narrators argued that payday muggings both resulted from and intensified racial animosity, while Black narrators denied that payday muggings reflected or created racial tension. None of these conflicting, oversimplified claims were fully accurate, but the salient ethnic and racial characterizations carried by the stories nonetheless influenced residents' views of and actions toward each other. Many Mexicans, for example, avoided Black residents in part because of stereotypes carried by stories like these.

The divergence between White, Black, and Mexican versions of payday mugging stories reinforced the divergence in their oversimplified claims about Mexicans' role in Marshall's decline. When talking about the first decade of

Mexican migration, White residents characterized Mexicans more often as victims and less often as causes of the town's decline. Both White and Mexican residents instead tended to see African Americans as the primary cause of that decline. When talking about the second decade, many White residents characterized Mexicans as responsible for a newly revitalized downtown. Blacks had ruined the town, they inaccurately claimed, and Mexicans were now bringing it back. Black residents, on the other hand, accurately characterized most African Americans as good citizens. They did not identify the Mexicans as victims who deserved extra sympathy. They sometimes characterized Mexicans' arrival as illegitimate, and they often told oversimplified stories that blamed Mexicans for the town's decline. As we will see later in this chapter, some Blacks mobilized against a Mexican political campaign in part to fight back against the inaccurate stereotype of Blacks as the problem and Mexicans as the solution to Marshall's woes.

As the Mexican community developed from the first to the second decade and it became clear that many of the migrants planned to stay in town, Mexicans' relationships with Black residents became even more important. The pathway followed by the Mexican community centrally involved both imagined and actual interactions with African Americans. In payday mugging narratives and other stories, White, Black, and Mexican narrators characterized these relationships in divergent ways. These divergent evaluations combined with other resources to establish pathways that solidified for individuals and communities. For example, evaluations of Blacks as violent and predatory in payday mugging narratives sometimes combined with widely circulating racial stereotypes of Blacks, together with ongoing racist discrimination against Blacks in housing and employment, to help keep many African Americans from moving "up and out" as others had done. In another example, in the first decade of the Mexican community, evaluations of Mexicans as passive victims in payday mugging narratives sometimes combined with other resources—like the presence of family in Mexico and the stress of being undocumented—to encourage some migrants to return to Mexico. For other Mexicans, the stereotype of Mexican migrants as passive and childlike from payday mugging stories combined with the difficulties of learning English and their systematic isolation in school, together with other resources, to encourage Mexican youth to accept careers as physical laborers who worked for others.

We now move on to describe in more detail how the development of Mexican businesses in the second decade generated different stories about the migrants—with White residents tending to characterize Mexicans as revitalizers and Black residents continuing to see them as invaders who worked hard but nonetheless changed Marshall for the worse. As the Mexican community developed, the stereotype of passive victims carried by payday mugging stories often gave way among White narrators to characterizations that emphasized hard work and revitalization. These new stories became important resources that—together with material factors like Mexicans' hard work, their mutual support, and their accumulation of economic capital as they started businesses—opened opportunities for some Mexican migrants to travel pathways "up and out," while also allowing some Whites to blame Black residents for their own continuing economic struggles. The move from passive victims to active revitalizers, as narrated by many Whites and Mexicans—despite its oversimplifications—did represent the experiences of some Mexicans in Marshall across the first twenty years of the migrant community.

Revitalizing Business in Town

Several entrepreneurs, including two of Juana Faccone's siblings and one of her cousins, started businesses in the first decade of Mexican migration. But in the second decade, more and more migrants planned to stay and raise their families in Marshall, and many of them became entrepreneurs. Their businesses included a landscaping company and a tile store, but most were small food stores or Mexican restaurants. In the mid-2000s, the rapidly growing group of Mexican entrepreneurs created the "Latino Business Council," which hosted Spanish-language conversations about shared concerns. This group partnered informally with other Hispanic professionals who served the Mexican community—a doctor, educators, and directors of social service agencies—and by 2010 they had gained some access to government leaders and began to have a voice in town.

As more and more Mexican-owned businesses opened along the major streets in Marshall, residents noticed. Father Kelly described the change:

> It's wonderful. You can walk around Marshall and see the shops or just the people walking through the neighborhood. A lot of them are Mexican ... I think [residents] see the positive side. I think they see it may be revitalizing the town a little bit. You'll see some Mexican restaurants, Mexican stores, and they see that as a good thing ... [Mexicans] own businesses up and down Main Street. It's like Little Mexico.

Figure 5.1 Mini-Mall catering to Mexican shoppers.

By 2016, several blocks on Main Street had more Mexican businesses than non-Mexican ones. An entrepreneur had rented out the entire second floor of a former office building and offered the perimeter offices for rent to small, start-up Mexican businesses. He called the development "El Zócalo" ("The Main Square") and signs in Spanish directed patrons upstairs. Between five and ten small businesses operated there at any given time. One of these was a grocery store and restaurant that had taken over one end of the space. This sort of business was relatively common—a one room store of anywhere from 300 to 1,000 square feet, with another room in the back that housed a small restaurant operated by the same owner.

Down the street from El Zócalo was another Mexican mini-market. Here too the products and customers were almost all Mexican, with bags of tortillas stacked high in several spots. Walking from El Zócalo to this establishment at the end of the commercial strip, you would pass a Mexican bakery that sold *pan dulce* (sweet bread), two other small Mexican grocery stores, a sign advertising the local *tortilleria* (tortilla makers), and the offices of AYUDA, a social service agency that we describe in the next chapter. You would also pass a hair salon run by Jamaicans offering braiding, a Korean-owned electronics store and several businesses owned by White residents—a hardware store, a used clothing store, a coffee shop, and an Irish-themed restaurant. By 2015, however, the Irish restaurant had become "El Ranchero."

The few larger stores and chain restaurants downtown remained White-owned, and in 2016 Mexican businesses had still not opened in the strip malls a mile or two from downtown—which had mostly Italian, Greek, and chain restaurants, along with other White-owned businesses. Downtown, however, many dilapidated buildings and storefronts turned into Mexican establishments. The fanciest restaurant downtown remained Korean, a holdover from the Korean migrant community that was almost entirely gone. Brigid Hannigan, who worked at the local Catholic church, described the change in ethnicities that she had witnessed:

> On Main Street, which is now kind of the section of Mexican restaurants and things, that was Korean ... There was Korean banks, everything there was Korean for a while. So that was the other group that came in. And I don't know what happened. They just kind of disappeared ... And then I think we spent probably 5 or 6 years of just having very, the transient groups who came here—some from Mexico, some from other areas. But ... they came here for jobs and they ... weren't into retail yet.

Here Brigid described the transition period from *solteros* to a more settled Mexican community. When the Mexicans first started arriving in larger numbers at the end of the 1990s, they were just "here for jobs" and not planning to stay. But by the early 2000s, they began to open businesses and settle more permanently.

When Juan Castro arrived in 2003, he told us that there were only three Mexican businesses on Main Street—though according to others there were up to twice as many. By the time we met him in 2006, he said that it was "almost all Mexican businesses." He told us optimistically that the future of the Mexican community was bright—that "they will own more businesses. Their children will be citizens and they will speak English." For Mexicans, the creation of more Mexican stores downtown was a crucial symbol of the community's growth, one that marked their movement beyond the era of transient, disempowered *solteros*. Julio, a Mexican altar boy at St. Joseph's, told us in 2010 that the size of the community

> has changed a lot—a lot. The population was not as big as it is. It was nothing compared to how it is now. There weren't many Mexican stores around here. The church didn't get full up to the balcony like it does now. It was never like this. The population has grown tremendously in the last years ... [There are] Mexican stores opening up all over the place.

Other Mexicans who had come in the first decade of the community told similar stories. Ingrid said that when she arrived "there was only one little Mexican store" that was the sole source for Mexican products when she wanted to cook. But "now, wow! There are three on Brooks Street. There are four on Main Street,

I think. So, you can tell the difference. There are a lot of Mexican people now." Another Mexican mother told us that when she arrived the downtown "area was African Americans. In 2000 there were little Mexican stores, two or three stores, two or three restaurants that were Mexican. Now there are a lot of Mexicans."

White and Black residents told similar stories about the rapid growth of Mexican businesses during the 2000s. James Smith, for example, described the "big influx of Latino stores on Main Street" and estimated in 2010 that "if you go up there now you'll see probably 90 percent of the businesses up on Main Street are Latinos." This was an inaccurate estimate, even for 2016, but it conveyed the sense among most residents that a large number of Mexican businesses opened up quickly and that a significant portion of the downtown area was suddenly dominated by Mexican stores and restaurants.

Ivan and Anastasia were originally from Eastern Europe, and they owned a coffee shop downtown, a popular meeting place. It was there that Juana Faccone and two of her sisters chose for their first meeting with our research team in 2007. Anastasia, herself a migrant, told us that, "for so many" of the Mexicans, opening a business "is such a dream."

> They've been dreaming about this ... Many of them are great business people, but many of them just don't recognize how it works, what business is all about. You need to file the taxes, you need to have the supplies, you need to have the fresh stuff. If you are selling vegetables and fruits, you can't sell rotten strawberries, for example.

As she said this, another local business owner walked into the coffee shop. Ivan exclaimed "Tony!" He introduced Tony as another migrant, from Korea. Tony owned the cell phone shop on the corner and he told us that "Spanish people" were now his primary customers. By the late 2000s, Main Street had business owners from Korea, Jamaica, Mexico, Ukraine, Puerto Rico, and Italy, as well as native-born Americans of various ethnicities. They had all noticed the rapidly growing Mexican community, and most of them marketed to these new migrants.

As the Mexican migrant community moved into its second decade, both the private experiences and the public image of Mexicans were changing. Most residents expected that Mexicans were now there to stay. Migrants were less often characterized as passive victims and more often seen as entrepreneurs working hard to improve their lives. Many were sought after as customers and respected as business owners. These stories about growth in the Mexican business community were accurate in many ways. Mexican businesses did proliferate, starting in the 2000s. Not all Mexicans were entrepreneurial or successful, but many visible businesses did open and thrive in the downtown business districts. In this way, many Mexican entrepreneurs followed a pathway described by classic migration stories. Each individual success, however, was contingent, emerging from a network of both familiar and unfamiliar resources. We describe how this happened for several businesses owned by members of Juana Faccone's family.

Martínez Family Businesses

Several of the earliest Mexican businesses in town were started by Juana Faccone's relatives. The very first store was started by a second cousin who had come to Marshall from California and slept on a couch in Juana's apartment for a while when he arrived in town. His business was important enough to the community that he merited the honorific title of "Don Sánchez" among many Mexican residents. When we first visited Marshall in 2005, people directed us to his establishment as the best Mexican restaurant in town, and to him as someone who would know the history of the community. Around 1990, Don Sánchez started his business by driving an hour to a more established Mexican migrant community, where he bought tortillas and other Mexican groceries from a store. He then drove from house to house in Marshall and made deliveries. In 1993, he had saved enough to rent a vacant store on Main Street across from the main Spanish-speaking social service agency in the region. A few years later, he rented an adjacent space and opened what was the first Mexican restaurant. Mexican residents who had been in Marshall at the time still described his entrepreneurial success with admiration.

Anastasia's coffee shop was right next door to Don Sánchez's store, and she described how they started their businesses at the same time.

> Usually migration starts with, you have somebody who is a center. Sánchez next door was dreaming about his own business. So he rented a store and he started to bring Mexican groceries to this store. Then he developed a list of people in area, Mexicans in [surrounding towns] … And they're used to Mexican groceries, and he was delivering to them, once a week. At this time, we both were here at five o'clock in the morning. I've been every day hanging my towels in the store, and he was in the street putting stuff on his truck. And we started approximately the same time. Then people started to talk, to come to him. And then he developed those tacos … They're so delicious. The people are coming from all over for those tacos now.

Don Sánchez opened his store in a part of Main Street that had housed "mostly African American businesses and bars," as Juana's nephew Edwin told us.

Together with the social service agency AYUDA, his store became the center of a Mexican community that was about to experience very rapid growth. Don Sánchez became successful through hard work, the accumulation of capital, and other factors—but it was also crucial that he happened to open his store the year before the surge in Mexican migration began.

Another Mexican migrant who arrived in the early 1990s, Pedro, confirmed that Don Sánchez was the first Mexican business owner. He added that Sánchez was followed shortly thereafter by others.

> From there it began to grow, and there were more and more. From there after a few years, another store opened, José and his wife. Then a restaurant, then another store, then a restaurant. So in this way it has continued expanding. And for us it's good, because we have all of our customs and we can continue them actively. And I have seen that the American people also … are accustomed to Mexican food.

Pedro and his wife were lonely and homesick in Marshall when they first arrived in the late 1980s. They craved Mexican food. For their first couple of years, the nearest place to buy authentic Mexican food was a store in another small town about an hour away—the same place where Don Sánchez initially purchased food for his deliveries. Pedro still remembered the name of the store, "Fiesta," because he traveled there often. When Don Sánchez opened his store, Pedro said that he felt much better about living in Marshall. He used the word "support" many times to characterize what the store did for him and his fellow Mexicans. Normally we would say that customers supported the store—and they did—but in this case Pedro claimed it was even more important that the store supported the Mexican community.

In 1998, Juana's sister-in-law Liliana opened her own store half a mile away on a more residential street on the East side. Liliana had started an informal grocery business a few years earlier in the same way as Don Sánchez. She built a customer base among people she knew, delivering Mexican food door to door.

> Everyone's working hard when you come from another country. I wasn't satisfied working every day … get up at six o'clock, had to work … I thought, no, I have to do something. I don't like this life … We can't save anything. We can't save money … I talked to my husband, but he's still working. What can I do by myself? Nothing! I spoke to him and said, I'm thinking of something. I want to sell something for the Mexican community. He said, but we don't have money. I said, no, we have to do something. And we got some Mexican products and we knocked on the door, *knocked on the door*, and said, do you need something?

Bread, sausage, tortilla. No, not today ... Okay, that's my telephone number. If you need something, *please* call me. Okay? I can bring anything you need. Okay. Sometimes people called me. Sometimes I was waiting all day.

When Liliana had saved $3,000, the family opened their first store, renting a vacant storefront and naming it "Liliana's." It was the third or fourth small Mexican grocery store to open in Marshall.

Liliana and her family faced significant challenges at first. The space they rented was in bad repair and they had to renovate it themselves. Each member of the family also had to continue working outside the store in order to make money to build up inventory. As Liliana described it:

When we rented the space, we'd open at twelve o'clock because I had to work too. My husband worked. My sons worked. And some people called me, oh, what happened? Your store is closed. Oh, I'm going to open at one o'clock. Because always you're scared. You lose money, you make money. When we opened, the business wasn't good. We made maybe thirty dollars a day, forty dollars a day, because it was far away from the community. [At one point] we closed, we had to close because no money ... One Saturday, I remember, I say I won't work today. I'm gonna open the store. I'm gonna open now, just for a little while. We have a little bit: chiles, tortillas, phone cards, maybe bread, cheese. A little, very little. And [that] day, five hundred dollars. I sell from twelve to eight. I called Edwin and I said "Edwin, guess what?" "What happened, mother?" "I sold five-hundred dollars."

It took two years in which members of the family worked outside the store, but in 2000 Manuel, Liliana, and their sons had saved enough to expand. First, they bought the building in which their initial store was located, and then they bought another store one block away from Don Sánchez's on the near West side.

Liliana's son Edwin told us the story of the second store.

In 2000 we were told that this store was up for sale. It's in Marshall, and it's on Aster and Main Street ... The owner wanted to sell it, I guess because he didn't have time for his family. So my brother saw an opportunity and said to me, this is up for sale. So I took the initiative to go with him and talk to the owner ... He wanted uh, I believe he wanted 70,000 dollars ... I said I cannot give you that much and you don't have a lot of merchandise, and if I check your inventory you're probably gonna come to half of that. And he said, but the store is already built, it's here, you're not gonna have to do anything. I said, well, I'll give you 65.

Liliana and Manuel established a successful business in their first store, and as the Mexican community grew they were able to loan money to their sons in order to start a second business. The second store also did well, and several years later they were able to open a third store in a town about ten miles away near another growing Mexican community.

Edwin described how the two family stores in Marshall—together with Don Sánchez's and one or two more—became a magnet for more Mexicans to move to town.

> That was the fourth market that was opened in Marshall. It was for Mexican products as well. And it still was- the area was still populated by African American people. But by having those two stores I guess more Mexican people populated that area. And the town started growing. And the African Americans started moving away.

The Mexican stores and restaurants served as magnets, he claimed, drawing more migrants to settle in downtown Marshall. He also credited his parents with proselytizing about the town to friends and relatives in Mexico and elsewhere in the United States. Their motivation for proselytizing about Marshall was not primarily to gain clients for their stores, he told us, but to reduce their social isolation.

> Because of our struggles speaking English, in the early times, of my dad and my mom not having friends … [They responded] by bringing in people that they need. By telling them, come over and see for yourself. But I guess it wasn't because they were inviting them to get a better life. They were inviting them to have those people close to them. To actually speak to someone in their language.

Manuel and Liliana came in the 1980s, before the Mexican community began to grow. At that time, there were fewer Mexicans and they were often lonely and desperate to speak Spanish. By the time they opened their second store in 2000, they had almost 2,000 fellow Mexicans to speak with, and many of those became customers who helped their businesses flourish.

Most members of the Martínez family followed a classic, upward migrant pathway in many respects. They all worked hard in menial jobs for years when they first arrived, and over time they accumulated capital and started businesses. Not all the businesses thrived, however. Juana's brother Paco's restaurant failed after four years. This was painful for them, as he and his wife went back to working for others at relatively low wages. Nonetheless, by the time we met them in 2007 all but one of the seven siblings in town either owned a business or had a college degree and worked in a professional occupation. All of them were American citizens. Half of them had moved "up and out" of Marshall, buying houses in more expensive surrounding towns. Among them, they had twenty children born in the United States. The pathways traveled by Juana and her siblings were contingent. They depended, for example, on Carlo's chance meeting with Juana in that store in Mexico when he was on vacation. Their successes were also facilitated by the fact that Carlo happened to live in a town where many longstanding Irish and Italian American residents remembered their own migrant ancestors and were thus more welcoming. But the shape of several siblings' pathways followed the familiar pattern of "up and out." Juana herself, together with two of her siblings, moved "up and in" and remained in Marshall. They valued the sense of community there, and Juana became an educator who served the children of Mexican migrants.

Revitalization

The Martínez family was unusual because they came to Marshall in the 1970s and 1980s, before rapid growth in the Mexican community, and thus they had more time to work, build capital, and start businesses before large numbers of Mexican migrants began arriving in 1995. Many other Mexican entrepreneurs followed them and opened stores and restaurants in town. These businesses changed the appearance and feel of downtown Marshall. Spanish appeared on signs in public spaces and could be heard on many downtown streets. Mexicans walked up and down Main Street, pushing strollers, buying groceries, and going out to eat. Mexican food and the Spanish language became familiar to many longstanding residents, and significant numbers of them started patronizing Mexican businesses.

In commercial spaces, as in residential ones, many White residents characterized this as revitalization. Brigid described Marshall for us in 2010:

> I think it's on an upward trajectory ... I don't think the revitalization actually took hold until you started seeing more of the businesses moving in. And I think it is when many of the Mexican restaurants started up, many of those Mexican businesses. I've driven through downtown on Saturday nights, down on Main St., and gone out and everything else, and it's alive. I mean, there is stuff going on. You can hear the music, you can hear everybody. People are out on the street and things like that. Fifteen years ago, I can tell you, I would have been more afraid to drive through Marshall.

This story about the town's recent history, the "upward trajectory" of Marshall, was commonly told by White residents. They described public and commercial space—the neighborhoods, the streets, restaurants, and stores—as dangerous and dilapidated "before" but as "revitalized" by the late 2000s. The community had become vibrant, they said, more like it used to be, and hardworking Mexicans were the ones who made it happen.

A local White businessman explained it this way in 2006:

> Now I think there's a little bit of resurgence ... where people are coming back to shopping areas in town and we have a lot of potential down on Main Street here. I don't know if you've been down that area ... They're going to put in a direct route from the interstate into town, which will help. And the train station is nice. It's new ... I think that [Mexicans] are a hardworking people. They're a faithful people. Yeah, I think they're doing a lot as far as helping bring back the business. That Main St. business district was a real vibrant part of the town back in its heyday in the '50s and '60s.

As described in the last chapter, both White and Black residents talked about a golden age of Marshall in the early and mid-twentieth century. They recalled or imagined shopping, entertainment, food, and vibrant community life. Several nearby towns had experienced similar histories, with an imagined golden age followed by significant decline as manufacturing went overseas in the second half of the twentieth century. Marshall residents often told us that these neighboring towns had successfully encouraged redevelopment and experienced a resurgence of investment and activity in the twenty-first century, while Marshall had continued to decline. Some White residents now felt that Mexican migrants were finally bringing vibrancy back to Marshall.

A few White residents told us explicitly that revitalization was happening because of the transition from *solteros* to families in the Mexican community. A school principal, for example, claimed:

> As I started to track some of the students as to who was staying ... more and more of them each year were staying. And so that kind of told me: wait, they're putting down roots here. And then I started thinking, that's when we started seeing the rise in a lot of the Mexican restaurants, and a lot of the other businesses.

Another educator said: "A lot of it is families coming and bringing stability and revitalizing the neighborhoods, and there are various Mexican business opening up." As Mexican families settled and made a commitment to Marshall by opening businesses, they helped both themselves and the town. The downtown business districts had more activity, and most White residents characterized this as revitalization.

The church secretary at St. Joseph's, Rosa, echoed the sentiments of many parishioners and added her own reflections:

> And in the town, here in Marshall, Hispanic businesses started to open up. That started attracting more Hispanics to eat because they have excellent food. And there are stores where they can find articles that they probably would not be able

to find elsewhere. Therefore, Marshall is growing and flourishing beautifully thanks to Hispanics ... This was a desolate town, but very pretty. I'm very happy. I like our people. I'm Mexican and I like tacos. I like to go to all of the restaurants around here, and I like socializing a lot with my compatriots ... There are many people who are here in America who don't want to work. They are- I don't want to speak about certain things that don't sound right. But Mexicans came here to work. They are excellent workers. For nothing they work. Therefore migrants have raised this town.

Like other White and Mexican narrators, the church secretary credited Mexican business owners with revitalizing Marshall. This common story about Mexican success was of course oversimplified. For example, Paco and many other Mexican residents continued to struggle in relatively menial jobs. As we will describe below, Mexicans continued to confront racial stereotypes and punitive immigration enforcement. Nonetheless, many Mexicans aspired to the classic migration story, some experienced it, and it dominated the views of White residents.

Rosa's story had a dark side, however, reflected in her claim that "there are many people who are here in America who don't want to work." White and Hispanic narrators often positioned Mexicans as model minorities, and in the process they implicitly or explicitly contrasted Mexican with Black residents— whom they characterized as lazy (Lee, 1994; Wortham, Mortimer, & Allard, 2009). Oversimplified and sometimes inaccurate stories about Mexican revitalizers and allegedly lazy African Americans further disadvantaged Black residents and also contributed to tension between Blacks and Mexicans. This tension influenced many Mexicans' pathways in Marshall.

Exclusion

Across the United States, many African Americans have expressed resentment when migrants make claims on economic or political resources that they only recently acquired through civil rights efforts (Camarillo, 2004; Morawska, 2001; Sontag, 1992; Waters, Kasinitz, & Asad, 2014). In his study of intergroup relations in a Southern California suburb dominated by African Americans and Mexican migrants, for example, Camarillo (2004) found increasing numbers of stories about Black-Mexican conflict in the media. He observed stereotyping by each group against the other, particularly among community leaders, but he also found evidence of cooperation and amicable relations among ordinary people. The situation in Marshall was similar. Many Black residents reported admiration for Mexican entrepreneurs and some wanted to create interethnic coalitions against racism, but many Black residents were also frustrated as the Mexican community developed. Because African Americans had not fully moved "up and out," their reactions to Mexicans were complex.

Before the Mexicans arrived, Keon told us, Black and Italian residents competed with each other.

> Main Street used to be Italian. It was Italian stores … It was a constant battle. I remember as a kid [in the 1980s] … it was definitely a dominant African American community, and there was a dominant Italian community, and there was always a struggle between the two. So like I said earlier, my analogy was, I guess, casualties of war? They [Mexicans] came in and there was a little animosity like, whoa, we fought for this and you came in and just took over businesses, took over things.

Throughout their time in Marshall, Black residents had to fight against poverty, residential segregation, and racism to accumulate economic and social capital. Because their experiences differed in some ways from earlier White migrants, their stories about Mexican successes also often differed from White residents'. According to many Black residents, Mexicans were not revitalizing Marshall. Mexicans started to take over residential and commercial spaces just when Black residents had begun to achieve a fair share of political and economic power, and this did not feel like revitalization to them.

Black narrators often coupled this story with the sort of nostalgia described in the last chapter. Doreena, Joyce, and Tiffany co-constructed a nostalgic account of a racially mixed commercial space that used to exist on Main Street:

> Doreena: They had Black, Black and White people were on Main Street.
> Tiffany: Yeah, my hairdresser used to be there and it's not there anymore.
> Doreena: Yeah, it was a mixed community on Main Street.
> Joyce: It was mixed but it was, it was Italians.
> Doreena: Italians.
> Tiffany: Yeah.
> Doreena: Italians, Blacks.
> Joyce: I don't know if it was the Black people were the owners or more like the hairdressers in the barber shops.
> Doreena: Right, right, yeah, and they, some of them had-
> Joyce: And worked at the nail salons.
> Doreena: A lot of them had businesses. They had businesses. They used to have second hand stores, and different shops, up there you know. Yeah, a lot of them moved on, a lot of them people moved on.

Despite their articulate co-construction of this story, these women's personal experiences of Marshall's history were very different. Doreena was in her seventies, Joyce was in her forties, and Tiffany was only twenty. When Tiffany was born, Mexican migration had already begun, as had significant economic decline in town. The three women nonetheless remembered Marshall as a place with a strong Black community. Doreena explained that Main Street used to be "wonderful," but "now there's no businesses down there." From White and Mexican perspectives, in contrast, business down there was booming.

One longstanding Black resident gave a specific date for the beginning of the decline: 1998, near the beginning of the rapid Mexican migration.

> Ninety eight it started changing. It started going downhill, you know. 'Cause uh, the [Black] community just like- I guess when the older ones passed on, the younger ones, they didn't do anything. They just let it go, you know. And now you got all these migrants coming in here. And, as far as I'm concerned, it made Marshall terrible ... Now you got the Mexicans coming in here. Some of them, I would say, not all of them, some of them are very good. They got jobs, they work, some of them have a business, and so on. But you do have some, they don't work, they just hang on the corners. It's just that, I mean, we have enough of our own people hanging on the corners without having somebody else. Now, the neighborhood is terrible ... What really started happening was drugs started coming in. And we had drug dealers on the corner and ... most of the people, they got fed up and sold and moved out ... Now, it's dominated, it's Mexicans now.

This older Black resident provided a more nuanced account of Mexican migrants, describing some of them as "very good" and others as problematic. He also characterized African Americans as a heterogeneous group, with some being industrious while others, especially "younger people," were lazy. He described the arrival of the drug trade as a turning point, one that he did not blame on Mexicans. The outcome of his story was familiar: longstanding Black residents no longer felt safe or welcome, so they moved out.

Joyce and Michelle described the transition from Black-owned to Mexican-owned businesses.

> Interviewer: What happened to the Black owned businesses on Main street?
> Michelle: They closed.
> Joyce: Yeah, a lot of them were, either, they closed or I don't know if they were bought out by- but there's just so many Mexican places there, on Main Street, you know.

Michelle:	It's just, I don't know. I hate to call it little Mexico, but it feels like little Mexico.
Joyce:	Yeah, I avoid it at all costs.
Michelle:	Yeah.
Joyce:	I don't even go up and down the street.
Interviewer:	Michelle, is that true for you also? Do you avoid it?
Michelle:	Yeah, I don't frequent Main Street at all … There's a lot of passing blame on others for things that Blacks aren't able to do or to achieve, or to buy or to own. It's always the White man keeping them down, or Mexicans coming over here getting treated differently.

Main Street, once home to businesses that catered to Black residents, became filled with Mexican stores and restaurants. By the late 2000s, Black residents who once went to Main Street to shop and socialize didn't "frequent Main street at all"—because it is "not nice anymore," "very congested," and filled with [Mexican] "babies, and strollers." Many African Americans like Michelle and Joyce felt as if they had lost their town. The increasing numbers of Mexican businesses were key symbols of this loss.

Michelle also mentioned stories that circulated in the Black community to explain the decline. Some blamed White people for the lack of economic

Figure 5.2 A storefront on Main Street advertising money transfer services to Mexico.

opportunity among African Americans, she said. But others blamed Mexicans. Mexicans were "treated differently" by White residents, given unfair advantages, and as a result they were now taking over streets that were formerly home to Black businesses. We only heard these stories of Mexicans' differential advantage from Black residents, although research in other locations supports some of their claims (López-Sanders, 2009). Fewer White and Mexican residents even knew about the loss of Black businesses, and we never heard them talk about it. Because almost no Whites lived in the downtown areas where Mexicans were settling, it makes sense that Blacks would be the ones feeling pushed out.

Many African Americans felt unwelcome in the new Mexican businesses. John, for example, was a community organizer in his late thirties who spent significant energy trying to solve what he called the "Black and Brown problem" in Marshall by reaching out to Mexican youth. We will describe his organization in the next chapter. John's mother was born in Marshall, and he moved back to the community as an adult. He said that when he walked down Main Street, "the disrespect was to the utmost … because they saw me as a Black man." He went on to recall a specific experience he had on Main Street when he encountered two Mexican women and their children:

> As I walked up, they pulled their child, and looked at me, stared at me, looked me up and down. I was dressed professional, like I am now—I'm pretty clean cut— looked at me as I walked by, looked back at me, continued to speak Spanish. So I remember I looked at them, nod my head, and they pulled her kid and look at me, like offended. And they just kept speaking Spanish and looking at me.

Some Black residents described how they had been prevented from entering Mexican-owned stores, where owners had installed door buzzers so that they could decide whom to admit. And they were frustrated when stores in their neighborhoods stopped stocking items sought by Black customers.

Language was also important. Black residents sometimes complained that Mexican businesses did not provide help in English. Doreena described this:

> Doreena: You go in the store, and you ask them a question, and they go-
> Interviewer: You're shrugging your shoulders.
> Doreena: Why you here? You don't know nothing … Why you here working? He's just there putting stuff on the shelf but you can't ask him a question 'cause, he go "Me no understand English." Why you here working then?
> Tiffany: Well- he has to make money as well.

Joyce echoed her mother: "It felt like an invasion of people who weren't really interested in socializing because, for one, they couldn't speak English, and weren't interested in trying to speak English ... on Main Street where it's just been bombarded with a lot of Spanish businesses." Mexicans' use of Spanish reinforced many African Americans' sense that their town had been invaded and that they were being excluded.

In the passage above, Doreena's granddaughter Tiffany empathized with Mexican workers, noting that the Spanish-speaking Mexican worker "has to make money as well." Black residents were not homogeneous in their views, and they characterized Mexicans in various ways. Sometimes they saw Mexicans as the "other," as coming in and creating an environment that excluded Black residents from spaces that were once theirs. At other times Black residents aligned themselves with the struggles of Mexican residents and praised their industriousness. James Smith, for example, described these conflicting attitudes:

> Well, it was a mixed feeling. Some [Black] people, they liked them. Because they said you know "Hey they are willing to work, you know. Who cares? Let them work, let them get their jobs." But then others felt that they shouldn't be coming over here. Some people had this thing where they said: "They come over here to take these jobs, they don't have to pay taxes." Everybody pays taxes. I don't know where they get this mentality that they come over here, they take the jobs and they don't pay taxes. That's what everybody keeps saying. "They're starting these businesses, they got these jobs, they're making money, they don't pay any taxes. They don't do this, they don't do that." This is what some people were saying. Like I said, it was a mixed feeling.

We often heard African Americans praise Mexicans for their hard work and success. One man, for example, talked about a rapid shift in the Mexicans' economic situations due to their industriousness: they "just arrived, just got here and [we] come back a couple of weeks later and [the Mexicans are driving] Escalades." As we describe in the next chapter, many young Blacks also worked hard to build solidarity between African American and Mexican youth. Black residents' views of Mexican businesses were divergent—including admiration, understanding, resignation, resentment, and anger—although feelings of exclusion were most common.

Despite this heterogeneity in their responses, most Black residents told stories about community decline that diverged from White residents'. Even after the malls opened and retail stores downtown started to close, our Black interlocutors reported that businesses still catered to their needs and their community felt intact. Many economically successful Blacks moved "up and in," staying in town and enjoying the sense of community. Many African Americans thus argued that the decline came in significant part from the arrival of Mexican "others." With Mexican migration came many Spanish-speaking people renting apartments in historically Black neighborhoods as well as the closure of some Black businesses along Main Street. The changes in public space that White residents described as "revitalizing" Marshall were viewed by most African Americans as accelerating community decline and instability.

Many Black residents also told less positive stories about Mexican work habits and economic contributions than White residents did. One longstanding Black resident told us:

> Most of the old Mexicans, the only thing they do, they work. They work all day, all week and they- I will say, they will drink on the weekends ... But the young ones, they're out on the corner, drunk, falling down in the street ... I don't know what they did in their country, but, I mean, you don't just pee out in the street.

James Smith also described some undesirable behavior by Mexicans and noted that their actions damaged the reputation of the whole community. At one public meeting called to discuss the Mexican community, he argued that certain actions portrayed the Mexicans in a negative light. He told stories about them holding events and then the next day there being broken bottles and beer cans left in public spaces. He then described how many Black residents complained about the messiness and "disgrace" of such behavior. While White residents emphasized the positive aspects of the recently arrived Mexicans, Black residents were more likely to tell stories about dysfunction and invasion.

Black residents were not the only ones who had ambivalent feelings about the growing Mexican community. Many White residents also reacted negatively to the growing Mexican presence in public space. One White educator we spoke with in 2006 expressed a sense that Mexicans had invaded: "It's been quite a change. You drive down the street and there are street corners where the people hanging out there were once Black but now they are Mexican ... This Mexican community sticks together a lot more than the Black community does." He worried that Mexicans were prone to gangs. "I don't get the feeling that they're going away any time soon, do you?" Other White residents also told stories about Mexicans as dirty and threatening. So not all White residents credited the Mexicans with industriousness and praised their revitalization of the town. Some agreed with Black residents that their town had been invaded.

Despite heterogeneity within groups, however, we most often heard divergent stories from Black and White residents about Mexicans' entrepreneurial efforts and their movement into commercial space. African Americans described it as invasion and decline across the twenty years of the Mexican community. Most White narrators told stories with a shift in the middle, describing decline and Mexican victimization in the first decade then revitalization in the second. Both stories oversimplified, but both nonetheless contributed to residents' pathways. Mexicans eyed Black residents warily, mostly expecting tension or hostility. Many Black residents did not think about Mexicans much, focusing instead on other challenges and opportunities. A few Black residents recruited Mexicans as partners in their work against racism, as described in the next chapter. But many Black residents also perceived Mexicans as a potential threat and mobilized against them—in cases like the housing ordinance described in the last chapter and the political campaign described below.

In some respects, Mexican migrants followed the classic migration story from struggle to success across their first two decades in Marshall. Many Whites' and Mexicans' stories clearly emphasized this classic pathway. But the story was also accurate, in some respects, in describing many Mexicans' experiences. A community of transient laborers in economically marginal positions, mostly *solteros* who were sometimes victimized by slumlords and criminals, became a community with many settled families and some successful entrepreneurs. Furthermore, the robust telling of the story itself, especially by White residents who controlled access to resources, opened economic and political opportunities for some Mexicans. The classic story was nonetheless too simple to describe the more complex reality. Mexicans traveled divergent pathways, and the community as a whole continued to face substantial challenges. The emerging pathway traveled by the Mexican community was influenced by resources that were pushing in different directions, such that it did not neatly conform to the story in which Mexicans moved "up and out." Their complex relations with African Americans were one important resource, and we will return to these below. First, however, we describe complexities introduced by Mexicans' interactions with federal immigration authorities.

Migration Enforcement

Mexicans were vulnerable to migration enforcement, both because of some migrants' undocumented status and because of the stereotypes and practices that were encouraged by this enforcement. The material and institutional realities of immigration enforcement blocked many Mexicans' pathways toward economic, academic, and commercial success. It was difficult for Mexicans to make the transition from victim to revitalizer while government agents were tracking down undocumented migrants. Accelerating immigration enforcement actions also kept alive characterizations of Mexicans both as invaders and as victims, despite the fact that many Mexicans were citizens or had official permission to live and work in the United States. Like other Americans, longstanding Marshall residents often characterized Mexican migrants through stories about their interactions with law enforcement. Migrants could not avoid these authorities because of institutional realities. Many migrants did not have driver's licenses, for example, yet they needed to drive and so were periodically detained by local police. Federal migration agents also increased their enforcement activities in Marshall around 2010, as they did elsewhere in the country, and these caught or disrupted many migrants (Brabeck, Lykes, & Lustig, 2013; Chishti & Bergeron, 2009; Horsley, 2010; Office of the Press Secretary, 2009). Simple stories about revitalization and welcome capture some aspects of the second decade for Mexican migrants' in Marshall, but immigration enforcement shows that the situation was more complicated. The Mexican community's pathway from invaders and victims to revitalizers did not follow the classic positive migration story in all respects.

In the late 2000s, the Marshall Police Department adopted a strategy common in the United States at that time, focusing on smaller "quality of life" crimes. Enforcing restrictions on underage drinking, loitering, littering, and loud noise was thought to decrease major crimes and increase quality of life. The department created a special unit for this enforcement, and the unit often investigated and detained Black and Mexican men. Black residents objected to this strategy, and senior police officers held several forums where they defended their approach. At one gathering at the Washington Community Center in 2009, for example, James Smith was a representative of the police department. He acknowledged that "most people say all they're doing is arresting Black people," but he argued that loitering is in fact against the law and that police are just doing their jobs.

In a subsequent interview, he explained how this policing worked.

> The younger generation, they want the fancy cars and the hip-hop and the music. And of course it wasn't loud enough for them. I mean, they wanted everybody in the town to hear the music. And of course the Latino community- they like the loud music, the fast cars, the audio packages that make some noise. The louder the better, you know. But it wasn't that you were going to stop any particular

> group ... makes no difference who ... A lot of times, you know, just by stopping somebody that has the music too loud, you might stop another crime ... They might have drugs lying right there on the seat. They might have a gun lying on the seat, sticking out from the bottom. You look in there, you can see it. And here you might be able to take a potential homicide off the street, stop it from happening because this guy got a gun. Just by stopping him, because he got loud music.

As part of this enforcement, the police sometimes cited or arrested undocumented migrants. James Smith insisted that they did not intend to do migration enforcement, but in fact their strategy of stopping people for minor infractions led them to detain some Mexicans for migration violations (Armenta, 2017).

> You can't go asking people if they are here illegally or whatever. I mean, when my guys ... stop somebody for a violation, they ask you for your papers ... and if you can't produce them, then you get written up for that. And it was tough for a lot of the Latinos, because a lot of them didn't have a driver's license. But they wanted to work and they would take that chance ... A lot of times, we'd stop the guy, a Latino that doesn't have a license. And it got to a point where [officers] knew a certain guy, "There's José, he don't have a license". ... So they would pull him over and write him up again or tow his car. And some of the Latinos thought that we were just picking on them ... We are not going to go around stopping every Latino just to check him out to see if he's here illegally. If he creates a traffic violation, we're going to pull him over ... We don't even know that a person is here illegally ... We would run him through NCIC, to check a warrant for that person. And they may come up as a hit. He's wanted by INS, you know, and we would call in the migration authorities.

Immigration enforcement may not have been the goal, but the police department's quality of life campaign nonetheless resulted in the deportation of some undocumented migrants. These enforcement actions produced resources that were central to constituting many Mexicans' pathways—for example, the fact that undocumented migrants sometimes had their cars impounded, the fact that even documented Mexicans could not drive without fear of police, and the fact that family members were sometimes deported. These realities made it more difficult to keep a job, graduate from school, and accomplish other goals— but the salience of any particular resource varied depending on the individual's pathway and the other resources available. Juana and her siblings, for example, were much less affected by these realities then Allie's parents.

The police interacted with the Mexican community almost exclusively through enforcement actions. As a secretary at the police department told us in 2008, "there's not a single policeman on the force who speaks Spanish, even though one third of the town is Spanish. There has been one detective who speaks Spanish." The lack of contact between officers and Mexican migrants led some officers to circulate inaccurate stories about Mexicans. Police officers often drew on widely circulating national stereotypes to characterize Mexican migrants as uneducated, illiterate, drunk, and dirty. We did not speak to any officers who characterized Mexicans as serious criminals. One told us that "we rarely have problems with them. They're hardworking, hardworking people. [It's] rare that you run into a Mexican or Latino that's disrespectful. They're hardworking. They drink. They get drunk. We can handle that. They don't shoot each other." Here, again, we see the contrast between an unflattering characterization of Mexicans and a tacit, more negative characterization of African Americans as violent.

Many in the police department did want to have better relations with the Mexican migrant community. A church staff member described how an officer came to St. Joseph's once with a plea for migrants to report crimes to police.

> We had a lieutenant from the Marshall police force come and talk to our parishioners. He explained to them that you have legal rights. Whether you are documented or undocumented you have legal rights as a human being in America, and you should not be afraid to call the police if you have been robbed.

This message was difficult for many migrants to believe, and most Mexicans did not call police except under extreme duress. Mexicans nonetheless told us that policing in Marshall was better than in other American cities they had experienced. Juan Castro, for example, told us in 2007 that "the police stop you for all kinds of reasons. Sometimes it seems for no reason at all. But they're not bad in Marshall. Elsewhere they are worse. If you get stopped there it can be trouble because they will ask for your papers and you can get deported." Life in Marshall was challenging for Mexican migrants, but most told us that it was preferable, in this and other respects, to many other places in the United States.

Marshall police behavior toward Mexicans changed around 2009, however. At that point the Obama administration began increasing enforcement of migration laws (Chishti & Bergeron, 2009; Horsley, 2010; Office of the Press Secretary, 2009). This involved more raids by ICE officers in Marshall and elsewhere. The raids were allegedly targeted at undocumented migrants who had committed crimes. We heard conflicting accounts about the degree of cooperation between Marshall police and federal immigration authorities. This was a contentious issue nationally, with many police departments refusing to cooperate, while others eagerly joined immigration enforcement efforts (Armenta, 2017; Coleman & Kocher, 2011; Donato & Rodríguez, 2014; Saunders, Lim, & Prosnitz, 2010). But

ICE clearly operated in Marshall, most actively in the early years of the Obama administration, and they swept up undocumented migrants with no criminal history other than immigration violations. A White resident married to a Mexican man summarized: "It seems often that the police try to find the bad people who are causing problems, but in the end they take away the good people who are hardworking and doing their part for the community, who only want a better life here, while the bad people stay." At one community forum about policing, the director of a local social service agency described one incident from this era, in which the police went to a residence looking for someone who had committed a crime. The criminal did not in fact live there. But police then asked for the documentation of the individual who opened the door. This father of three was taken to jail, and his family ended up being evicted from their apartment because their breadwinner could not work. The Puerto Rican agency director argued that these actions tore apart families and brought down the entire community, especially "good" migrants who were working hard. The police chief responded to the story by claiming that police were not concerned with immigration status. He claimed that they only intervened if people broke the law. He added, however, that ICE had given them a protocol and that Marshall police did not have any say in how ICE acted.

ICE raids created fear in the Mexican community. One elementary school teacher described how she and fellow teachers tried to calm children by saying that "they are only looking for bad people." But the children would correct her by saying that when ICE came after one person, if there were other undocumented people living there, they would all be taken away. Some students in her school had lost a parent in this way. Other educators told similar stories. One described a day when "it was rumored that an ICE van showed up and, you know, I couldn't believe it. [There was] large absenteeism that day. And the kids were deathly afraid." Mexican parents would communicate by text message when they heard of immigration enforcement activity, and information would spread rapidly. In response Mexicans would sometimes skip work, school, or church, or sometimes leave town for the day. Allie's parents, Hernán and Mariana, used these occasions to explore more of the country, going sightseeing with their children out of town. Brigid Hannigan described the consequences at church.

> The rumors start filtering around Marshall that ICE is around and they are doing raids and they are picking up people and the police are involved … Rumors like that go around in cycles every couple of years, and you just have to calm them down because when those rumors start filtering is when we see the attendance at

mass is low and I get a multitude of phone calls from the Hispanics saying they are not going to faith formation or youth group.

She was correct about the drastic decline in attendance on such days, but she underestimated the frequency of these alarms. They occurred at least every couple of months from 2010 to 2012. She also failed to appreciate the reality of the raids for those directly impacted, because they were not just "rumors."

The enforcement actions had severe consequences for the people deported and their families, and they created a climate of fear (Coleman & Kocher, 2011). They also had an impact on Mexican businesses, because customers would stay away. Juana's brother Paco described the consequences for his restaurant.

> But one day, suddenly in the morning, the immigration officers came to Marshall and the people don't go out for many days. If the people don't go out, we don't have business. ... Some people asked or called because "Hey, I saw the police, I saw ICE in your restaurant"—because in another place, in a Mexican restaurant, they went over there. They got 5 people. But the people were scared. From that day, the business broke ... Outside of Marshall there are other businesses, good businesses, Mexican food, and they got customers. People go out for a Mexican restaurant in other places, but not Marshall because they scared of the police. Immigration and the local police—it was a combination with ICE.

The threat of immigration enforcement made life difficult for undocumented migrants, and it reduced the vibrancy of downtown businesses owned by Mexicans.

Migration enforcement complicated the simple picture of revitalization and upward mobility that many White and Mexican residents described when they talked about the development of Mexican businesses in Marshall. Many Mexicans' situations were improving, both materially and ideologically. As Mexicans saved money and opened businesses, many accumulated significant economic and symbolic capital during the second decade of the community. More young families settled in town, more Mexican ventures succeeded, and more Mexican children did well in school. At the same time, however, the threat of deportation severely constrained many migrants' behavior and wore them down emotionally. The stereotype of "illegals"—which was reinforced by enforcement actions as well as national media—also made them seem alien and threatening to some longstanding residents. Depending on the particular case, these stereotypes and associated microaggressions could influence migrants' pathways.

Some residents overemphasized one story or another—arguing either that Mexicans would mostly move "up and out," following oversimplified pathways attributed to earlier migrants, or that they were victims of racism and entrenched institutional structures that must be overthrown. Some academic accounts oversimplify in these ways as well. Neither of these stories is accurate, although both capture some realities. Nor is it sufficient simply to posit a "hybrid" reality that includes both elements. Instead, individuals and communities travel divergent pathways. Realities about revitalization and realities about racism are in some cases crucial resources influencing an individual's pathway, but for other individuals they are not. Just because revitalization or racism exists in a context does not mean that it becomes crucial to all pathways traveled in that context. From this Latourian perspective, it becomes clear that the reality of immigration enforcement affected individual Mexicans differently. Members of the Martínez family, for example, did not fear deportation. They nonetheless confronted stereotypes about Mexicans and microaggressions that were intensified by migration enforcement and claims about "illegality." But these realities were not salient enough to divert most members of the family from their pathways toward personal and commercial successes both "up and out" and "up and in." Families with undocumented members, however—especially ones who were deported—confronted migration enforcement as a crucial reality that could suddenly and dramatically change their lives. Most Mexicans were affected by the institutional realities or the ideologies associated with "illegality." This complicated the community trajectory from struggle to success, such that Mexicans' actual pathways diverged from this simple story to a greater or lesser extent. Even in 2016, the pathway of the Mexican community had not yet solidified, because of resources that pushed in different directions.

Politics

Mexicans became involved in town politics as they accumulated economic and symbolic capital and, as one might expect, they encountered resistance (Prieto, Sagafi-nejad, & Janamanchi, 2013; Rangel-Ortiz, 2011). Juana Faccone's nephew Edwin was the first Mexican candidate to run for city council. We followed him throughout the campaign, as he went door to door and participated in various public events. His opponent was African American, and longstanding Black residents mobilized against his candidacy. This was typical of relations among migrants and longstanding residents throughout Marshall's history, in some ways, with an established group resisting newcomers' attempts to obtain political power. But the complex interethnic relations in this particular town in the early twenty-first century made some aspects of Edwin's experience unusual. Black residents both positioned him as an outsider and reached out to him as a potential ally. Edwin's experiences illustrate how contingent resources from various timescales can influence an individual pathway.

After the election, Edwin sat down with us and narrated his experiences across the campaign. He felt that his success as a business owner pushed him toward politics. The store he owned with his brother was small but thriving, and it brought him into contact with many Mexicans.

> It all happened because having a market I saw people. I saw the needs and the people. People that do not speak English. People that need some type of form to be filled out … First, you start helping people. But then it is so many people that need help that you cannot help them all … Running the store, I couldn't do that. So I guess my name got out there. People started knowing me.

Edwin was known as a community leader among many Mexican migrants. He was a successful businessman, an American citizen, fluent in English and Spanish, and he cared about helping Mexicans in need. As he helped more people, it became clear to him that he could have a bigger impact by advocating for the Mexican community through the political process.

Edwin became central to an emerging group of Mexican business owners. By 2010, Edwin told us, Main Street was "becoming a Hispanic business district. We call it now an international district. But it's a Hispanic business district. There are Mexican restaurants, hair stylists and all that, owned by Hispanic people." These business people felt that the town of Marshall was creating regulations that disadvantaged them. Just as town government had enacted the housing ordinance that disadvantaged some Mexican tenants in 2005, Edwin and his colleagues felt that the town was now passing unreasonable ordinances directed at their businesses.

> The town started being hard for us. By making regulations that probably they thought that we weren't going to notice. We weren't going to be able to fight back, because we were Hispanic … So they came up with some ordinances about parking. So that's how we started. I … started talking with other business owners saying, "we can't have this. We have to go to the town." So the town people heard our needs. And I said to the President of Council, "how come you do this to us without giving us a form or sending a letter to the businesses of the changes you are going to make? I mean, don't you think we have the right to know?" … Suddenly I'm known to them. And some of them invited me to be part of Council. Because I'm Hispanic. And because I can- we need representation now in the town. That's how I decided to run for election.

A sitting member of Council encouraged Edwin to run—an Italian American woman named Mariam Desantis—and she volunteered to include him on her slate of candidates as a "teammate." Desantis offered to help Edwin and their other teammate by contributing connections and resources. In the end, however, she ended up hurting Edwin's candidacy more than helping it. But it was primarily because of her encouragement that, in 2012, Edwin became the first Mexican to run for political office in Marshall. Desantis told him that he "wouldn't need to do much [work] to run for Council." As he told us after the election: "I found out she was very wrong."

Edwin as a Hispanic Candidate

The "team" running as a slate for several council seats included Edwin, Mariam Desantis—a current council member who had moved to Marshall as an adult—and a woman from the Dominican Republic named Sandra Solis who owned a business and had volunteered for town organizations over several years. Sandra and Edwin identified themselves as "Hispanic" or "Latino" candidates and emphasized the importance of representation for the growing Mexican community. Mariam Desantis and her staff emphasized this even more than Edwin did. Mariam's partner told us:

> This is important for the Latinos here because, one, there's never been a Latino on Council. So this is history-making itself. It's important because Latinos need representation ... so that they can have a voice, and they don't have to be so silent ... They are regular people that have jobs, and they have businesses, and they have homes, and they send their kids to public schools, and they are regular normal people, just like everybody else. Period. And if you look around Main Street, you will notice there is a huge Latino presence here. I would say 80% of this area is Latino. So I think it's time that they have somebody who represents them.

The team's White campaign manager also emphasized the importance of having two Hispanic candidates on the team: "Sandra Solis and Edwin Martínez, both of them are Latinos. If they win they will be the first Latinos on Council." Dominicans and Mexicans did not interact much in Marshall. In fact, only a handful of Dominicans lived in town. But for political purposes, at least at the beginning of the race, Edwin and Sandra presented themselves as fellow Hispanics.

Edwin himself regularly talked about the importance of representation for the Mexican community. He was well known among Mexicans in town, but this was not a significant advantage because most Mexican residents were not citizens. Edwin, as he told us, "was well supported by them, but they cannot vote." He received solid support from Mexican Americans who could vote, but it became clear that this would not suffice. In order to win, he would need some Black votes—because the majority of residents in his district were Black and Mexican. In order to campaign for Black votes, however, Edwin had to engage with the complex interethnic relations that we have described. A narrative about Mexicans moving "up and out," allegedly just like the Italians, might have appealed to White residents, but it would not have been a successful political strategy for reaching Black voters. The narrative of revitalization was important for Edwin's own sense of self, however, and this made his campaign for Black votes challenging.

One of the team's campaign staff members was a Black resident named David. He canvassed with Edwin, and he was cautiously optimistic about Edwin's potential to attract Black voters.

> An older African American gentleman, if I pulled 10 of them off the street, four of them might have an issue with a Latino running for Council. But that's only four out of 10, ... only if you have a vested interest in the belief that Marshall will always be an African American municipality. I don't think that anyone else is really that bought into the idea that Latinos can't be a part of Council. There have been African American members of Council going all the way back to the 1990s ... The Council has been African American dominated for a while now. So the idea that Marshall needs to stay Black, kind of falls on deaf ears. It's been Black for a while. There's a demographic change that everyone can see.

Black residents of Marshall, David claimed, were familiar with Mexican food and customs, and they accepted the presence of the newcomers. He hoped that they would be willing to elect a Mexican man to Council. It turned out, however, that he underestimated some Black political operatives' ability to position Edwin as an outsider.

Black Pushback

Edwin was running for the Democratic nomination in one district of Marshall, while his teammates ran in other districts. He had been told that the Black incumbent in his district was not going to run again. Unbeknownst to him, however, there had been conflict between Edwin's ally Mariam Desantis and this incumbent Councilwoman, Linda Nelson. Nelson decided to enter the race against Edwin at the last minute, and she rushed to file her paperwork in time. There was a dispute about whether she submitted all her forms by the deadline. Desantis asked Edwin to join her in a formal complaint that Nelson had not filed her documents appropriately, and he did so. The election authorities ruled in their favor, and thus Edwin appeared alone on the primary ballot as the only Democratic candidate in that district. This initially seemed to be a victory, but in the end it hurt Edwin.

The complaint against Nelson mobilized several Black political operatives in town, who created a write-in campaign for her. A longstanding Black resident named Wayne told us what happened.

> In the fifth District we had Miss Linda Nelson. Linda Nelson has been in Marshall for a long time. I think she's raised 3 sons here. Not naturally from Marshall, but she has roots here. Her kids were raised here, went to school here. She's done a lot of local youth things. She's involved in a lot here in Marshall. Not all Marshallites are from Marshall and not everyone that is from Marshall is a Marshallite, is something that I always say, and Miss Linda is one of them. Unfortunately, because of a slight error ... Miss Linda forgot to turn in a paper that she had to turn in—didn't turn it in on time, so she was challenged by this group of people because they're for the first time in Marshall as well. Edwin was a Mexican that was running for a seat in Marshall. Edwin was connected with this group. Unfortunately for him, it was the wrong group.

Mariam Desantis was disliked by many African Americans in Marshall, and Edwin's connection to her damaged him. When Desantis filed the complaint seeking to remove her colleague Linda Nelson from the ballot, Black community leaders were outraged. They set about educating Black voters on how to vote for her as a write-in candidate.

Wayne went on to say, about Edwin: "now, that he was a Mexican didn't help his" candidacy. The Mexican community was growing, and their "time is coming ... I just don't think that time is right now in Marshall." Over the prior two decades, African Americans had achieved representation and then majority status on Council. From an African American perspective, they had only recently achieved their rightful place in the political power structure. Mexicans should wait their turn, Wayne claimed. Many successful African Americans had moved "up and in," and the Black community was not yet ready to yield power. In retrospect, Edwin told us, the relationship between Black and Mexican communities was "tense" and his joining with Mariam Desantis and filing the complaint against Linda Nelson made things worse.

> The town is run mostly by African Americans ... And it [has been] a very tense election. My opponent is an African American ... and she took it very personally

when I said I was running against her. Because we were both Democrats. And she used to speak to me, but now she doesn't speak to me because I wanted her seat. But I remember she said she wasn't running, and she said to me that I could have the seat, that she wasn't going to be up for reelection. I don't know if she was told that she needed to run. That's how much African American power there is, I guess.

Edwin and his teammates identified him as "Hispanic." They emphasized the need for Hispanic representation on Council, given the growing Mexican community. But, in the end, his Mexican identity was not the only important factor. Contingent realities about Edwin's candidacy made a big difference in the election: he was enlisted by an ally who was widely disliked by Black leaders, and he joined this ally in using a technicality to keep his Black opponent off the ballot; he was also running at a time when there was substantial tension between some Blacks and Mexicans, as we have described.

From the outside, it might appear as if Edwin made the mistake of challenging the incumbent Black power structure. But this is not how Wayne and other Black community leaders saw it. They cast the election of 2012 as the triumph of a newly energized Black electorate overthrowing outsiders—mostly White—who did not care about local Black residents.

> Until now our local government was outsiders, not Marshallites. But then in the last elections Marshallites were, you know, they were more engaged. Two of them won in the primary, for the upcoming election here in November. We got the people of the town involved and very engaged ... 2012 was anticipated to be one of the biggest years for Marshall elections, because after the [Obama] presidential election, which engaged so many people ... we were going to have 4 open seats on our local governmental council. We were having 4 open seats on our school board. Here was an opportunity for all the disgruntlement you had, for all the talk back, all the disdain you had for the local politicians or the local school board officials, here was your chance to get involved. And the local people of Marshall stepped up to the plate.

After Barack Obama's election in 2008, and during his reelection in 2012, many Black Americans felt empowered to participate in politics. Wayne was able spontaneously to give us names of a dozen Black Marshall community members who ran for office or helped organize others' campaigns in the 2012 cycle. He contrasted these with three White council members whom he also listed by name. "None of these [White] people that I have mentioned are from Marshall, at all. But they were on the Council. The problem was ... they weren't thinking in the way of a Marshallite ... and we were pissed off because they had ruined our town." From longstanding Black residents' perspectives, the election of 2012 was about Black residents consolidating their power and ousting incompetent White politicians. It must be said that Wayne was correct in his harsh assessment of some White leaders from earlier decades—some were incompetent, some were corrupt, and a few had been charged with crimes.

In the end, Edwin lost the primary election in significant part because of the team he joined. Black political leaders cast Mariam Desantis as not a "native Marshallite," and they applied this "outsider" characterization to him as well. African Americans worked hard to defeat both Mariam and Edwin. Rebecca Culver, a former Council member and part of a Black family that had been in town for three generations, told us that he might have been successful if he had run on his own.

> I remember him just being a nice person, and he owned a business. And that's all I knew of him. Our daughters go to the same school. So we have that in common. I thought that he ran a good campaign. He was out knocking doors. He was very visible. I think that he should have run on his own, by himself as an individual … You have to know who you are associating yourself with … I think he would've been a valuable asset to the Council based on his exposure and his position in our community as a business owner and a Latino.

If he had approached the election differently, without antagonizing the Black political establishment by aligning with Mariam Desantis and trying to keep Linda Nelson off the ballot, Edwin might have won.

Figure 5.3 Polling station during municipal elections.

"Native" or "Natural Marshallites"

As we have described, Mexicans had arrived in town with complex internal divisions and divergent group histories—they came from different parts of Mexico, they were from different social classes, and they had various beliefs and aspirations. The longstanding Marshall community was also heterogeneous and changing. One cannot understand interethnic relations in Marshall by analyzing two groups, allegedly homogeneous Mexicans and allegedly homogeneous longstanding residents. Black residents in Marshall were in a different position than White residents, and longstanding middle-class Black residents were different than the working-class Black residents who had arrived more recently. In some contexts, like church, Irish Americans were positioned differently than other White residents. In order to understand the pathways Mexicans took, we must examine the diverse interethnic relations that actually existed. These included some material and institutional resources, like incumbent Blacks' control over several Council seats and their political apparatus. They also included stories that Black residents told about Edwin and his allies, stories that characterized him as a Mexican outsider with shallow roots and no warrant to a leadership position in Marshall.

A group of longstanding Black residents unified during the 2012 election under the banner of "Marshall Natives for Change." They told a story about themselves as the "natural" governors of Marshall, telling nostalgic stories about their families' deep roots in town. These stories only partly captured the town's history and its future, but they became a powerful motivating force in driving Black turnout and victory in the election. Wayne explained Edwin's defeat as a consequence of his failure to align with these natives. "What went wrong for Edwin," he told us right after the election, "was that he aligned himself with the opponents of 'Natives for Marshall,' ... the Marshallites born and bred, raising up and fighting to bring back to Marshall what we know Marshall to be—small town life, family orientated, home ownership, things like this." Edwin's teammates, he went on, "don't understand us, they don't know us, they are not one of us. Edwin, where he went wrong, was getting against that."

Wayne then explained to us who "Natural Marshallites" were.

> Natural Marshallites, we know each other. You know your family. If you are a Marshallite you can ask somebody their last name and you can go back 3 generations. Oh, I know your mom, I know your dad, I know your grandma, I know your uncle. Are you what's-your-name's boy? Oh that's your family? I know your family. That's how Marshallites are, and we are a tight group. We're a tight-

knit family and a lot of people are related, you know, right here within the town, whether through marriage or not. So the problem is the influx of outsiders. So you hear commonly, "Oh, they are not from Marshall, they don't know what's going on." That's part of the problem that our local government has. They are not from Marshall. They don't think like Marshallites think. So decisions they make, they all commonly knock heads with Marshallites because that's not what we do, that's not how it is here.

By "Natural Marshallite" Wayne meant Black residents like himself, descendants of the earlier wave of migration from the South in the early and mid-twentieth century. The White council members whom Wayne and his allies defeated did live in Marshall. Some of them had family roots in earlier waves of migrants to the town, although Mariam Desantis herself was a relative newcomer. But according to Wayne, these people had abandoned the town by moving "up and out" and were trying to govern it in a way that disadvantaged the growing Black population. From his perspective, African Americans had only recently achieved the political power they deserved, as Italians moved out and left the town to the remaining Black residents. He naturalized this claim with a story about an allegedly stable, robust Black community that stretched back generations. His story was partly true and partly false, but it was nonetheless politically effective.

African Americans' newfound political power was threatened by the rapid growth of the Mexican community. Mexicans, too, were starting to feel that they did not have sufficient political representation and that their community was being ignored and disempowered. In making these arguments, they used the same claims that African Americans had used in their struggle to overcome White domination. This created an uncomfortable situation for many Black residents, because most of them remembered when they or their ancestors had been disempowered in the same way. Black residents often responded to Mexicans' claims in one of two ways. Sometimes they denied that Mexicans were disempowered in the same way African Americans had been, often by characterizing Mexicans as illegitimate interlopers who were receiving unfair advantages. At other times, they claimed that Black residents' time in power had just begun and that it was unfair for them to be pushed aside so soon. Some Black residents seemed to feel uncomfortable keeping Mexicans down with rhetoric similar to things that had been said about them by Italians and other White residents. Wayne and his allies overcame that discomfort and built a powerful story that helped propel a successful campaign.

Edwin tried to adopt this story told by longstanding Black residents, by identifying himself as a "Marshallite." He worked hard to communicate this during his campaign. When he knocked on doors, all over his district,

I was telling them a little bit about myself. That I've been a resident in Marshall for like 25 years. That I went to Marshall High School. That I attended the local community college. And that I have a business in Marshall. And that I have investments in Marshall. And things like that. And when people heard that they probably thought, well he's a resident of Marshall so I can probably vote for him.

Edwin maintained this optimistic view until right before the election, believing that many longstanding residents would consider him one of their own because of his long history in town. "When I was a candidate I didn't hear any opposition until right before the election. The 'Native Marshallites.' We ... had public meet and greets, where all the candidates met an audience and told a little bit about us. And it was then that I learned about the 'Native Marshall' group." At one of the community forums—in which candidates gave short speeches about themselves and community members asked questions—Edwin first heard the term "Native" or "Natural Marshallite." Some of the Black candidates presented themselves in this way, claiming that their opponents were outsiders who did not understand or care about longstanding Marshall residents.

A Black former Council member explained why natives would make better Council members.

> I think that Marshallites are very hard, are very difficult at trusting outsiders, people that are not originally from here ... Being from here the level of trust is more sound, because you know that that person has been here as long as you have, so you know that they know what the real issues are ... The Council members are supposed to be members of the community ... They're supposed to get [policies] from what the residents want to happen. The reason why natives would be better at that is because they're actually going to hear the voices of their cousins, family members, relatives.

According to this story, "Native Marshallites" had a much easier time communicating with constituents because of existing networks. A newcomer like Edwin might have heard things in his store, but he did not have the deep family and neighborhood ties that Native Marshallites did.

David, Edwin's African American campaign staffer, described the rhetoric of the "Natural" or "Native Marshallites."

> There is a group that is calling themselves the Native Marshallites. They are promoting the idea that Marshall should be run and operated by locals ... The reasoning isn't wrong. It's the way they're going about doing it. [Interviewer: But does "Marshall Native" have any ethnic implications?] See, this is the really ugly, sticky wicket part of this that I really don't like. Yes. Unfortunately, yes, it does. I don't like it ... It hurts me when I see stuff like this.

This staffer was himself a Black native of Marshall, but he saw the idea of "Native Marshallites" as a problem. It pitted the Mexican migrants against Black residents, and in his view it divided people who had common experiences and interests. The pathway David envisioned for the Black and Mexican communities involved collaboration and not competition. He acknowledged that important parts of the story told by Native Marshallites were accurate. African Americans in Marshall had in fact been unjustly excluded from the political process. But they were engaging in a familiar political move that distorted the reality of a changing town. We have of course often seen this move nationally—imagining an idealized, more ethnically homogeneous past and building political support for one group's candidates by positioning newcomers as threats to this community. This has been done over and over by White Americans in an effort to exclude African Americans and other groups (e.g., Phillips, 1969), and in Marshall it was done by Black residents to exclude Mexicans. In this way, Linda Nelson's victory over Edwin and the stories about Mexicans not being "Natural Marshallites" repeated a familiar pattern in interethnic relations when the prior migrant group struggled to keep the new migrant group out of power.

Edwin's campaign enacted a conflict over whether the Mexicans were Marshallites or not. The "Natural Marshallites" told a story about their town that did not include Mexicans as part of "us." But Wayne and many other Black residents were ambivalent about this stance. It helped them win the election, and the Marshall City Council—as we write this book several years later—has five Black members, two White members, and no Mexicans. Wayne worried that there would come a reckoning in the relatively near future, as the Mexican community grew, where Black and Mexican residents would have to choose between being rivals or allies.

> The Mexican population is still growing in Marshall. Up until this point it's just like been this new thing. There have been problems, maybe, here and there, but nothing specific as far as racial groups against groups, as of yet. Now I do anticipate that there will be problems, because I think the Mexicans, as they continue to grow, I think they'll grow in strength and they'll start to demand. Right now I think they are in a humble way, like "this is yours, we're just here." But they're getting tired of that. They're getting restless. They want their voice to be known. They want their presence to be understood. And I think they'll start establishing territory ... I think they'll stand up and want to establish their own. Hopefully we can create or establish a good enough relationship in this transition where that doesn't happen. But if we as Blacks don't reach out and take

their hands and pull them in as brothers and sisters, then there will be turmoil in the future. I do believe that.

This was a compelling analysis of the situation. As new migrants came to Marshall across two centuries, the preceding groups mostly moved "up and out" and their influence waned. The English and other Protestants marginalized the Irish for many decades, but eventually the Irish moved into the most desirable neighborhoods and took over key town institutions. The Irish marginalized the Italians, who lived in the East end with recent Black migrants, were forced to bury their dead in the undesirable back of the Catholic cemetery, and had to establish their own separate Catholic church. But by the late twentieth century, many important businesses and residential properties in town were owned by Italian Americans. The Irish, and eventually the Italians, marginalized African Americans. When the Mexican community began in the 1990s, however, African Americans were becoming the largest group in town and they began to gain political power. Wayne wondered how this next transition between ethnic groups would go, and he envisioned a growing Mexican community that would bridle against entrenched Black politicians who treated them as threats.

Wayne raised a possibility that had not happened in earlier cycles of migration, one also envisioned by David and some other longstanding Black residents. They imagined that Black and Mexican residents could both move "up and in" and form an alliance, instead of one group moving out and the other taking over. James Smith articulated a similar view. As the Mexican community stabilized, making the transition from *solteros* to families, he saw an opportunity to create a strong, ethnically diverse community.

> There's more of a stabilization and the community is starting to be more settled ... I think Marshall is special because of our diversity. We have a great mix of people here, and whenever we get together, we get along. And I'm not saying that everything is always peaches and cream, but you know we have a way of being able to survive as a town. I don't think there are too many towns that have survived the way we have.

James envisioned a future in which African Americans, Mexicans, and others would all contribute to the community and get along. Instead of recurring cycles in which newcomers supplanted longstanding residents—who moved "up and out" after a period of interethnic conflict—he hoped that Blacks and other longstanding residents could welcome Mexican migrants and create something new.

> To deal with the next wave of migrants I think first of all you have to visualize and realize how you were treated, you know, put yourself in that position. When

> I came here, how did I feel? How was I treated? I didn't like it … We gotta make it easier for them so they don't have … to go through the problems that we went through … We've got a mixture of everything here, and in order for us to keep it going we have to welcome the people with open arms.

James, Wayne, and David envisioned a diverse community that would work together to improve the town for everyone. Many longstanding Black residents felt that Marshall was special. In an earlier era when they were excluded from neighboring towns because of redlining and racism, Marshall had accepted them. There were tensions and mistreatment, but Black residents contributed to building a community where they felt at home. Drawing on this positive experience, James, Wayne, and David imagined that Marshall could perhaps be a new kind of community in which Black and Mexican residents could work together in a new way. They hoped that it could become a flourishing town built on interethnic solidarity, an outcome not envisioned by familiar stories about migrants either assimilating or causing decline.

As the Mexican community developed across its first two decades in Marshall, the migrants faced at least three possible pathways with respect to African Americans—both in the realities of their relations and in the diverse stories told about them. First, in some ways African Americans treated Mexicans as earlier "host" groups had treated newcomers. Many Black residents responded like the English, Irish, and Italians. They felt that Mexicans were encroaching on their neighborhoods, their businesses, their jobs, and their political power, and they fought back. Thus, many Mexicans had to struggle against Black residents. Second, African Americans like James and Wayne wanted to establish solidarity with Mexicans, to encourage them to move "up and in," and to work together to build a stronger town. Some, like James, envisioned this as an integrated community that would welcome members of all groups. Others, like some of the young African Americans who created community organizations, envisioned this as "Black and Brown" people uniting to fight White racism. On this pathway, some Mexicans joined together with Black residents. Third, as we have seen in White stories of commercial and residential revitalization, most White residents imagined Black residents as an exception to the usual migration story of moving "up and out." Many White and Mexican residents imagined the migrants moving past many African Americans and following Irish and Italians' earlier successes.

As we ended our time in Marshall in 2016, we saw evidence of all three pathways. Mexicans who spent time in different spaces found different pathways opening up—with St. Joseph's being different than town politics, for example, and both being different from community organizations run by Black residents. Institutional spaces, divergent stories, and other contingent resources—for example, Edwin's choice of a hated teammate, Martínez family members' access to economic and cultural capital through Carlo, or documentation status—shaped Mexicans' diverse pathways, and individual Mexicans moved in different directions. Despite David's best efforts, for instance, Edwin did not ally himself with African Americans in solidarity. His family continued to have modest entrepreneurial success, but he spent most of his time with other Mexicans as his political career ended.

The struggles in Marshall over public space—which we have described with respect to crime, commerce, migration enforcement, and politics—involved both typical and atypical pathways, and they illustrate both the inaccuracies and the power of simple stories. Mexicans did change across the first two decades from a collection of transient, vulnerable outsiders to a more stable community that was developing economic, political, and symbolic power. Narratives of revitalization captured some of what actually happened. But the realities of migration enforcement together with stereotypes of illegality and otherness made the reality more complicated. So did the complexities of Black-Mexican relations, which were a contingent factor present in this town but not in some similar ones. Father Kelly, Doreena, Marco, James, and others observed similarities between Mexican migrants' experiences and the migration stories told about their own ancestors—stories centered around despair and struggle, then hope and success. We have seen how, in residential and public spaces, Mexicans did follow this familiar pathway in some respects. But the host community in which this oversimplified story imagined they were assimilating was itself fractured and changing. Instead of seeing newcomers simply becoming like their hosts, we have instead described two internally complex, moving entities interacting and changing. As the newcomers and longstanding residents developed together, both individuals and communities followed contingent pathways that we can only understand by attending to the diverse resources that made diverging pathways possible. The emerging pathway of the Mexican community itself had not yet solidified, and heterogeneous resources continued to pull in different directions. Some individual Mexicans found themselves on more stable pathways—sometimes classic pathways involving struggle and success, while at other times tragic stories of struggle and exploitation or deportation—but the community as a whole was still in flux.

6

Community Organizations: Three Imagined Mexican Pathways

The last four chapters have illustrated in detail the core elements of our argument about the diverse, contingent pathways that migrants travel. First, we have shown how individual Mexicans and the Mexican migrant community sometimes followed familiar storylines that either describe struggle and ultimate success or focus on hostility and exclusion. But we have also shown how individual and community pathways were sometimes unexpected. Edwin's commercial success, for example, in many ways fit a simple, positive migration story, but his political career did not. In school, Allie was positioned for academic and perhaps economic success, although her extensive duties at home were a significant constraint. Nancy and Sara, despite having similar backgrounds, traveled different pathways from Allie and different pathways from each other. The Mexican community as a whole was in some ways on a familiar pathway, but in 2016 there remained significant indeterminacy and it could well end up moving in unexpected directions.

Second, we have shown how both typical and atypical pathways emerged over time and solidified as diverse, contingent realities took hold. Edwin's choice of a political teammate and Sara's decision to go on that fateful date, for example, turned out to be pivotal, contingent events that influenced their pathways. Father Kelly's dispositions toward bridge-building, together with his Spanish fluency and his arrival at the same time as more young Mexican families were settling in Marshall, were crucial to the development of the Irish-Mexican community at St. Joseph's.

Third, we have shown how migrant pathways are shaped by resources from at least four interconnected timescales. Realities about cycles of migration and interethnic relations, about the development of the Mexican community over two decades, about the details of individual lives, and about particular events all played crucial roles in migrants' pathways. But no one set of resources is always crucial. In different cases, heterogeneous resources from different scales turn out to be central. Juan, Edwin, and Allie, for example, ended up on different pathways because of somewhat different configurations of resources that became relevant in their particular cases.

Fourth, we have described the important roles that migration stories play in individual and community pathways. Even when they are inaccurate, stories can be crucial resources that influence the realities of migration. The systematic erasure of Black migrant successes in White migration stories, for example, helped foreclose opportunities for many African Americans. At the same time, White and Mexican narrators' stories about Mexican "revitalization" helped open opportunities for some Mexican migrants. And many Black narrators' emphasis on the Mexican "invasion" contributed to Black flight, encouraging longstanding black residents to move out of town.

Finally, we have shown how both realities of and stories about interethnic relations play an important role in migrant pathways. The past two chapters have illustrated how relations between Mexican and Black residents became crucial resources—both as members of the two groups encountered each other politically, economically, and relationally in neighborhood and public spaces, and as White residents told stories about and reacted to Black-Mexican contact. The complex, yet-to-solidify relations between Blacks and Mexicans derailed Edwin's political career, but they also provided opportunities for interethnic solidarity in two community organizations we describe in this chapter.

Thus, we have shown how diverse migrant pathways solidify over time as contingent resources from multiple scales—centrally including migration stories and interethnic relations—coalesce. This chapter describes how resources from six nonprofit community organizations also contributed to emerging migrant pathways in Marshall. Our descriptions of these organizations allow us to review several common pathways traveled by and imagined for Mexican migrants. These community organizations envisioned Mexicans having different optimal futures. Either explicitly in stories that they told, or tacitly in their practices, organizations mapped out divergent pathways—some toward stereotypical "assimilation" into an allegedly homogeneous America, some toward or away from solidarity with Black residents, and some with a vision of maintaining Mexican culture while also building connections to longstanding residents. We use these organizations to summarize several pathways that different Mexicans followed in Marshall, and we show how contingent resources available in the organizations contributed to these emerging pathways for various migrants. As we have also shown for schools, churches, neighborhoods, and public spaces, when individual Mexicans happened to spend time in one particular community organization, resources from that particular space often influenced their pathways. Like other spaces, the community organizations changed over the course of the two decades and provided different resources at different moments in the development of the migrant community.

Community organizations played an important role in Marshall, influencing the pathways taken by individual migrants, the Mexican community, and the town itself. The organizations provided material and psychological support, circulated stories about migrants, and became sites where interethnic relations developed. In this chapter, we explore how six organizations influenced Mexicans' pathways. We trace how these six organizations were positioned within the cycle of migrant arrivals in Marshall. They were heterogeneous in their histories, clientele, and areas of expertise. Some existed long before the Mexican population grew, some changed as the Mexicans arrived, and others were created to serve the Mexican migrants. The Washington Community Center, Marshall Men for Progress (MMP), and Y-Achievers were founded by Black residents, but over time they included Mexicans. AYUDA, Club de Padres, and Arte, Tecnología, y Educación del Pueblo (ATEP) were created to serve Spanish-speaking residents. AYUDA was created to serve the Puerto Rican community in the region, around 1970, but it shifted to serving Mexicans as their numbers increased. ATEP and Club de Padres were new organizations, created to serve Mexicans in the second decade of the migrant community. Some of the organizations focused on educational success for underrepresented children, some provided recreational and out-of-school learning opportunities, some celebrated Latin American cultures, and some provided a broad range of social services. All but one changed significantly with the arrival of the Mexicans and with the development of the migrant community across two decades.

In this chapter, we trace how these organizations contributed to Mexicans' heterogeneous experiences and pathways in Marshall. The six organizations facilitated different positions for migrants and longstanding residents because of their diverse histories, missions, and practices. Crucially, the organizations adopted divergent stories about exemplary migrant lives. AYUDA emphasized assimilation, encouraging migrants to adopt American norms and celebrating successful instances of Mexicans who moved toward an imagined mainstream American life. ATEP celebrated Mexican culture, displaying Mexican-inspired art to the broader community and encouraging young Mexicans to embrace their roots. MMP and Y-Achievers expanded to include Mexican youth in their efforts to empower marginalized Marshall residents, working toward "Black and Brown" solidarity. These divergent stories about the migrant community imagined different pathways for Mexicans. In this chapter, we describe how the various organizations contributed to divergent pathways for the Mexican migrants who frequented each one.

Members of our research team became deeply involved in several of these community organizations across our eleven years in town. In addition to our observing many classes and workshops at AYUDA, two research team members taught English there as volunteers during our first few years in town. Stanton Wortham and several members of our team created the Club de Padres, attended every meeting, and supported the group financially throughout its existence—in a joint effort with educators and Mexican parents to empower Spanish-speaking parents in their relationships with teachers and administrators. Briana Nichols led several team members in interviewing and spending time with the African American founders of MMP and Y-Achievers. Half a dozen team members participated in events and programs at ATEP, across its history. We gathered intensive data there, spending hundreds of hours volunteering in various educational programs, participating in reading groups, and attending public events.

The Washington Community Center

The Washington Community Center was a longstanding Marshall organization that served Black residents and could have served Mexicans if the migrant community had developed differently. The Center was founded in response to a tragic event. The official Center history tells the story this way:

> In 1947, the Washington Community Center was incorporated in response to a tragedy within the community. On July 6, 1945, five youth from the community went swimming in a swimming hole. Marshall's African American community frequented this area because Marshall's public swimming facilities were segregated at the time. Misfortune struck when one of the youth became caught in an undercurrent; she went under at least three times. Her friend jumped in to rescue her; however, he only knew how to "doggie-paddle," a skill he learned at Boy Scout camp. His valiant rescue attempt failed: that afternoon, both children tragically lost their lives. The death of these two children prompted Marshall's African American community to organize a grassroots fundraising effort to build a facility where all residents could safely swim and enjoy other recreational activities.

Virtually every Black resident whom we spoke with knew of the Washington Center, but members of other groups often did not. Even Black Marshall residents who were born long after this event had heard about the tragedy in 1945 and the racial segregation that caused it. When asked about his memories of the Black community in Marshall, John—a resident in his thirties—told us:

> How I would describe it? What I heard wasn't always pleasant. Like the Washington Community Center, like the reason why that was started. There were issues swimming with, you know, "the other." There was a lot of segregation, and they had issues with Black folks swimming with other people, so they had to start the Center ... How it started was, some young folk went swimming in the creek and they drowned because that was the only alternative they had. They couldn't swim in the public pool, so they went in the creek and they died.

Leaders of the Black community in Marshall began to raise funds immediately after the tragedy, and a decade later the Center opened. According to the Center's history, it was named for Booker T. Washington because his spirit "was reflected not only in the courage and selflessness of the young people who perished that day in 1945, but also the caring and sense of community imparted by all those whose contributions helped build the facility." The Center had an air-conditioned gym, a stage, a kitchen, and a pool. It lived up to its founders' hopes, providing recreational, cultural, and educational opportunities to Black children and families across generations.

The Center provided "youth and adult recreation, police-community relations, community safety, leadership development, financial literacy, political action, neighborhood improvement, and social services." During our time in town, the Center hosted programs including a summer camp, a financial literacy seminar series, a summer lunch program for children, and Thanksgiving events including turkey giveaways. The pool was particularly popular. During the summer months, it was full of Black children and families enjoying the facility. By the end of our time in town, however, the pool had closed due to lack of funds needed for maintenance. The Center building remained open and hosted occasional events and programs.

Despite the fact that the Washington Community Center was not intended only for African Americans, other residents rarely used it. It explicitly welcomed "all residents of the greater Marshall community." Its official mission said that

> the low-income residents of Marshall have limited resources. The BTWCC provides programs and opportunities that address residents' needs and improve their quality of life. Through its activities, the BTWCC will stand at the forefront of Marshall's revitalization.

The emphasis on "revitalization" was important. As described above, many Marshall residents told stories of decline and revitalization. White residents most often blamed the decline on African Americans and credited Mexicans with revitalization. Black residents told a different story. They recounted how African American residents arrived in Marshall during and after the Great Migration of Blacks from the South, from 1910 to 1970, eager to work and build better lives for their families. They described the racism that excluded their ancestors from jobs, neighborhoods, and public spaces. But these ancestors came together to build their families and institutions like the Washington Community Center, and thus African American residents credited these ancestors with revitalizing their community in the face of significant challenges.

As described above, this history of Black revitalization and intact community was erased from other groups' stories. Most White and Mexican residents did not know that many Black residents' aspirations, contributions, and successes were similar to those of other migrant groups. Many Italians who lived together with African Americans in the East end in the first half of the twentieth century had respect for their Black neighbors. By the time the Washington Community Center was completed, however, Italians were beginning to move "up and out," while most Black residents remained in the downtown neighborhoods. Starting in the 1960s and 1970s, residents of Irish, Italian, and other European ancestry often told stories that emphasized high crime rates in Black neighborhoods and characterized Blacks as dangerous. They no longer lived close to the Washington Community Center, and they never used the facility.

The Center was located in a neighborhood on the near East side that remained mostly Black until the second decade of the Mexican community. But as the number of migrants grew, Mexicans settled in that area as well. Mexicans did not use the Center at all, however, with the exception of occasionally renting the function room for private events during the second decade. In 2012, two Mexican youth gave us their perspective on the Center. Valeria and Gloria were friends of Nancy's who attended Marshall Middle School. When Katherine Clonan-Roy asked the girls if they ever went swimming in the summer, Gloria said, "No, Marshall does not have a pool." Katherine said that she had driven by a pool the previous summer and it looked crowded. Valeria said, "Oh, yeah, but that is a Black pool." She said that they don't go to that pool because "all the Black people go there, and it's nasty." Many Mexican children would no doubt have enjoyed the pool, but the two communities missed an opportunity to connect because of ethnic boundaries and stereotypes.

Mexicans had been exposed to negative stereotypes about African Americans while they were still in Mexico—largely from Hollywood movies and other media, but also from Mexican ideologies that favor whiter over darker skin—and most had never met an African American person before coming to the United States. These stereotypes often intensified when Mexicans arrived. Many Mexicans felt excluded and misunderstood by Blacks, whom they accused of bullying and racism. As described in Chapter 2, however, two years after making these racialized comments Valeria and Gloria had several Black friends and were more sympathetic to Black experiences. Valeria herself fell in love with and dated a Black classmate. But the story about Blacks as threatening nonetheless persisted among both Mexican and White residents. For their part, Blacks were occupied with their own struggles against racism and efforts at advancement. Until the second decade of the migrant community, fewer Blacks focused on Mexicans' situations or their potential either as allies or as competitors. At MMP and Y-Achievers, however, this separation and wariness between the two communities began to change during the second decade of the Mexican community.

In 2014, the Center had to close the pool due to lack of funds, as described in local media.

> It's a first in 61 years. The gate to the Booker T. Washington Community Center pool in Marshall will be closed this summer, leaving over 1000 kids without a pool on hot days. The Center, which relies on donations, doesn't have the money for repairs … and hope to open this summer is gone. "It's sad, it really is," said one mother. "The children don't have any place to go."

The Washington Community Center struggled because of declining government funds for community services and what we have called "Black flight"—the migration of middle-class Black families out of Marshall into surrounding suburbs, which left fewer potential donors with the means to support the Center. The Center continued to run a few programs, and it rented out its gym for events, but attendance was much lower than in prior years.

Mexican families looking to rent an inexpensive hall occasionally held events in the Center during the second decade. In 2014, for example, we observed a party there.

> It is 8 p.m. and the walls of the Center are shaking with sound. Violins, trumpets, and guitars create a loud, exuberant melody. Inside, 100 adolescents and their families gather—dancing, drinking, eating, giving gifts. The music stops. From a back hallway, Brenda makes her entrance into the main gymnasium. All eyes are on her. She is wearing a tiara and a strapless blue ball gown with ruched

organza. The crowd begins to cheer. As the cheers die down, the music picks back up and Brenda's *chambelanes* [male escorts] surround her. They begin to engage in a choreographed, ceremonial dance. Brenda is turning 15 and this is her *quinceañera*.

Although the pool had closed and by 2014 the Center ran relatively few programs, Mexican families began to rent out the space for *quinceañeras* and other events. Valeria and her peers had once characterized this as a "nasty," "Black" space, but in later years it was used and valued by the Mexican community. Such events did not bring together Black and Mexican residents, however. As middle-class members of the Black community moved away from downtown and Mexicans moved in, the Washington Center space was repurposed. Ethnic segregation continued, and Mexicans held their own ethnically homogeneous events there. The Washington Center represented a missed opportunity, a place where Black and Mexican residents could have interacted but did not. This contrasts with St. Joseph's, for example, where Irish and Mexican residents successfully built hybrid activities and stronger relations. The differences between the two spaces emerged in part because of contingent realities—for example, the presence of a leader determined to create interethnic community in one case but not the other, and the historical connection of Mexicans but not Blacks to the Catholic church.

AYUDA

In Chapter 4, we described how Juan received a legal summons from his landlord for alleged failure to pay rent. Confused and apprehensive, he asked us for help. We connected him to a community organization called AYUDA. The agency found him a lawyer named David who successfully supported Juan in the legal process, pro bono. AYUDA was founded around 1970 to serve the needs of a small Puerto Rican community in Marshall and surrounding towns. In the 1980s, some Cuban refugees moved to the area for a few years, and AYUDA served their needs. The founding director, himself Puerto Rican, told us in 2005 that many Puerto Ricans had resented it when the agency shifted its focus to Cubans. He felt that it had been the right thing to do, however, because "the most recent migrants always have the most pressing needs. Right now that community is the large Mexican population." As the Mexican community began to grow rapidly, AYUDA made another transition and focused its services on Mexican migrants.

Pastor Dave described this transition in 2006, telling us that the founding AYUDA Director

> was there for 35 years. When AYUDA was founded, the Latino population in Marshall may have constituted 5% of the population, and I think it was all Caribbean. With the [Mexican] influx, it's now a third of Marshall and it's 80, 90% Mexican, which has just blown away all their intake structures, support structures. [The AYUDA Director] is trying to increase the staff and all ... to just keep his head above water. Most of his staff is Puerto Rican. You know that there are major cultural differences.

In fact, the Hispanic population in Marshall was less than 2 percent in 1970. This very small Spanish-speaking community changed over time, from Puerto Rican to Cuban and then to Mexican. AYUDA accommodated these changes. The agency was challenged starting in the late 1990s by the rapid arrival of Mexicans, as more and more people needed services. It was also challenged by the cultural differences between Puerto Rican staff and Mexican clients, as second-generation staff who had no experience with lack of legal status encountered clients who spoke a different dialect of Spanish and faced different challenges. The organization nonetheless served crucial functions for many newcomers like Juan.

AYUDA was located on Main Street in Marshall, in an old bank building. The founding Director had served on a community development board convened by the bank's parent organization. When the bank decided to close the branch on Main Street, during the era of economic decline in Marshall, he convinced them to let AYUDA have the space. The following field note describes our initial impressions of the building.

> Inside, the walls are painted a dull, bank-like beige and the space is dark. The old bank vault sits in the middle of the large main room, with the door wide open. We ask, irreverently, if it's an important person's office, or if they ever lock anyone in there, but the Director tells us that it's used to store office supplies. Two secretaries and the Director's wife are there during our visit. One of the secretaries answers the phone in Spanish, as does the Director. He speaks to both secretaries in Spanish, but one responds to him only in English. To the left of the entrance is the computer lab, which has many computers and a few tables. To the right of the entrance is one of the classrooms, which provides a sharp contrast to the rest of the ground floor. It is large and spacious, with big windows, carpeting, and lots of colorful children's supplies. Upstairs are two similar classrooms which are clean, orderly and filled with clear plastic boxes that contain colorful blocks and other materials. In the classroom there are displays of books—all in English, though a few have Hispanic authors. A Mexican flag hangs below one

of the clocks, but there is no Spanish text anywhere. There are signs in English on the walls, including one about what we can do to realize "our goals." Though the classrooms are spacious, warm and welcoming, the staff offices are small and cramped. The computer equipment in the offices looks relatively new, however. The Director tells us that he has had to move his office twice already, to make room for new classrooms as the agency expanded.

This description highlights two notable aspects of AYUDA. First, after it almost closed due to lack of clientele in the early 1990s, it grew rapidly when the Mexican community arrived. In the mid-2000s, AYUDA secured government funds as well as donations from charities and individuals to expand its programming for the growing Mexican population. Virtually every Mexican in Marshall knew of AYUDA, and most non-Mexicans had heard of it. The organization's growth stalled after the economic downturn in 2008, however, as funds became more scarce. Second, AYUDA's educational programming for children was largely in English. Staff spoke Spanish when serving adults. But they encouraged a transition to English for Mexican children. This fit with AYUDA's preferred story about "assimilation" to mainstream American culture.

Despite tight budgets and the needs brought by Mexican migrants, AYUDA had broad, ambitious aims. Its mission was to "provide education, social services and health access to Hispanic and other low-income people, helping them succeed and become productive … We believe that they, too, can achieve the American Dream of success." It offered a broad range of services. It supported education, providing after-school programming for about twenty-five elementary and middle school children daily, including ESL classes, computer lessons, and homework help. It offered a preschool and parenting program for young children and their mothers—a program that had increasing demand as the number of young Mexican children grew. In the first decade of the Mexican community, the agency offered guidance for high school boys who had arrived as adolescents, encouraging them to stay in school. In the first decade, it offered English classes for adults, but it was unable to continue these because of limited funding.

AYUDA also supported the health of Mexican migrants by connecting them to health providers that served the uninsured. Some migrants had psychological or substance abuse issues, and AYUDA sent them to local agencies that had bilingual staff. The biggest health challenge for Mexican children was often dental. Both AYUDA and school staff told us of many cases where migrant children—even as far along as middle school—had seen a dentist only once or twice in their lives. Mexican parents worked at time-consuming and difficult jobs in order to provide for their families, and because of economic, cultural, and linguistic barriers they struggled to support their children's schoolwork and get them medical care. Dental care was sometimes beyond their reach. AYUDA helped by educating parents about the importance of dental hygiene and arranging for families to use a free, mobile dental unit that visited town.

The Director of AYUDA also served as an advocate for the Mexican community, informing town leaders about the realities of migrant life and pushing back against negative stories circulating in the press. When the town passed the ordinance against overcrowding in 2005, the local paper printed editorials disparaging Mexicans. The director described how local newspaper editorials complained that "illegal aliens"—he said the word "Mexicans" was never used—broke the law by living in enormous groups. He told us that claims about overcrowding were exaggerated. Mexicans wanted to save money and were willing to endure what others would call crowding. The problem was also aggravated by that fact that landlords turned a blind eye to extra tenants in an apartment. The director wanted to get involved and told us that he had drafted many rebuttals to these letters, but he was afraid that speaking out could cause AYUDA to be targeted and might result in loss of funding. Because the Mexican community was so new, there were almost no Mexican bilinguals with enough social capital to advocate for this community in public. The Puerto Ricans who ran AYUDA sometimes adopted that role. They did not have to fear deportation, because they were legal residents, and they understood American society. But the founding director was nonetheless cautious in his advocacy.

AYUDA also helped Mexicans deal with migration enforcement. The new director, who took over in 2006 after the retirement of his colleague, became a more active public advocate for Mexican migrants. In the late 2000s, as described in the last chapter, federal migration authorities began to target Marshall with periodic raids. In 2009, St. Joseph's hosted a "summit" where town leaders came to hear about the needs of the Mexican community. After the government officials made their presentation and asked for input, the new director of AYUDA—also Puerto Rican—was the first to speak. He emphasized the fear that many Mexican families felt with increased, unpredictable migration enforcement. He told the crowd: "It is no longer about if you commit a crime. Just walking down the street the police can pick you up because you look Latino." He told stories about Mexican families being evicted because they were breaking codes by having too many people in the house. When authorities detained Mexican migrants, AYUDA provided them with legal assistance and translation services. They also connected relatives of deportees to agencies that helped with food, housing, and mental health. Many Mexican residents knew of and appreciated these services.

The advocacy and support provided by the Puerto Rican leadership of AYUDA were crucial for many Mexicans throughout the first two decades.

Across its half century, AYUDA adjusted to the needs of Spanish-speaking residents in Marshall. It moved from serving its original Puerto Rican clientele to Cuban refugees and then to Mexican migrants. As the Mexican community faced new challenges—like the increase in families with young children needing preschool and the need for legal advocacy because of increased migration enforcement—AYUDA responded by providing new services. The agency focused mostly on addressing urgent needs and seeking resources to meet them. It differed from some of the organizations discussed below, however, by telling stories that cast assimilation as a desirable goal for migrants. The second director told us that Mexican migrants should "become part of the citizenry, assimilate. At AYUDA we emphasize to families that they should start to attend meetings and wider community events … and become part of their own solution." On its website, AYUDA presented success stories that featured assimilation. One story talked about Rosa, praising her command of English—good enough to direct an English-language version of the school play that year, the story emphasized—and noting that her five-year-old son was already reading fluently in English. When AYUDA ran parenting classes in tandem with its preschool program, staff assumed that Mexican migrants needed to learn how to parent in the "right" way. That is, Mexicans needed to adopt mainstream American practices, which were assumed to be superior.

Sometimes, as with dental hygiene, this was surely the case. But assimilation encourages migrants to give up their own traditions and misrepresents heterogeneous, changing mainstream practices as stable, "natural," and superior (Moll, 1992; Valencia, 1997). In its explicit advocacy and its practices, AYUDA most often presupposed that migrants needed to change and conform to mainstream American culture. Many Mexicans who spent time there were encouraged to think of themselves as on the same pathway as familiar, oversimplified positive stories about earlier migrant groups—Puerto Rican, Irish, Italian, and others—who had moved "up and out," achieving the "American Dream." The four organizations described below also helped Mexican migrants, but they adopted divergent stories about Mexicans and the larger community. Instead of arguing for assimilation, ATEP—an organization founded by a Mexican migrant—celebrated Mexican culture, encouraging people to read Mexican literature in Spanish and to adopt Mexican artistic traditions. It created connections among White and Mexican residents, in spaces that celebrated Mexican artistic achievements. Club de Padres and MMP encouraged Mexicans to become politically active and to advocate for their own visions of the town's future, working to change existing structures without losing their identities as Mexicans. MMP explicitly aimed to transform American society by empowering Black and Mexican youth. These organizations told divergent stories about American society and envisioned diverse places for migrants in that society.

As Mexican migrants became involved with these organizations and their varied stories about migration, their pathways often diverged. Clients often came to AYUDA for basic help with food, health care, and the law. AYUDA helped them to stabilize their lives and raise their families, while encouraging them to adopt practices from mainstream American culture. Youth who became involved with MMP or Y-Achievers were introduced to a different set of stories and practices—ones that included critiques of the existing American system—and were encouraged to challenge the status quo. The different organizations told varied stories about optimal Mexican migrant lives and how their particular services facilitated these diverse pathways, and the organizations' stories shaped the kinds of services they offered and often influenced the pathways taken by migrants involved with a given organization. The contingent fact of involvement with one organization or another was often a crucial resource causing migrants' pathways to solidify in one direction or another.

Club de Padres

Mexican parents were deeply concerned with their children's futures, and most paid close attention to their children's schooling. Educators consistently told us that Mexican parents were committed to education. Many monolingual Spanish-speaking parents, for example, regularly attended school events that were delivered only in English. They went to parent-teacher conferences, and they responded quickly to school concerns about discipline, even when they struggled to understand what educators were saying. Mexican parents often told us that they wanted their children to move beyond their own physically demanding, relatively low-paying jobs. Despite their attendance at events, however, Mexican parents generally did not feel connected to the schools. Marshall schools struggled to recruit Spanish-speaking staff, in part due to the scarcity of highly educated Spanish speakers in the region, and many parents had difficulty communicating. Parents were also unfamiliar with the American school system, and this hindered their attempts to advise their children and intervene at school.

In response to such concerns, our research team worked with district administrators and Juana Faccone to create bilingual resource rooms, places where parents could come once a week and find bilingual staff who offered advice and homework assistance to Mexican parents and children. By 2009, four of the six district elementary schools had developed such resource rooms. In one room at Grant Elementary, on a day that we observed, six families attended a ninety-minute session. A district specialist and the school's math coach offered guidance about the math curriculum. The school's bilingual community liaison—a young paraprofessional from South America named Patricia—translated into Spanish for the parents. The school's two certified ESL teachers also attended and worked on homework with individual children. One of them spoke Spanish and was able to interact with the parents, and a member of our research team worked with individual families in Spanish as well. Toward the end of this session, the parents began speaking about the need for Mexican parents to have a greater voice in the school district.

Patricia and the parents became very animated while discussing the possibilities, agreeing that Mexican parents needed to take initiative about their concerns. As Spanish speakers, Patricia said, "we have to join together and have our voices heard." The parents went on to discuss the concerns that led them to this conclusion. One mother told a story about an attempt to visit her son's class. She had arrived at school one day and asked to observe how he was doing and learn about the activities in his classroom. But the school turned her away and would not let her into the building, for reasons that she did not understand. One of the fathers said that, if they worked together as parents, they could make such visits possible by agreeing on logistics with the school. Another father brought up the problem of translation, saying that "most parents from here, if they have a question, they go and speak with 'el presidente' of the school, but if you want to do that you have to try to find someone to translate." The parents were frustrated, but they told us that they wanted to make positive change instead of just being angry.

After hearing concerns like this, in 2009 we worked with the school district, Juana Faccone, and a group of parents to create "Club de Padres." This "Parents' Club" was formed with the support of a grant that our research team obtained to increase opportunities for Mexican parents' involvement in their children's schools. It provided an informal opportunity for Spanish-language conversation about the schools and was open to any district parent. Juana moderated the discussions herself, and school district administrators—sometimes including the Superintendent—attended the meetings. We recruited parents by distributing flyers at elementary schools and inviting parents that we knew personally. Our goal was to create a Spanish-speaking space where Mexican parents could talk with each other about their concerns and share those concerns with district administrators. The meetings were billed as *charlas informales*, informal chats. One Saturday morning every month we reserved a room at the local public library. We provided food as well as childcare in an adjoining room. The District welcomed this initiative, and several bilingual school district personnel attended each meeting. Members of our research team facilitated, helping with childcare and logistics.

The first event attracted about fifteen families, almost all with elementary school children. We continued to host monthly meetings throughout the winter and spring of 2009, and we resumed in the fall. Attendance increased moderately, reaching thirty-five to forty Mexican parents and children per meeting. Several members of our team, plus Juana Faccone, Patricia, and the District ESL administrator, attended every meeting through the end of 2009. A group of about half a dozen families also attended every meeting, with other families cycling in and out. The superintendent attended a few meetings, and she was eager to connect with the Mexican parents even though she did not speak Spanish. A school district administrator translated for her.

A typical meeting would start with tamales. Juana Faccone's brother Paco owned a restaurant where he and his wife made wonderful Mexican food. He would arrive with an enormous pot or two and unveil the tamales to the crowd of children gathered around. As in many Mexican gatherings, the atmosphere of these events started out warm, communal, and energetic, with people greeting each other and engaging in supportive conversation about their lives, and with children playing all around the room. Juana would call the meeting to order and a couple of graduate students or school district volunteers would gather the younger children and take them to an adjoining room. In the first five or six meetings, the parents were relatively quiet and looked to school personnel for direction. Juana would ask open-ended questions about their experiences in school, and the parents did share experiences and concerns when prompted.

As organizers we had no agenda. We simply asked parents to share what was on their minds. Many expressed a desire to learn English. They felt growing distance between themselves and their children, as their children learned English and moved along in American schools, and they felt that their speaking English might help overcome this. From the first meeting, parents also asked about how to help their children with homework and support their progress in school. The parents were not familiar with some of the subject matter being taught, and few could understand homework in English. Furthermore, they had no experience with the grading system and other aspects of American schooling. This—together with the fact that most could not speak English well enough to communicate comfortably with their children's teachers—made it difficult for them to support their children's academic work. District staff heard this concern, and they pressed the District to make available Spanish-language versions of students' homework. Some of the curriculum packages they used already offered Spanish translations of homework assignments, and for one or two subject areas the schools were subsequently able to send home assignments in Spanish. The schools also translated more of their communications into Spanish as time went on.

Parents appreciated the opportunity to communicate with school personnel at Club meetings. One of the bilingual paraprofessionals—whose job was to help teachers in working with Spanish speaking students—summarized parent perspectives during the second meeting of the group by telling everyone about parents' concerns with communication. She said that parents wanted to know when things were going badly with their children—especially in regard to discipline problems—but that the parents weren't really involved when things are good. She suggested that both parties were responsible for keeping communication open, including when children are succeeding at school. "You don't need to schedule a conference when things are good" was the typical attitude, but she argued against this. This paraprofessional proposed that schools should communicate consistently about successes as well as challenges. District personnel embraced this idea in principle, and the monthly Club meetings allowed for some communication along these lines. However, given the tasks of daily life, communication remained a challenge. Some parents took charge and showed up at school regularly, building relations with teachers and other staff, but most Mexican parents were not as connected to their children's schooling as they would have liked.

In other areas, parents made more progress. District administrators asked at the first meeting about something they were considering—purchasing headsets to allow simultaneous translation at school meetings. Parents were enthusiastic about the idea, and so the district bought some. At a subsequent meeting, a district administrator introduced the day's speaker in English, and parents wore the headsets while a staff member provided simultaneous translation. Parents were also enthusiastic about another idea, suggested by Juana Faccone, where several might pool resources and hire a teacher to tutor their children after school. Parents were interested in this and discussed the logistics—how many hours, how many days, how to group kids into similar grade levels. They asked Juana how much it would cost, and she offered to connect them with potential tutors. She also suggested that school buildings might be open and willing to offer space. Several ideas like this were discussed at club meetings. The gatherings brought together parents in ways that had not happened before, and along with school personnel they made some progress.

At one meeting, several parents expressed concerns about other students bullying their children, forcing them to give up seats on the bus or beating them up at recess. One mother was particularly upset about this, but she hesitated to identify the perpetrators. When pressed, she eventually whispered that they were "*morenitos*," meaning "little Black children." This created an awkward moment for the translator, because the Black superintendent was eager to understand what this parent had just said. After hearing the translation, the Superintendent said this was the first she had heard about bullying on the buses and she promised to investigate. We have described similar stories about interethnic relations that shaped perceptions and behaviors, and we have documented how these stories sometimes contributed to distance between groups. But Club de Padres provided a space where Black, White, and Hispanic educators could interact directly with Mexican parents and devise solutions. They did not solve all the problems raised, but they engaged Mexican parents' concerns respectfully.

Only a small fraction of Mexican parents in Marshall attended the Club de Padres, however. Most attendees understood that other parents were busy, and some occasionally explained that most parents worked very hard, sometimes at more than one job, such that it was difficult to find the time. Other attendees, however, drew distinctions between themselves and other Mexicans. One mother asked: "There are lots of Latino parents in our community; where are they today?" In response, some parents drew invidious distinctions between themselves and parents who did not attend—claiming that they were less educated, less cultured, less committed. A member of the research team argued that more parents would come over time. She compared these early club meetings to a seed, saying that out of this group a larger organization would grow to include many more parents. The distinctions drawn by Mexican parents between types of Mexicans illustrate the diversity of positions and pathways among migrants. Divergent stories were told about different kinds of Mexicans, even among Mexicans themselves, and demographically similar individuals had different experiences with schools and in town.

The Club de Padres envisioned a different role for Mexican parents than AYUDA did. Instead of urging them to assimilate, the Club empowered them to ask for change. Spanish-speaking school staff encouraged the parents to communicate and assert themselves. Juana Faccone implored parents not to be intimidated by their lack of English. If your child is sick and you have to write a note to school, she said, write it in Spanish and the school will find someone to translate. "Un grupo de padres es una fuerza" [a group of parents is a force], she told them, and another staff member added that you have to "defender sus derechos" [stand up for your rights]. Some Mexican parents took this advice to heart and confronted educators with serious concerns during Club meetings. One mother was upset because her fourth-grade daughter had been reprimanded for speaking Spanish in class while she was helping a fellow student who had just arrived from Mexico. District administrators agreed that this was completely inappropriate. They promised to add this topic to future professional development in the district, together with cultural sensitivity training for teachers.

During the eighteen months we worked with the club, two significant changes occurred. The first was a switch, after a few months, to a discourse of "rights." The parents initially asked for favors and deferred to educators' expertise. Over time, however, encouraged by Spanish-speaking district staff at the meetings, they began to foreground their "rights" as parents. In one spring meeting, for example, the parents engaged the issue of undocumented status. The lone mother from Puerto Rico urged all parents to speak up. She had urged other parents to complain about things that happened at school, but they responded that she can do that, while they could not, because *no tengo papeles* [I do not have papers]. She emphasized that "in the school, it does not matter. The school is not the migration authorities. With documents or without, you have rights as a parent." Later, someone gave an example of a secretary in a neighboring school district who asked for a student's documentation and then refused to sign her up for school because she did not have a social security number. The ESL director explained that this was illegal: children have the right to attend school, and schools cannot ask about migration status. Parents were surprised, saying they had not known this and that the Club de Padres was important to help them learn such things. Juana emphasized that they as parents had the same rights in school as any other parent. This turned into a long conversation about the district's responsibility to translate important information into Spanish. For many of the parents, this was an empowering moment—learning that they and their children had equal rights to be served by the schools regardless of their status.

Similar conversations about rights happened at subsequent club meetings. On another occasion, one of the White, bilingual ESL teachers brought up the topic of parents' rights. She said that it was parents' right to have a conference with their child's teacher. A parent asked if it should be an obligation of the parent, instead of a right. This generated a discussion of rights and responsibilities of both parents and teachers. A parent summarized a popular view that it was the responsibility of the teacher to keep the parent informed, but it was the obligation of the parent to be involved. In the middle of her summary, a paraprofessional interrupted her, and the parent responded by referring to the paraprofessional as "La Hermana Pérez" [sister Pérez]. The use of "sister" here indexed an empowering political solidarity. Where previously they had felt like outsiders without rights—depending on the goodwill of educators and longstanding residents who would help when they chose to—some parents in the Club began to feel like members of the community who could demand their rights.

This conviction that Mexican parents had rights in school went along with a transition we have seen elsewhere, in the second decade of the Mexican community, in which some migrants began to feel empowered. At St. Joseph's, for example, Mexican parishioners took charge of some church events once Father Kelly provided spaces for their voices to be heard. In town politics, Edwin and fellow Mexican business owners created the Latino Business Council, and Edwin felt empowered to run for City Council. Some students also felt empowered to participate in demonstrations against racism and injustice at the high school in the early days of the Black Lives Matter movement. The Club de Padres was part of a change in the migrant community experienced by some Mexicans, a change toward positioning themselves as people whose voices and agency could in some spaces have an impact.

The second transition in the club happened at the end of 2009. A group of parents approached us at the beginning of a meeting, led by José Luis López, an articulate and forceful parent who had attended all the meetings. They expressed their gratitude that we had started the Club. They then explained that they would like to run the Club themselves. They had already elected officers, with José Luis as the president, and they wanted to organize the meetings from that point on. Because the goal of the Club had always been to empower Mexican parents in their relations with the school district, we were pleased with this intervention and happy to let them take control. Starting on that day, they set the dates and ran the meetings. We continued to provide food and attend meetings for another few months, but the Mexican parents ran the organization.

One individual whose pathway was particularly influenced by participation in the Club was José Luis, the president of the group. He had been a leader in Mexico, serving in the army, but in the United States he had not felt empowered to step forward. When speaking Spanish, he was forceful and articulate, and he inspired other parents with his claims and exhortations during Club discussions. He and his wife subsequently became fixtures at Mexican community events, especially ones that involved political mobilization around a cause. We would see them in the audience or helping to organize various gatherings that built a sense of community and empowerment among Mexicans. We saw them participating actively in their children's schools—in fact, on most of the occasions where we visited their children's school either José or his wife was there speaking to educators or volunteering in class. The opportunity to join and then lead the Club de Padres helped José feel as if he could participate actively and advocate for change. He and his wife subsequently became more involved in the community and the schools.

After José Luis and other parents began to run the meetings at the end of 2009, some things stayed the same. Parents continued to discuss their aspirations and concerns, and school district personnel continued to listen and respond. Our research team partnered with the parents on one successful project: the production of a film for teacher professional development. We had noticed that many teachers in the district circulated a negative stereotype about Mexican parents—that they only wanted their children to learn English and get jobs. This was clearly untrue. One only had to speak with Mexican parents for a few minutes to hear about their high hopes for the children's educational and vocational success. But the vast majority of teachers could not speak with Mexican parents because of the language barrier. The research team and Club leadership decided to make a short film in which parents could articulate their hopes and concerns about their children's education, in their own words (Gallo & Wortham, 2012).

We introduced this idea at a club meeting, explaining that we would like to show such a film to teachers so that they could hear directly from parents. We showed a short film made by a Hispanic advocacy organization in another town, as a sample so that parents could understand the genre, and we asked for volunteers. There was silence for a while. Then one parent named Laura broke the ice, joking that she'd do it but that she would have to visit the beauty salon beforehand. Eventually, twelve mothers or couples agreed to participate in the film. Bilingual doctoral students conducted the interviews, inviting parents to share their experiences and perspectives on local schools. Many parents were excited about the opportunity to describe their experiences for local educators, although some were nervous about being on camera. All of the interviews were conducted in Spanish in settings chosen by the parents. After explaining the purpose of the film and gathering some basic background information, researchers invited parents to describe good and bad experiences with their children's schools. They were also invited to share advice for newly arrived parents about local schools, advice for teachers about working with Mexican families, and ideas about how to improve the relationships between local schools and Spanish-speaking families. Stanton Wortham provided the funding required to produce the film, and graduate students volunteered their labor. Over the next several years, we showed this film to central district personnel, at school faculty meetings and district professional development sessions, as well as to educators in other districts.

In summer 2010, the funding we had been using to provide food ended and the meetings became less frequent. We hoped that the group would continue under its new parent leadership, but unfortunately it did not. The abrupt demise of the group resulted from a contingent misunderstanding. In the next academic year, the new principal of one school heard about the group and decided that she would like to host a parents meeting early in the fall. She publicized it to parents from her school, but a core group of participants from the prior year also heard about it and planned to attend. They thought that this was the same Club de Padres, starting up in the new academic year. When José Luis entered the school—together with his wife, carrying food she intended to share with everyone—the principal told them that they were not welcome because it was a closed meeting only for parents with children in her school. He was shocked and upset, and this event fragmented the group. Parents with children at that one school continued to attend the school-run meetings, but the majority of participants lost touch and did not continue.

This illustrates the impact of contingent events. The principal intended to create a parents group for her school, and she did not realize that the Club de Padres had been a group for all District parents. By turning away José Luis and other longstanding members of the group from that meeting, however, she effectively ended the Club. Despite this unfortunate outcome, the Club had an impact on some Mexican parents. The dominant story at Club meetings, after the first few months, positioned Mexican parents as having the right to demand services for their children in school. Parents who participated in this space created opportunities for leadership and had access to educators who listened to their concerns. Many parents also began to think of themselves differently. Through the Club, these parents' efforts contributed to some changes in the school district—with a few educators attending Club meetings and others hearing Mexican parents' perspectives on the film, and with many educators responding to Mexican parents and children more effectively than they had in the past.

Over the eighteen months of the Club's existence, we witnessed a transition to more effective interventions by Mexican parents and more alignment between parents and White, Black, and Hispanic educators. Somewhat similar, positive changes happened in the second decade with the development of the Latino Business Association and the Irish-Mexican community at St. Joseph's. Mexicans who participated in these organizations often had opportunities to take leadership and feel more in control. In some cases, like with José Luis, this had a significant impact on their pathways. Next, we describe two community organizations that hoped to build solidarity between Black and Mexican residents and work toward a different kind of collective empowerment.

Marshall Men for Progress and Y-Achievers

MMP was founded by five Black alumni of the Marshall schools in 2011. Their literature described the group:

> MMP is a group of men who strive to serve the greater Marshall area. In serving as positive male role models and citizens, MMP strives to promote a thriving and successful community ... MMP is made up of a diverse group of Marshall High School Alumni that have strong ties to the Greater Marshall community. Each individual brings a particular skill set, aspirations and desire to build a better future for the community and its residents ... Members were born and/or were raised in Marshall, attended Marshall Schools and now reside within the greater Marshall area where they have committed themselves to the greater cause of the community ... Marshall Men for Progress strives to promote and support a healthy, vibrant, and flourishing community. We will accomplish this by supporting and promoting community-based programs that encourage community involvement, economic development, youth opportunities, cultural awareness, and community health and welfare.

The organization ran scholarship fundraisers, a football clinic, an annual turkey drive, after-school clinics, and an awards banquet. These programs provided youth with educational opportunities, supported families in need, and celebrated successes by members of the community.

Harrison, the founder, was motivated by the contrast between the wealth of the surrounding suburbs and the lack of resources in Marshall.

> There have been things removed from our community since [we were growing up]. Technically there is only one community center, which is the Police Athletic League, where before there was the Washington Community Center, the Y, the Salvation

Army ... Everything is down. And it's hard for me to believe that [this is happening] in the richest county in the state.

When these relatively young men were growing up in the 1980s and 1990s, Marshall had more resources for youth, including several community centers that had closed. Marshall in that earlier era was not as wealthy as surrounding towns, but it provided various opportunities. The members of MMP had all gone to college, and most had successful careers that allowed them to move "up and out" of Marshall. Many of them in fact lived in surrounding towns and not in Marshall itself, but collectively they nonetheless wanted to move "up and in," contributing to their old community in a time of need.

Since their childhoods, Marshall had become more impoverished. MMP literature attributed this to spending cuts: "With drastic cuts in funding by municipal, state, and federal authorities for education and social programs, the need for a service organization like the MMP is greater than ever before." Harrison decried the decline of Marshall. He and his friends decided to provide some of the support that they experienced growing up in Marshall—creating spaces where youth could find sympathetic mentors with high expectations, where youth accomplishments were recognized, and where young people could receive services ranging from free meals to homework help.

YMCA Achievers was a national program run by the YMCA that aimed to help youth succeed academically. Literature from the regional YMCA described the program:

> The YMCA Achievers program of the YMCA of the USA is an academic achievement/career development initiative purposed to help teens set and pursue high educational and career goals, resulting in graduation and acceptance to an institution of higher learning. At the [Marshall area] YMCA, Y-Achievers expands on this goal by offering developmentally based, extracurricular mentorship and workshop activities, designed to give 5th–12th grade youth the tools they need to succeed in college and beyond. Research shows that teens are more motivated to succeed academically when supported and guided by adults. The Y-Achievers program addresses these issues by pairing students with successful mentors and providing academic and career-related advice and support.

YMCA branches in different regions create their own chapters of YMCA Achievers, receiving guidance from the national organization. John created a chapter at the YMCA near Marshall in 2005. John's mother was Black and his father was from Spain. He identified himself as mixed race, but he socialized largely with Black residents. When John started the YMCA chapter, he initially called it "Black Achievers," specifically aiming to serve Black youth. About five years after founding the chapter, however, he changed the name of the organization to Y-Achievers and he began to invite Mexican youth as well.

Like Harrison, John was motivated by the visible discrepancy between the wealth of surrounding towns and the poverty he saw in Marshall. Like Harrison, he claimed that the county was the richest in the state. It was in fact not at the top, but he was correct to place it among the wealthiest.

> Per capita it's wealthier than Beverly Hills. But Marshall is the poorest community in the county, and it had the highest truancy rate. So I started a college prep program, education program and started seeing why there were some problems with truancy. Some students want to go to college, why weren't they following up? … When there's a program that will help us financially get into college, or teach us how to understand some financial things to get into college, it gets people's attention … You start bringing more people in and like, more things spawned from there. We had like financial summits, stuff like that.

John witnessed Black youth in Marshall, whom he identified with, dropping out of school. He had been successful in college and career, and he wanted to provide other young people with an opportunity to achieve a similar future through his chapter of Y-Achievers.

Both MMP and Y-Achievers were started by Black men hoping to support Black male youth. The organizations served dozens of youth at any given time and were known by some in the Black community but were unfamiliar to most other residents. These organizations told a story about Marshall's history similar to the ones described in Chapters 4 and 5, in which the town had declined from its glory days and needed revitalization. The Black community in Marshall had been robust, according to these stories, providing a good place for them to grow up when they were younger. But it had declined—allegedly due to lack of resources and the unequal distribution of income—and this disadvantaged contemporary Black youth. As Black residents, they did not see substantial signs of revitalization yet. White residents credited Mexicans with revitalization, but these Black men did not see revitalization that benefited poor Black residents. They created MMP and Y-Achievers to create a more nurturing environment for Black male youth.

The founders of these organizations knew about the Mexican migrant community. They remembered the era of *solteros*, and their initial understandings of Mexicans were mostly drawn from that era. Like many Black residents, the founders were sympathetic to the hardships and discrimination faced by Mexicans, but they did not identify or align themselves with the migrants. As the Mexican community grew and became more settled in the second decade, however, the men running these organizations noticed an increase in Mexican youth who faced some of the same challenges as the Black youth they were serving. They did not see Mexicans as revitalizers to be celebrated. Instead of focusing on the success of Mexican businesses along Main Street, they focused on Mexican youth who were struggling in school. Their narrative of town history emphasized the disadvantages faced by Mexicans instead of the "revitalization." They expanded their organizations to serve Mexican youth together with Black youth, because they came to see Mexicans facing disadvantages similar to those encountered by Black youth.

In one conversation, Harrison discussed challenges faced by Black people in America. He explained why he could understand that Mexicans might feel shortchanged because of the lack of bilingual education in Marshall schools. This frustration was compounded by the ironic fact that private schools and wealthier surrounding school districts offered more Spanish than the Marshall schools, even though Marshall had many more Spanish-speaking residents.

> And I can't blame them [for being upset] ... For example at [a local private school serving wealthy children], in a 3 year old class you learn 2 languages, day one. We have more Latinos in our district than they do in their little school, and they're learning 2 languages. So they claim there's an issue between Latinos and African Americans. Now, there's been stuff, and I was telling someone about this recently, maybe when there was some robberies, and saying stuff in the neighborhoods where [Mexican] guys would come off the truck with wads of money. But I think that the guys who robbed them would rob anyone with a wad of money. So I don't really want to say it was because they were Mexican men.

Here Harrison alluded to the "payday muggings" described in Chapter 5. Like other Black residents, Harrison argued that these criminals did not have any particular negative feelings toward Mexicans. Black criminals were not being racist in robbing Mexicans, but just expedient, and they would have robbed anyone with money. He went on to say that the alleged divide between Black and Mexican residents was in fact much less important than the similar histories of struggle shared by the two groups.

> To me, if you integrated language in the school, because language is sometimes a bigger barrier than- you know, a lot of things. That's even what happened in slavery. This is the history, man, if you think about it. They conquered us and made us speak their language because they took- they got rid of your language because if you don't, if you know something they don't know, you can conquer them. So if you want to quote, unquote, combat any issues that we have in the district, teach both languages all the way through.

Here Harrison advocated a transition in relations between Blacks and Mexicans. In the era of *solteros*, Blacks and Mexicans may have interacted in negative ways, as in payday muggings. But as the Mexican community developed and many Mexican youth were entering high school and struggling academically, Harrison imagined a different possibility for Black-Mexican relations. He presented Marshall, after the influx of Mexicans, as a "strong, diverse population." He empathized with Mexicans' struggles. Black youth in Marshall had to deal with inadequate funding and support, despite the wealth of the surrounding area. Similarly, Mexicans had to deal with inadequate bilingual support because of limited resources in Marshall schools. When Blacks were enslaved and brought from Africa, they were denied access to their own languages. Similarly, he claimed, Mexicans in Marshall were being denied education in Spanish. Like Father Kelly, Doreena, Marco, and James Smith, Harrison saw parallels between his ancestors and current Mexican migrants—but, in his case, the similarities did not involve the classic, positive migration story. Instead, he saw similar histories of exploitation and struggle.

Around 2012, both MMP and Y-Achievers expanded their missions to serve Mexican youth. This was the time when John changed the name of his organization. "It originally was an African American program. It was the 'Black Achievers,' but we opened it up to all groups. Marshall at the time it was a big, huge Hispanic population so we said, we wanted to have inclusion, so let's drop the Black and let's have the Y-Achievers." MMP also expanded its mission to serve a broader community. Their materials were changed to say:

> MMP community-based initiatives and activities aim to support the community as a whole, while promoting unity, success, growth, revitalization and a great quality of life within our municipality. MMP programs, events and collaborations are diverse and reach a multitude of residents across various demographics. MMP initiatives focus on the servicing of youth and adults in the region.

Both organizations aimed to serve youth "across various demographics," which in practice meant Black and Mexican young men. This transition happened as the first group of Mexican children born in Marshall were approaching adolescence.

Members of MMP advocated for more Spanish-speaking staff in the schools. At one meeting among the founders, they described their rationale.

> Darrell: You talking about in the '60s and '70s, most of Marshall was Caucasian, and then you know, '80s, '90s, that's when more African Americans came and the Caucasians started moving out ... and there was more of us than anything. And now the Latinos came and the African Americans are moving out [agreement from others] and it's more of them, so-

Jamar:	I was at some sort of school yesterday, the all kindergarten school, and no lie, maybe out of a class of twenty or twenty-five, more than half is Latino and Mexican.
Darrell:	Yeah, most definitely.
Interviewer:	In Marshall?
Jamar:	In Marshall, and I'm just sitting there like- the teacher's gotta speak both languages.
Darrell:	Most definitely.
Harrison:	And they don't.
Darrell:	They have to!
Harrison:	But they don't. At the kindergarten center there's more, I believe, because it would be almost crazy not to, but throughout the district, which- this has been going on for the last ten years, even more, because ten years ago was '05, so it's definitely been since '05. They haven't adjusted the staff demographics.

As their conversation continued, these men argued that the lack of Spanish-speaking teachers was part of a larger pattern that affected Blacks as well as Mexicans—the continued predominance of White employees in organizations that served children from non-White communities.

Jamar:	I think our community and our county, where even the child services, many of the cases that come across their desk need bilingual services, but there are not enough workers. I don't think the counties and the towns have come to the realization that the demographics have changed.
Darrell:	Or just don't care.
Jamar:	But at the same time they don't come to the realization that, you know, our jobs and our livelihood can come into jeopardy, you know, because, we may not be equipped to serve our population.
Interviewer:	Right.
Jamar:	So there is a, there is like a pushback of people still trying to- the county departments, if you look at a county department that serves, you know 70 percent 80 percent of their clients are minorities and then their workforce is-
Interviewer:	White.
Jamar:	Yeah, White.

In the early years of the Mexican community, Black Marshall residents did not typically feel solidarity with the migrants. Sometimes Black residents were unhappy about being displaced from residential and commercial spaces. Sometimes they felt that Mexicans were competing with them for jobs and starting businesses that excluded Black residents. Many Blacks were sympathetic to the challenges Mexicans faced and admired their hard work. But calls for solidarity like those made by Harrison, John, and their friends became much more common in the second decade of the migrant community—especially among younger Black residents. As the Mexican community changed, these formerly Black organizations changed in response, including Mexicans in their stories about residents who were being unjustly treated by society.

This story about Mexicans and their possible futures was fundamentally different from the revitalization narrative. Instead of Mexicans being hardworking, uncomplaining model minorities who would move "up and out" because of their own efforts, MMP and Y-Achievers characterized Mexican youth as struggling victims of discrimination who should align with Blacks to demand better treatment. This story also differed from the assimilation narrative offered at AYUDA. Instead of being migrants on their way to joining Irish, Italian, and other previous migrant groups in becoming part of the American mainstream, MMP and Y-Achievers characterized Mexican youth as fundamentally different than Irish, Italian, and other White groups. Instead of pursuing the "American Dream" through hard work and obedience, these organizations argued that Mexican youth should critique racial injustice and demand more resources. Mexican youth who participated in these organizations thus tended to imagine themselves and their pathways through American society differently than those who spent time at AYUDA and ATEP. Nancy and her friends were inspired through a similar story catalyzed by the Black Lives Matter movement—a contingent, historical set of events that happened to occur when they were in high school. Some adolescent Mexican males were influenced at MMP and Y-Achievers by a story that also positioned them alongside Blacks demanding social justice.

Once the founders of MMP and Y-Achievers expanded their mission to include Mexican youth, they had to confront tensions between Black and Mexican residents. John described these tensions as serious.

John: A gentleman ... brought it to my attention. He said in Marshall there's a Black-Brown problem. And because my father is of Hispanic descent [from Spain] and my mother is African American he was like, might be something good for you to be able to address both sides of the issue. So I thought it was a challenge, I took it, and did a lot of talking. It was very bad when I first got here, very, very bad.

Interviewer: Can you describe to me what you mean by that?

John:	Um, the disrespect was to the utmost. When I would go into the stores, there's a section of Main Street that's predominantly Mexican. So when I go into the stores, it was very hostile, disrespectful.
Interviewer:	Towards you?
John:	Towards me. Because they saw me as a Black man, and it was, it was prevalent. And it was just a lot of different—I think it was ignorance on both sides.

John claimed that the situation had improved during the second decade of the Mexican community. He focused his work on building connections between Black and Mexican youth, pointing out similarities between their situations.

John:	I focused on commonalities … Once I got involved in [Marshall] the people saw that I wasn't going anywhere, and I wasn't taking any messes … so let's see what he got to say … There's more commonalities—to be honest, I'm gonna take the gloves off, like listen, both you communities are being oppressed.
Interviewer:	right
John:	So let's stop talking BS and fighting against one another and start working together and try to bring both of us up, instead of fighting each other while someone else is just looking at us and laughing.
Interviewer:	And was that message well received?
John:	Yes, it was well received … There was a lot of animosity. An African American community that was always here and then you had an influx of the Hispanic population. And they were like, oh we fought for a lot of things, and you guys just came in here and took what we fought for. And I've heard—I sat in on these conferences and [Mexicans] were just like, you know you're lazy. You guys don't do anything. And we're like, whoa, we fought a battle. We're tired right now, there's a lot of casualties and you came in and just picked up all the pieces so …

As described in the last chapter, many Blacks resented Mexicans for not appreciating the struggles that African Americans have gone through. As a Black man, John understood this resentment. But he did not feel resentment himself. Instead, he worked to convince Mexicans that they shared a common struggle with Blacks. He acknowledged Mexicans' unhappiness about the mistreatment they received from some Blacks, and he acknowledged Black resentment at being pushed aside by Mexicans who did not appreciate their history of struggle. By listening to both sides, John convinced some Black and Mexican youth to focus on their common challenges and demand change in the larger society.

MMP and Y-Achievers thus provided an alternative story about Mexican migrants, one that placed them in solidarity with Blacks working against oppression. This story, like the stories about assimilation, revitalization, and upward mobility, accurately described some Mexican experiences but misrepresented others. All Mexicans experienced racism, and the vast majority had limited access to resources and experienced economic hardship. But most worked hard and improved their economic conditions, as many Irish, Italian, and Black migrants had before them. Many Mexicans aspired to move "up and out" of Marshall, as described in classic positive stories about migration, and some perceived themselves as "White." Through their entrepreneurial efforts, Mexican businesses and customers also brought some economic and social revitalization to downtown—although this may have disrupted the former sense of community among some Black residents. Stories that focused either on oppression or on upward mobility oversimplified migrants' experiences. But these oversimplified stories nonetheless influenced individuals' pathways. Mexicans who spent time at AYUDA were more likely to imagine themselves assimilating, while youth participating with MMP were more likely to imagine themselves engaged in a struggle for justice. The stories told by the organization that an individual happened to frequent often became important resources that helped constitute the pathway traveled by that particular Mexican migrant.

Arte, Tecnología, y Educación del Pueblo

As the Mexican community developed across its first two decades, many migrants stopped positioning themselves as transient guests and began asserting their rights as longstanding residents. Participants in Club de Padres moved toward having more influence in their children's schools, and some Mexican youth involved with MMP and Y-Achievers positioned themselves as activists fighting for justice. A different type of story was told at Arte, Tecnología, y Educación del Pueblo (ATEP), an organization that celebrated Mexican culture. Noé, the founder, came to the United States from Mexico in the 1990s. He had been a journalist, an artist, and an instructor at a prestigious university there. His wife was American and they returned to the United States so that she could enroll in graduate school. Noé did further graduate study himself, and he began teaching at a local college. In the early 2000s, he started to spend time in Marshall as a journalist. He received a contract from a network in Mexico to produce stories about the experiences of Mexican migrants in the United States, and he interviewed many fellow Mexicans in Marshall.

He admired the energy and hard work exhibited by many Mexicans, but he was concerned about the challenges they faced—particularly about the difficulties Mexican youth were having in school. He envisioned a migrant community in which people supported each other, preserved important aspects of their Mexican traditions, and launched young people on pathways where they could succeed in American society but still consider themselves Mexican. In 2005 he, his wife, and some friends planned a nonprofit organization. As Noé envisioned it:

> I was amazed when I saw the whole potential of the immigrant community ... That's what triggered my idea and made me say, OK, I see everybody opening businesses. I see everybody making new things in the Mexican community. But what about education? What about art? How can we help the challenges that the school district has? How can we help the kids to succeed in school? How can we take the kids to college? What can we do so that the new generation can do better than their parents?

Three years later, the organization was incorporated, with a board of directors and Noé as director. For the first several years, there was insufficient money to hire staff, and Noé ran the organization as a volunteer in a small space provided by another organization. He obtained several modest grants to offer services to the community. The first major program was created in conjunction with a local community college, providing college counseling to Mexican schoolchildren. The second program, launched in 2011, was a technology room that had eight sophisticated computers where Mexican middle school students came after school for homework help and to take classes in web design.

Like AYUDA, ATEP was designed to serve the needs of Spanish-speaking residents in Marshall. Unlike AYUDA, but like Club de Padres, it was created in the second decade specifically to serve the Mexican community. Club de Padres, however, was started by White allies, while ATEP was started by a Mexican. Noé explicitly intended to celebrate Mexican culture while helping Mexican youth succeed in American schools. He created activities that included Mexican art and literature, and he recruited Latin American artists to participate in ATEP activities and teach young people about their traditions. He worked hard to overcome what Valenzuela (1999) calls "subtractive schooling" by connecting Mexican children to their own cultural traditions (cf. also Moll, 1992; Yosso, 2002). A broadly educated person himself, Noé designed multidisciplinary activities that included aspects of Mexican culture while preparing young people to master job skills or build a pathway to college. For example, he offered classes in filmmaking in which he encouraged Mexican youth to create videos that explored their cultural traditions. He also recruited a local artist to teach Mexican residents mural painting in the tradition of Diego Rivera. Noé envisioned ATEP as a partner with both Mexican migrants and the broader community, supporting healthy school performance, job training, and cultural celebration. ATEP was initially known by a relatively small group of Mexican and White activists, but toward the end of the second decade it became visible to a large segment of the Mexican migrant community and to some longstanding residents as well.

ATEP explicitly challenged the alleged choice between assimilating to American culture and planning a return to Mexico. As the organization's literature put it:

> Whereas ATEP realizes the importance of acclimating to North American culture, and making successful transition to a new country, we also want to sustain the cultural roots of our Latin American countries ... In addition to pursuing economic stability, our Hispanic families also seek to develop the artistic talents of our youth. Today Hispanics represent the youngest population group in the US, and our children have rich talents in music, drama, visual arts, crafts and dance, among other areas. ATEP considers it a priority to provide programs which demonstrate the artistic talents of the new generation. In this way, the growth of our Hispanic community can be accompanied by the artistic expression of our values and ideas.

Noé envisioned a community where well-educated youth were prepared to attend American universities and have successful careers, but where they also participated in community life that included regular engagement with Latin American art and cultural traditions. The organization hosted shows in which Mexican youth displayed their Mexican-inspired artwork both to migrants and to interested longstanding residents.

As ATEP grew, Noé created activities for adults as well as schoolchildren. Beginning in 2014, they hosted a book group, for example—a "círculo de lectura"—in which community members gathered to discuss Spanish-language literature. Briana Nichols participated in this group. Octavio Martínez, Edwin's brother, told her why he joined the group.

> Just a month before the book club I was sitting bored at home, and I was thinking why isn't there something, an activity, like to socialize that isn't the same thing that Hispanics always do, like watch soccer ... There aren't other things that

bring lots of people together ... We can talk on the phone about a movie and say if we liked it or didn't like it, and things like this, but ... it's very superficial—like I'm going to give you my summary of the movie and my thoughts and something like that. And so with this feeling that I was missing something, and then two weeks later I see an announcement for this book club, and so I said, I need to do this.

Many migrants were lonely. They worked hard at their jobs and took care of their families. They often did not feel welcome in public activities. Outside of church and work, they found limited spaces to interact with others. The book club and other events at ATEP provided a welcome alternative, where Mexican migrants could speak Spanish and connect with others in a culturally familiar setting.

Octavio described the typical activities in the book club, and he explained how the event helped build community and overcome loneliness.

Octavio:	Every week we are exploring a Latin American author. This book has the most complete anthology of Latin American authors—so we have already read authors from Chile, Argentina, Nicaragua, and Mexico, and today we are going to read José Revueltas, who is writing about a theme that is both universal and very local ... It is important that it's in Spanish, though it's not important that the authors are Hispanic. But it's definitely important—Spanish is my first language, so I definitely do understand more in Spanish, and it also helps my writing and my reading.
Interviewer:	I've noticed that the topic of immigration comes up a lot in book club. Do you think that this is a space that is particularly good for talking about that topic? Do you think there is a value to having this as a space where most of the people who are book club members are immigrants?
Octavio:	Absolutely. I mean it's probably more to share stories. I don't know how much, I think we are mostly sharing stories.
Interviewer:	What's the value in sharing stories? What do you think it gives?
Octavio:	A common ground—you know, not to feel like a loner. It's just sort of like, something in common.

Through the book club and similar activities, ATEP provided opportunities for migrants to connect with others and reconnect with their cultural traditions. The book club even created transnational community. Noé used social media to include friends from Mexico in their discussions, and these Mexicans brought a perspective that deepened migrants' ties to their country of origin.

By participating in activities like this at ATEP, migrants imagined themselves on a pathway that was both Mexican and American. ATEP told a different story about migrant futures than the other organizations. Like AYUDA, Noé believed that accommodation to American culture was important. But he argued that full assimilation was undesirable. He advocated what Gibson (1988) calls "accommodation without assimilation." Mexican children needed to learn English and succeed in the American educational system, but this was only part of a flourishing Mexican American life. Like MMP and Y-Achievers, Noé believed that fighting for migrant rights was important. But ATEP's activities did not center on demanding rights and confronting those in power. Instead of emphasizing either assimilation or struggle, ATEP worked to celebrate Mexican art and culture. Noé's goal was for Mexican and Mexican American children to learn about and value their cultural traditions, for them to be proud of and benefit from their history. He imagined these children on a pathway toward becoming global citizens who had competence in more than one cultural context, toward having the ability to prosper in the United States along with the ability to participate in and value Mexican traditions.

Figure 6.1 Mexican folkloric dance exhibition.

ATEP did not always live up to its ideals, of course. In 2013, for example, one of Nancy's friends was struggling. She had a much older boyfriend who was pressuring her for sex, and she had begun cutting herself. She went to ATEP, hoping for a safe space to find support. At first she enjoyed participation in art activities and she began to build connections with members of the group. But she was emotionally raw and quick to anger. She acted out several times, and she was given second chances. But then one day she gave Noé the finger, and he banned her from the organization's activities. She was thrown back on less robust supports and continued to struggle. From Noé's point of view, there were substantial challenges in running his programs and they could not tolerate chronically disruptive students. He wanted to project a positive image of Mexicans to the community, and he expected participants would follow his vision. As a result, some Mexican youth did not find the organization a welcoming space. Nonetheless, the organization prospered.

By 2015, ATEP had five paid and volunteer staff members and ran a dozen activities—including computer classes in the technology room, after-school homework help, art projects like mural painting, visits to museum shows of Latin American artists, mentoring for youth, Red Cross training, book clubs, summer camps, art shows, and soccer. They had just moved to a new building, one that used to house a local arts organization in a prominent downtown location. This location was symbolically important. The downtown area had declined, and this formerly active arts space had been vacant. It was notable that a Mexican community organization was able to bring its flourishing programs there, helping to revitalize downtown with Mexican programming that was both visible by and open to the larger community. As we write this book, ATEP is completing a move to an even larger space, in order to accommodate its expanding programming.

While ATEP was developing, the organization recognized that the Mexican community was also changing. They did not intend to preserve an allegedly static Mexican culture, nor did they oppose themselves to an allegedly static American culture. They saw that both cultures were evolving, in part through contact with each other. Noé hoped to contribute to a new, emergent hybrid culture in Marshall. As part of this process, participants at ATEP began to envision the kind of community they would like. They wanted opportunities to practice Mexican artistic traditions as well as opportunities to develop skills that would help them succeed in the United States. Many participants also began to feel as if they had the power to work toward these goals. Only a small fraction of the Mexican community participated, and in 2016 ATEP was still a small nonprofit organization vulnerable to unforeseen changes in external funding, but Noé and his colleagues had begun to provide an alternative story about what it meant to be Mexican in Marshall. This story involved some accommodation to America and some demands for recognition, but it was not a simple combination of assimilation and protest. ATEP tried to intervene, at a small scale in its early years, as host and migrant traditions in Marshall influenced each other and created something new.

At an ATEP book club discussion that took place in 2014, one member mentioned that it is hard to change a community, that inertia is strong, and that change takes significant work. "The changes in history are made by many people, including those who have dedicated their lives to it." Another remarked that "we have to plant the seed and work for change." José Luis, the former president of the Club de Padres, argued that change happens when people decide to change. He described how, in the house he grew up in, his father hit his mother, and he decided that he did not want the same thing for his children. So, he said, when someone wants to break the cycle, they can. "A ninety-degree change is very difficult. I would love to do a full turn, but it is very hard, very hard. But you can do it if you choose to." Another member agreed, claiming that we can decide for ourselves what is good and what is bad.

By the end of their second decade in Marshall, Mexicans participating in this ATEP book group imagined that they had the power to change the town for the better. They were no longer just trying to earn money for a return to Mexico, as most *solteros* did a decade earlier. They were not trying simply to assimilate to American culture, keeping their heads down and working hard in others' businesses. They were telling a story that positioned themselves as empowered to change their community by creating hybridized Mexican and American beliefs and practices. These book club participants felt as if they had opportunities to create a more ideal community in Marshall. This would not be identical to the Mexican communities they grew up in, but it would include important elements of those cultural traditions. ATEP provided a space in which a small but substantial group of migrants could imagine this sort of alternative future. As one of them wrote during an activity: "It's the objective of ATEP to be this space, free for personal discovery as much for children as adults. I hope that this is what it will be, without being perfect, when here we can freely express and define our social beings—not based on the expectations that they have for us but through a genuine search for self."

The organization continued to focus on young people, helping Mexican youth navigate the challenges and opportunities they found in Marshall. As Juana Faccone's nephew Octavio put it, the organization's goal was to

> help the community. Noé has a passion for kids, and that's good, that's what I respected a lot. Because, it might sound like a cliché, but if we can get the kids to triumph it's good. Especially being a minority, you know, I came here as a kid, and I needed a lot of help myself. I needed a lot of help with homework, and I couldn't go to anyone. My parents didn't speak English. None of my teachers spoke

Spanish. I couldn't go to my friends ... My family was one of the first Mexican families in Marshall, so I had to swim. It was really like sink or swim for me.

Octavio and Juana's family and the Mexicans who followed them to Marshall faced many challenges—ranging from the language barrier, to poverty, to racialized hostility from some longstanding residents, to predatory landlords and bosses, to loneliness, to the difficulty of creating a sense of self in a new place. At ATEP, some Mexicans found space to work toward a new vision of who they and their community could be.

Community organizations and other institutions in Marshall told various stories about and facilitated divergent pathways for Mexican migrants. At St. Joseph's, Father Kelly created an environment in which Mexican migrants could take leadership and bring their own traditions into the regular life of the church, while changing the church and some of its practices in the process. At ATEP, Noé created an environment in which Mexican children and adults could also build pathways that combined Mexican and American traditions. For some Mexican migrants in Marshall, one or the other of these two spaces helped them create transnational selves and communities that embraced their home cultures while incorporating elements of mainstream American life. In contrast, AYUDA and the classic, positive migration stories told by many White and Mexican residents envisioned a different pathway for Mexican migrants, one in which they would follow Irish and Italian migrants and move "up and out" into the American mainstream. For some Mexican residents, the growing Mexican business district and expanding opportunities for their children in school opened up this sort of classic migrant pathway toward assimilation. MMP and Y-Achievers, and Club de Padres in some respects, offered a third alternative. They imagined Blacks and Mexicans joining to demand fair treatment for "Black and Brown" residents. These spaces facilitated pathways in which Mexicans would work for social change through critique and protest. They imagined Mexicans following some African Americans by moving "up and in" to create a more just, interethnic community in town.

Each of these three stories oversimplified the complex realities of Mexican lives. We have described how Mexican experiences and pathways in Marshall exceeded these stories, and other work on race and ethnicity in similar towns has described further complexity (Brown & Jones, 2015; Jones, 2012; Rodríguez, 2012; Smith, 2014). However appealing one might find stories about migrant assimilation and success, resistance and solidarity, or emerging hybrid communities, many individuals and migrant groups do not travel any of these three simple pathways. We have shown how divergent migrant pathways emerge as contingent, heterogeneous combinations of resources come together in particular cases, and we have shown how some pathways do not conform to these ideal types. Despite their oversimplifications, however, we have also shown how each of these three stories came together with other resources to facilitate both typical and unexpected pathways that migrants actually traveled.

7

Powerful, Limited Stories

We began this book with two widely circulating stories about migration in America, stories that are often used to justify political positions. Each of these stories juxtaposes and evaluates ethnic groups differently. According to one story, migrants and their families typically overcome initial struggles to achieve success—moving "up and out" of places like downtown Marshall while revitalizing their new contexts. In Marshall, versions of this story were commonly told by White, Mexican, and other Hispanic residents, and it often positioned Mexicans as model minorities who would ultimately move past African Americans to follow the imagined pathways of earlier Irish and Italian migrants. According to the other story, threatening, dysfunctional migrants take "our" resources and cause a decline in "our" communities. In Marshall some White residents told this story, sometimes imagining Mexicans as drunk or hypersexual while at other times casting them as hardworking but with limited intellectual capacity and leadership potential. Black residents also told

Figure 7.1 An aerial view of Marshall at sunset.

a version of this story, blaming White policymakers for "dumping" migrants in downtown Marshall and blaming Mexicans for disrupting a stable Black community.

In addition to these two familiar stories, we have described additional stories that also circulated in Marshall. According to one of these, Mexican migrants were building hybrid identities and pathways, changing the longstanding community and creating something new. At St. Joseph's and ATEP, these stories mostly envisioned new connections between White and Mexican communities. But some Black residents like James and David also imagined new hybrids that included Black, White, and Mexican residents living together in diverse, flourishing communities. According to a fourth story, told especially at MMP and Y-Achievers, Mexicans would join African Americans to struggle against the White racism that affects both communities. This story imagined solidarity between Mexican and Black residents and joint demands for justice.

We have distinguished between such stories—which are told by academics, policymakers, and residents in Marshall and many other places—and more empirically adequate descriptions of the pathways actually traveled by migrants in America. It is difficult to maintain this distinction between stories and empirically warranted accounts, for at least two reasons. First, each of these stories does capture some migrants' and longstanding residents' real experiences. None of them is false, even though each of them is incomplete. Each story also contains some defensible ethical judgments. We cannot condemn migrants who aspire to move "up and out," for example, or those who hope to assimilate. Nor can we blame Black residents for working to maintain a community that was in fact disrupted in part by Mexicans' arrival. Many stories told about migrants are inaccurate, and some are unethical. We are not arguing that all stories are equivalent. But many diverse stories that circulated in Marshall were nonetheless partly accurate. Second, these stories are powerful facts in the world. Judging them simply on scientific or ethical grounds—by citing evidence that they cannot explain or by condemning their moral judgments—misses the fact that they will continue to influence thought and action regardless of whether we disprove or condemn them. Despite their inaccuracies and questionable moral judgments, we need simultaneously to treat these stories both as theories of and facts in the world.

This chapter builds on our empirical descriptions to sketch a more complex and adequate approach to understanding migration in places like Marshall. Before adopting one or another of the stories as a favored explanation, we must empirically examine the heterogeneity of migrants' actual lives. Our analyses have shown how diverse resources from many scales became relevant to Mexicans' pathways in

Marshall, and we have argued that processes at four timescales were particularly important: the cycles followed by successive migrant groups over Marshall's 200-year history and the interethnic relations among these groups; the changes within the Mexican migrant community across its first two decades, including the changes within diverse institutional spaces in town; the ontogenetic development of individuals within these two interconnected contexts; and discrete, pivotal events. For both individuals and communities, we have described some pathways that conform to familiar migration stories—of struggle and success, or of decline and exclusion—and others that diverge from such oversimplified stories. In this chapter, we first review the pathways traveled by communities and individuals in Marshall, describing processes at each of these four scales, in order to summarize our central argument. Migrants follow both familiar and unfamiliar pathways, which solidify when a configuration of contingent resources from various scales—often including, but not limited to, migration stories and interethnic relations—coalesces.

Pathways across Four Timescales

Cycles of Migration across Centuries

Mexicans followed several other groups that had migrated to Marshall over the past two centuries. The history of migration to the town was crucial for two reasons. First, descendants of prior migrants continued to live or work in Marshall, and these descendants were gatekeepers and interlocutors as Mexicans lived their lives in town. Interethnic relations that Mexicans developed with the descendants of Irish, Italian, and African American migrants influenced both community and individual pathways. Second, experiences with and stories about prior groups shaped how longstanding residents and migrants imagined their own and Mexicans' likely pathways. Some residents and some institutions expected Mexicans to move "up and out" as described in simple, positive stories about prior migrants, but these expectations were complicated by the more complex position occupied by African Americans.

Many Irish, Italian, and African American migrants in Marshall had experienced central elements of the classic positive migration story over the past century or more. They had faced hardship because of poverty, linguistic and cultural differences, and the absence of networks. They had experienced exclusion as longstanding residents steered them away from certain neighborhoods, exploited their labor, limited their business opportunities, and circulated racial stereotypes. Most prior migrants worked hard and accumulated economic and cultural capital over time. They took control of some trades and businesses, moved into positions of political power, and over time the dominance of the prior group eroded. In every group, there was individual variation, but many migrants and their children moved "up and out"—often literally, leaving Marshall and settling in wealthier suburbs while sometimes retaining economic or personal ties to the town. As they remembered their own and their ancestors' experiences, most residents described how migrants had followed the classic narrative that moves from struggle to ultimate success. Despite the somewhat diverse realities of actual migrant pathways, this story was almost universally applied to understand and position Irish and Italian migrants and their descendants, and it was also applied by African Americans to describe the experiences of many Black migrants.

This recurring cycle of migrant groups' struggle and success—both the reality that many migrants had experienced over prior centuries and the ubiquitous story that shaped people's evaluations of migrants—was partly broken by African Americans, however. Black migrants began to come from the South to Marshall only slightly later than Italians, but they did not move "up and out" as fully or as quickly. This happened for several reasons. African Americans have always faced exceptional challenges in America, because slavery and Jim Crow robbed them of cross-generational capital and because they face more intense racism than other groups (Jaynes, 2004; Massey & Denton, 1998). In Marshall, two other realities played an important role. First, Blacks arrived in two waves, and many in the second group moved out from "truly disadvantaged" situations (Wilson, 1987) in urban areas in the 1970s and 1980s. These migrants sometimes did not have the same experiences, expectations, or assets as the group of African Americans that had migrated earlier. Second, Black residents began to succeed socioeconomically just as changes in the broader economy made it harder to achieve economic success. In the 1970s, manufacturing jobs decreased and Marshall's downtown withered. This happened at the point in their cycle of migration when Blacks could have begun to build political and economic power, and at the same time as civil rights laws finally gave them more opportunities. Some Black residents succeeded economically, but much of the African American community remained disadvantaged.

Furthermore, many Black residents who could have moved out of downtown Marshall chose to remain. As we have described it, they moved "up and in." For most African Americans, despite the economic downturn, Marshall in the 1980s and 1990s was a good place to live. They did not have as much capital as other groups had accumulated at the same stage in their migrant cycles, and they were often discouraged from moving to wealthier towns because of continued housing discrimination. But they had a sense of community, several Black churches, some Black-owned businesses, and a belief that their time in Marshall may have finally come. At the same time, however, as we have shown in detail, densely circulating stories told about Blacks systematically erased their successes. Non-Black residents never told stories about the many African Americans who had in fact followed pathways "up and out" just like other migrants, or "up and in" to comfortable situations in town. Non-Black residents did not recognize the sense of Black community in downtown Marshall, and they did not see moving "up and in" as a viable possibility. Non-Black residents also often told stories that characterized Blacks as lazy, violent, and predatory. This systematic erasure of Black success—in stories that cast them as an aberration from the typical cycle of migrants moving "up and out"—was another important resource that hindered Blacks from following pathways toward socioeconomic success. Because of contingent realities characterizing the particular historical moment and the unique situation of African Americans in general, and because of these powerful stories that erased Black success, the recurring cycles of migrant community "progress" from struggle to success partly broke down for Black residents.

Mexicans also entered a town in which Irish and Italian Americans still played a prominent role in important institutions. Mexicans' relationships with these earlier migrant groups in many ways mirrored interethnic relationships from earlier cycles. Initial hostility gave way in some places to acceptance and even welcome. The police and federal migration enforcement often treated Mexicans literally and figuratively as aliens, for example, and some employers and educators imagined that Mexicans were diligent but not capable of higher-level work. On the other hand, many Mexican business owners succeeded with their restaurants and shops, and they began to advocate successfully for their needs with town politicians. School officials began to solicit Mexican parents' input, and educators helped many in the growing cohort of Mexican students succeed in school. At St. Joseph's, the Irish American community welcomed the migrants and integrated some Mexican Catholic practices into their own worship. After twenty years of increased Mexican migration to Marshall, hostility and challenges remained. In many ways, however, Irish, Italian, and other White residents imagined and sometimes treated the migrants as if they were following in their own ancestors' footsteps.

Mexicans could not participate in this more typical cycle of interethnic relations with African Americans, however, because Black residents were in a different position than earlier migrant groups. In some ways, Blacks behaved toward Mexicans in the same way that earlier migrant groups had. They resented Mexican settlement in "their" neighborhoods and urged town government to enact regulations restricting the number of Mexicans who could move in, through housing ordinances, for example. They worked against Edwin's candidacy and tried to maintain control over political institutions. Thus, Mexicans sometimes had to struggle against Blacks in the same ways as earlier migrant groups had struggled against their predecessors. But, in other ways, Mexicans found in African Americans a prior migrant group that had not moved "up and out," with many Blacks still living in downtown neighborhoods and relatively fewer Blacks owning businesses. Coupled with stories about Blacks as unsuccessful, these realities gave Mexicans an opportunity to move ahead of many Black residents—and to be identified as revitalizers who responded to the decline allegedly created by African Americans—while following Irish and Italian American residents in moving "up and out." As of 2016, many Mexicans were following such a pathway. Other Mexicans, however, participated in organizations that created Black-Mexican solidarity and encouraged protest against unjust social conditions and White racism. Still others chose to join neither Whites nor Blacks, but instead worked to maintain Mexican culture. The classic, imagined migrant pathway from struggle to success was fragmented in Marshall, and thus Mexicans faced divergent opportunities and challenges.

The two-century cycle of migrant group arrival, struggle, and success in Marshall was both familiar and unfamiliar. If African Americans had never settled in Marshall, Mexicans might have followed Italians in much the same way as Italians had followed Irish migrants. If Marshall had never experienced substantial Catholic migration from Ireland and Italy, such that Mexicans entered a town that had only White Protestant and African American residents, the situation would also have been different. For contingent reasons, Mexicans encountered both somewhat more welcoming Irish and Italian residents as well as a Black population that had only partly moved "up and out." As a result, the pathways open to Mexican migrants in Marshall were more diverse than they might have been.

The Mexican Community Developing across Two Decades

In this historical context, the Mexican migrant community itself changed substantially over its first two decades. In some ways, the development of this community followed a familiar pathway. The transition from *solteros* to families brought an increase in Mexican children who spoke English fluently and who began school with White and Black peers in kindergarten. In the second decade, many Mexican parents worked hard and built businesses, striving to support their families and give their children opportunities for further education and future success. Juan, for example, was able to finish high school and pursue a career repairing appliances instead of doing the more physically demanding labor that his father and brothers did. Allie was able to focus on school and dream about college. Juana's siblings opened stores, restaurants, and other businesses. All seven siblings built social and economic capital, and all of them had children and grandchildren who attended college and expected their own children to have successful careers. Many Mexicans also experienced opportunity and empowerment in other spaces. At St. Joseph's, Father Kelly invited migrants to lead celebrations drawn from their Mexican traditions. In the Club de Padres, Mexican parents sometimes successfully lobbied school district administrators on behalf of their children. These experiences resembled the classic migrant story of struggle and ultimate success.

Mexican residents did not uniformly move along this pathway, however. Many longstanding residents continued to believe that Mexicans were hardworking but perhaps not capable of the same commercial or academic success as White residents. In 2016, it was too early to tell whether the Mexican community would continue to develop as described in the classic migrant narrative—with Mexicans eventually becoming recognized as competent businesspeople and successful students capable of going to college and beyond. Various stories were being told, and individual Mexicans were in fact following divergent pathways. Some of the stories about Mexicans as academically less promising had real effects. Nancy, for example, chose the high school vocational track and pursued a career in the restaurant business. She did this in part because she saw a more academic or professional pathway as inappropriate for people like her. Her imagined future was constrained by lingering stories about stereotypical Mexican academic and vocational outcomes and by practices of tracking in high schools that disproportionately affect lower-income students (Oakes, 1985).

In some ways, then, Mexican residents were on the familiar pathway of a migrant group partway through the process of making it "up and out." In other ways, however, they did not follow this familiar story. The typical migrant story emphasizes assimilation, ignoring the changes that migrants bring to host communities. In Marshall, we have described the limitations of this story at St. Joseph's, where Father Kelly worked with many Mexicans and some Irish Americans to create new events and a new space—one in which emergent hybrid practices drew from both Mexican and American traditions. In 2011, St. Joseph's had twice as many Mexican as White families, and by the end of Father Kelly's tenure that year the church felt very different than it had a decade earlier. We described similar hybrids at ATEP, where young people used Mexican artistic genres to create shows and objects that spoke both to Mexican and to American audiences. Noé simultaneously emphasized to young Mexicans and Mexican Americans the richness of Mexican traditions and the importance of combining these with successful academic and vocational pathways in America.

Marshall was different than many other migrant-receiving destinations in part because of the contingent fact of its recent and recurrent experiences with migration. Leo, Carlo, and many other children of Italian migrants played a central role in politics, commerce, and other town institutions. Father Kelly and some key parishioners still remembered their Irish migrant ancestors. James Smith pledged to treat Mexicans better than his parents had been treated, because he remembered the challenges Black migrants had faced. Some children and grandchildren of migrants were hostile to Mexicans, of course. The local newspaper editor, for example, periodically wrote op-eds that vilified Mexicans as people who flouted the law and should be deported—once ironically publishing such a screed on the same pages as romanticized features about the migrant ancestors of Irish and Italian residents. But people in Marshall were nonetheless more often sympathetic to Mexicans than Americans in many other towns, in significant part because they still remembered and valued their own migrant histories.

Occasionally an unexpected configuration of resources makes possible a new pathway for individuals or groups. We have seen how contingent factors made something new possible in Marshall—for example, when Father Kelly's arrival coincided with the transition from *solteros* to families and his work with Mexican parishioners made possible the hybrid practices emerging at St. Joseph's. Another unexpected configuration of resources happened when the national racial politics surrounding the Black Lives Matter movement reached Marshall just as Nancy entered high school. This was a potential moment of change, where new pathways may have begun to open. Nancy and her friends were upset by the police shootings of unarmed Black men across the United States, and they began to feel solidarity with African Americans. All along there had been both similarities and differences between Mexican and Black youth, but up until this point most Mexicans had focused on the differences. Organizations like MMP and Y-Achievers had been working to develop narratives about common experiences of racialization shared by Mexicans and

Blacks and the need to struggle against these, but they had reached relatively limited numbers of Mexicans. With the Black Lives Matter movement, however, nationally circulating discourses about potential "Black and Brown" solidarity began to gain traction among Black and Mexican youth in Marshall. It was too early to tell in 2016 whether these movements toward Black-Mexican solidarity would take hold and spread among young people in Marshall, or whether stories of and pathways toward assimilation, hybridity, or other goals would dominate.

Mexicans in Marshall faced opportunities and challenges that pushed some of them to move past many Black residents and follow Irish and Italian migrants "up and out." Others confronted resources that pushed them toward solidarity with Blacks against Irish, Italian, and other White residents, and perhaps toward moving "up and in," toward maintaining a separate community in which they would celebrate their own cultural heritage. These and other pathways emerged and solidified because of contingent configurations of resources—because of Marshall's combination of Irish, Italian, and Black migrants, because of the emergence of the Black Lives Matter movement at a particular historical moment, because of increased immigration enforcement that came with political pressures in the 2010s, as well as other factors. Some of the resources that contributed to both familiar and unfamiliar two-decade pathways for the Mexican community in Marshall came from town's 200-year cycle of migration and interethnic relations, but not all of them did. Some relevant resources came from longer-timescale processes involving European colonialism and the history of US-Mexican relations. Others came from shorter timescales, like contingent events in which certain politicians were elected. But in this town and many others, resources emerging from centuries-long town history and decades-long migrant community history intersected and played crucial roles in facilitating the pathways migrants actually traveled.

Individual Pathways across Years and Pivotal Events

Individual Mexicans followed pathways that were shaped but not determined by the emerging histories of the town and the migrant community. In almost every case, something about Marshall's history of migration played a role in Mexicans' ontogenetic pathways. For Allie and her siblings, for example, participation in church events exposed them to Irish American residents who were somewhat open to Mexican individuals and traditions, and this facilitated positive interethnic connections. For Nancy's friend who fell in love with a Black classmate in high school, the presence of the African American community turned out to be crucial. Realities about the migrant community's own development also usually played important roles. The arrival of Juan, Nancy, and Allie at different points in the Mexican community's development was important to their opportunities, for example—with Allie having a potential pathway to educational success that had been closed to earlier cohorts. The proliferation of Mexican businesses in the second decade also allowed younger Mexicans to image themselves as successful in ways that would have been harder for their older peers.

Different resources were crucial for different individuals, however. Nancy and her friend Sara traveled different pathways, for example—because national stereotypes about Mexican girls that touched both of them had much more influence over Sarah's life due to her decision to skip school and go on that fateful date. Juan's experience also illustrates how contingent resources can combine to produce divergent outcomes. It mattered that he came to Marshall, a town in the New Latino Diaspora, instead of arriving in an area of traditional Hispanic settlement like California or Texas—where stereotypes and opportunities would have fallen into more familiar patterns. It mattered that he came to a town with a history of Irish and Italian migration, where many landlords and bosses felt somewhat sympathetic toward Mexican migrants and where positive accounts of migrants circulated more densely than in many other similar towns. It mattered that he arrived relatively early in the history of the Marshall Mexican community, at a time when the high school had limited experience with Spanish speakers and when there was a sheltered ESL program that segregated Mexican students. It mattered that he came as an adolescent, instead of earlier in his own ontogenetic development. And it mattered that he chose to stay in school, because that institution was different than many other spaces in town. This set of resources combined to push Juan down a different pathway that he might have had under different circumstances.

Every individual was also influenced by realities from scales both broader and narrower than the town and the migrant community. Nancy and some of her peers became involved in the Black Lives Matter movement, for example, and this emerged out of a centuries-long struggle against the effects of slavery and ongoing racism against Blacks. At a much shorter timescale, Allie's pathway toward becoming a successful reader and excellent student was made possible in part by her relationship with a supportive teacher who recommended the Reading Olympics, a relationship that developed over a couple of months while she was in elementary school and that depended on events like the assignment of Allie to that particular teacher and the teacher's recognition of Allie's potential in particular interactions. Despite the importance of these and other realities from various scales, processes emerging across Marshall's 200-year history and the two-decade development of the Mexican community were crucial to the ontogenetic pathways that almost all individual Mexicans experienced.

The influence of town and community processes on individual Mexicans was often mediated through the institutions they spent time in. We have shown how schools changed across the two decades of the migrant community, such that Mexican students who attended elementary school in the second decade found their language welcomed in ways that contrasted with the deficit view of Spanish that persisted in the high school. Town politics were challenging for Mexicans, with Black residents maintaining their power and keeping Mexican candidates out, while St. Joseph's was more welcoming and open to Mexican traditions. Spending time at AYUDA could encourage assimilation, while time at MMP and Y-Achievers encouraged resistance and time at ATEP encouraged celebration of Mexican culture. Different institutions foregrounded different resources and circulated divergent stories about town and migrant histories, and these often pushed individual migrants' diverse pathways in one direction or another.

An adequate account of individual and community migrant pathways will describe contingent networks, not discrete variables. Stories of migration that treat groups as monolithic and describe similar outcomes—for all Mexicans, all migrants who came at a certain age, all who arrived in certain locations, all who persisted in school, or all who arrived in a certain era—inevitably oversimplify. These various resources do influence migrants' lives, but they have effects only as contingent resources that partly constitute networks through which particular pathways emerge. As Latour (2005) argues, the social world is made up by configurations of resources that coalesce into networks which make possible particular outcomes for individuals and groups. Within such a network, resources take effect only as part of a larger configuration. Individuals and communities follow varied pathways made possible by somewhat different networks, with similar resources configured differently and unexpected resources changing otherwise familiar configurations. As analysts we should describe contingent configurations of resources and the pathways that they make possible, instead of settling for oversimplified models. Latour's claim about contingent resources and networks must be qualified, however. Sedimentation does occur. Some configurations of resources become stable in certain places and times such that we can describe regularities. In Marshall, we have described both familiar and unfamiliar outcomes. Many Mexican migrants followed familiar pathways traveled by earlier migrants, much of the time, although many also diverged in some respects.

What are migrant and host experiences in contemporary America actually like, and what can we predict about migrants' future pathways? Those pathways will be both familiar and unfamiliar, simple and complex, with different migrants and different communities moving in various directions. Any adequate account of migration must attend to diverse, contingent resources and the emerging, solidifying pathways that these resources make possible. We have described how intersections between town, community, and individual resources facilitated migrant pathways in Marshall that were sometimes familiar and sometimes unexpected. Whatever their scientific or political inclinations, scholars, policymakers, and residents should move beyond oversimplified stories to recognize contingency and change.

Stories, Ideologies, and Theories

We have also argued that oversimplified stories about migration are not merely correct or incorrect, however. They oversimplify and often distort, but they are also part of the phenomena that we need to explain. Although inadequate as scientific accounts, simple stories influence how longstanding residents and migrants position themselves with respect to each other, and thus they have real effects. In order to trace the heterogeneous pathways that migrants and their communities travel in contemporary America, we have to describe the role that widely circulating overgeneralizations about migration play in shaping those pathways.

For example, we have shown how many Marshall residents told a story about Mexicans revitalizing both downtown and St. Joseph's parish with their entrepreneurial spirit, devotion, and hard work. This story left many things out—for example, the fear of deportation and the vulnerability created by undocumented status, the ongoing racialization of Mexicans as either invasive and dangerous or passive and victimized, and the fact that many Black residents had experienced a strong sense of community in downtown neighborhoods right up until the Mexicans' arrival, such that "revitalization" was not an accurate description according to many African Americans. But the revitalization story nonetheless had power. The normative force of the characterizations in this and related stories positioned Mexicans as positive contributors, as part of the solution for Marshall's woes. Just as the Italians had moved "up and out," many expected the Mexicans to build businesses and gain power in the coming decades. These expectations led many residents to accept Mexican business owners as legitimate participants in policy discussions about downtown, and they helped some Mexican youth to imagine themselves having successful careers.

We have shown how stories about Black and Mexican residents distorted reality in various ways. Despite the widespread evaluative characterizations in payday mugging narratives, for example, few Black residents were violent criminals and most Mexicans were not helpless victims. Many Black families did in fact succeed in moving "up and out," despite the erasure of their stories from public discourse, and many others chose to move "up and in." The distortions in these and other stories notwithstanding, however, they influenced people's behavior. Many Mexicans took on the role of revitalizers willingly and energetically. Having this role available gave Mexicans an opening that had not as readily been available to most Blacks. They were able to rent space and start businesses, and some White residents started to venture downtown to patronize Mexican businesses in ways they had not done with Black-owned ventures. Oversimplified stories helped create a reality that resembled those stories in some respects—with some Mexicans flourishing and many Black residents feeling pushed out.

We have described three broad types of oversimplified stories. First, many residents positioned migrants as either assimilating to or resisting a stable host "culture." Many scholars have criticized this type of theory (e.g., Glazer, 1993; Kearney, 1995). We have shown in detail how the host community was not stable. Even if Mexicans had not arrived, Marshall's economic situation, its ethnic makeup, and other aspects of the community would have been changing. Mexicans, by migrating, were opening themselves up to change, and they did change through contact with American residents and institutions. The migrants' changing pathways intersected with an already changing host community, and the arrival of the migrants altered that community's pathway. Marshall residents adopted simple stories about assimilation and resistance, but these did not accurately describe what was happening in town.

For example, we described in Chapter 5 how Black residents had only recently acquired significant power in town government when they were confronted with an electoral challenge by Juana's nephew Edwin. African Americans understood their situation against the background of historical relationships with Italians and other White residents, and their responses to the Mexican candidate were colored by this history—a history that until recently had had nothing to do with Mexicans. In order to understand what happened in that election, and Black-Mexican relations in general, we have to move beyond limited stories about assimilation and resistance to describe how changing communities shaped each other's historical pathways. These pathways were nonetheless influenced by those oversimplified stories. For example, many Black residents' stories about the invasion of their spaces were incomplete, but they influenced the actions of Black voters and helped keep Mexicans out of political power. Similarly, many Mexicans' stories about Blacks as violent or racist were inaccurate, but they nonetheless led Mexicans to interact less frequently with Black residents despite living in the same neighborhoods.

Second, we have moved beyond simple stories of antagonism and welcome to describe more complex, shifting positions attributed to and occupied by Mexicans across varying spaces. Migrants were credited with revitalization and blamed for decline, at different times, in different places, and by different people. They were sometimes racialized and excluded, but at other times longstanding residents identified with and embraced them. Marshall residents positioned themselves with respect to Mexicans in various ways that differed across institutional spaces, ethnic groups, individuals, and historical eras. But powerful, widespread stories about revitalization, decline, and invasion nonetheless sometimes intersected with various other resources to position Mexicans in coercive ways. For example, many Whites welcomed the growth of Mexican businesses along Main Street, seeing this as revitalization of what they perceived as a dirty, dangerous area. They characterized the Mexican migrants as hardworking, uncomplaining, and a boon to the community. But others—mostly African Americans, but also some White residents—saw Mexican businesses and neighborhoods as exclusionary and felt invaded and pushed out. We have described how these stories about revitalization and exclusion changed over the two decades, with different reactions to the single men who dominated the first decade and the intact families that dominated the second. In order to explain longstanding residents' reactions, we must acknowledge both the power of revitalization, exclusion, and invasion narratives and the fact that each of these failed to capture the complex configurations of resources that constituted the varied, emerging migrant and community pathways actually traveled.

Third, we have in some ways moved beyond dichotomous stories about longstanding residents and newcomers to describe heterogeneity among both Mexicans and other ethnic groups. Labels like "Mexican," "Spanish," "Black," "Italian," and "White" shaped people's experiences and opportunities while ignoring important differences. Such labels are salient in many political and academic contexts, but they direct attention away from the many other similarities and differences individuals embody and the varied experiences and beliefs within groups. We described Juana and the first Mexican family to settle in Marshall, for instance. Her siblings, their relatives, and friends came from a middle-class background in Mexico and became successful entrepreneurs and professionals relatively early in the history of the Marshall Mexican community. We contrasted this group with more recent migrants from working-class backgrounds, like Hernán and Mariana, many of whom continued to struggle economically. We also described complicated relationships between different groups of Black residents—some that had been in Marshall for several generations and more recent arrivals that tended to be poorer—and between Black residents and the Italians who preceded them. Mexican migrants on different pathways and with different resources encountered a complicated set of changing relationships among various groups of longstanding residents. Emerging pathways traveled by the migrants intersected with pathways being traveled by other residents. Interconnections among these pathways yielded a diverse, changing set of models, experiences, actions, and habits. Because of this complexity, an adequate analysis must move beyond dichotomous stories about encounters between migrants and longstanding residents and about allegedly homogenous ethnic groups. We cannot understand Black-Mexican relations, for example, without understanding the history of White-Black and White-Mexican relations, and we must also keep the internal complexity of these communities in mind.

With respect to these three types of oversimplified stories—assimilation to and resistance against allegedly static host communities, allegedly dichotomous reactions of welcome and antagonism toward migrants, and oversimplifications of hosts and newcomers as homogeneous groups—we have explored both their power and their limitations. Some Mexican migrants followed pathways similar to the stories about earlier migrant groups like Irish and Italians, in some aspects of their lives, but others did not. Simple stories were one crucial resource that shaped the development of individuals—contributing to the networks of resources which allowed migrant pathways to solidify in different directions, with various outcomes and sometimes ongoing indeterminacy across individuals and institutional spaces.

Migration stories are told by residents and outsiders, by politicians and academics. Too often, we treat stories as entirely true or entirely false. Both everyday actors and academics sometimes treat stories as accounts that stand apart from and can describe the truth about migrants and host communities. One can of course adopt an overly simple story to achieve a political end, and this is sometimes warranted. But we must keep in mind the incompleteness of and inaccuracies in all migration stories. On the other hand, both everyday actors and academics sometimes treat stories as mere ideologies, as falsehoods used to dupe people into supporting the interests of some group or other. Stories do influence the realities of migration, sometimes powerfully, but they are not simply falsehoods used to manipulate the unsuspecting. Stories are more and less accurate and more or less influential. Instead of exalting them as truths or condemning them as manipulation, we must carefully examine migration stories' accurate and inaccurate claims as well as their intended and unexpected effects.

We have, of course, ourselves been telling stories about Marshall in this book. Scholars, like all humans, are condemned to tell relatively simple stories about complex, changing realities. Life always includes divergence, contingency, and change across multiple scales. Stories fail to capture the full reality, in principle, because of limited time and the fact that stories themselves often change realities. The human condition involves the struggle to tell accurate stories while knowing both that those stories always fall short and that the stories may also be used to change the world being described. We cannot give up our attempts to describe the world accurately, however, because we all inevitably make claims about reality that we urge others to accept. Nor can we pretend that some stories simply describe the world without themselves being actions that intervene in it. When making sense of complex phenomena like migration, we must be humble—expecting all stories to be too simple, looking for unexpected, heterogeneous resources that may well be relevant to any given case, and acknowledging the limited scope of our generalizations. We must carefully attend to diverse evidence and multiple points of view, doing the best we can to represent a complex, changing reality.

Imagining Our Migrant Future

Migration occupies a central place in the American imagination. Most Americans are descended from migrants, and many tell stories about migrant experiences. Almost everyone is familiar with archetypal migrant narratives, and most of us find them moving. These stories describe migrants coming to America, experiencing hardship, working diligently, and building successful lives for themselves and their children, as many of our ancestors did. But other stories—just as American—characterize migrants as fundamentally different than longstanding residents, as bringing danger and dysfunction, and urge their removal or domestication. Some stories characterize migrants as agents who work to improve their lives, some present them as dangerous, some portray them as victims of circumstance and exploitation who deserve solidarity, charity, or pity, and there are other narratives as well.

Despite the passion with which these stories are often told, we have shown that none of them accurately describes how migration in America actually happens. Even demographically similar migrants have divergent experiences—despite the fact that our simple stories of migration are often powerful enough to obscure this complexity. We have seen that the actual pathways traveled by migrants and their communities are contingent and diverse. Individuals have varied dispositions. They arrive in host communities at different historical moments and different points in their ontogenetic development. Host communities have particular histories that predispose them to receive migrants in varied ways, and these communities change over time as migrants settle. Migrant communities within host towns are themselves heterogeneous and often change rapidly. Institutions within communities differ in their responses to migrants, and these organizations respond to contingent factors and change over time.

Recognizing these complexities is crucial if we hope to respond intelligently to the politically motivated stories that oversimplify migration in America. Despite stories told on the right, migrants are not wrecking our country by bringing change to a formerly stable, homogenous whole. The country was changing anyway, and it has been formed by many prior, ongoing cycles of migration. Despite stories told on the left, migrants are not simply racialized and oppressed. In some ways, many migrants are eagerly following familiar pathways "up and out," and we have no right to judge them for this aspiration. Black-Mexican relations are complex and varied, and Mexicans cannot be seen as part of a monolithic struggle envisioned for them by elites with an oversimplified view of social conflict. Instead of adopting such simple stories, we must simultaneously attend to familiar challenges and appreciate divergent possibilities. Some struggles and opportunities recur for migrants, and we should learn from experience and more effectively facilitate the contributions that they will continue to make to our country. But we must also appreciate migrants' heterogeneous goals and the diverse yet often fulfilling pathways being traveled all around us.

254 *Migration Narratives*

Figure 7.2 Clouds parting after summer rain.

References

Agha, A. (2007). *Language and Social Relations*. New York: Cambridge University Press.

Alba, R. D., & Nee, Victor. (2003). *Remaking the American Mainstream: Assimilation and Contemporary Immigration*. Boston, MA: Harvard University Press.

Allard, E. (2013). *Latecomers in the New Latino Diaspora*. Doctoral dissertation, University of Pennsylvania.

Allard, E., Mortimer, K., Gallo, S., Link, H., & Wortham, S. (2014). Immigrant Spanish as Liability or Asset? Generational Diversity in Language Ideologies at School. *Journal of Language, Identity, and Education*, 13, 335–3.

Armenta, A. (2017). Racializing Crimmigration: Structural Racism, Colorblindness, and the Institutional Production of Immigrant Criminality. *Sociology of Race and Ethnicity*, 3(1), 82–95.

Badillo, David A. (2006). *Latinos and the New Immigrant Church*. Baltimore, MD: Johns Hopkins University Press.

Bakhtin, M. (1935/1981). Discourse in the novel (Trans. by C. Emerson & M. Holquist). In M. Bakhtin (Ed.), *The Dialogic imagination* (pp. 259–422). Austin: University of Texas Press.

Barrett, J. E., & Roediger, D. (2008). How White People Became White. In P. S. Rothenberg (Ed.), *White Privilege: Essential Readings on the Other Side of Racism* (pp. 35–40). New York: Worth Publishers.

Bauman, K. (2017, August 28). *School Enrollment of the Hispanic Population: Two Decades of Growth*. United States Census Bureau. https://www.census.gov/newsroom/blogs/random-samplings/2017/08/school_enrollmentof.html

Behnke, A. O., Gonzalez, L. M., & Cox, R. B. (2010). Latino Students in New Arrival States: Factors and Services to Prevent Youth from Dropping Out. *Hispanic Journal of Behavioral Sciences*, 32(3), 385–409.

Behnken, B. D. (Ed.). (2016). *Civil Rights and Beyond: African American and Latino/a Activism in the Twentieth-Century United States*. Athens: University of Georgia Press.

Berry, B. J. L., & Dahmann, D. C. (1977). Population Redistribution in the United States in the 1970s. *Population and Development Review*, 3(4), 443–71.

Blommaert, J. (2005). Situating Language Rights: English and Swahili in Tanzania Revisited. *Journal of Sociolinguistics*, 9(3), 390–417.

Blommaert, J. (2007). Sociolinguistic Scales. *Intercultural Pragmatics*, 4, 1–19.

Bluestone, B., & Harrison, B. (1982). *The Deindustrialization of America*. New York: Basic Books.

Bonilla, F., & Girling, R. (Eds.). (1973). *Structures of Dependency*. Stanford: Stanford Institute of Politics.

Bove, V., & Elia, L. (April 18, 2017). *Why Mass Migration Is Good for Long-Term Economic Growth*. Harvard Business Review. Retrieved from: https://hbr.org/2017/04/why-mass-migration-is-good-for-long-term-economic-growth

Brabeck, K., Lykes, M. B., & Lustig, S. L. (2013). *The Psychosocial Impact of Detention and Deportation on U.S. Migrant Children and Families. A Report for the Inter-American Human Rights Court*. Retrieved from: https://www.bc.edu/content/dam/files/centers/humanrights/doc/IACHR%20Report%20on%20Pyschosocial%20Impact%20of%20Detention%20%20Deportation-FINAL%208-16-13.pdf

Brown, H., & Jones, J. A. M. (2015). Rethinking Panethnicity and the Race-Immigration Divide: An Ethno-Racialization Model of Group Formation. *Sociology of Race and Ethnicity*, 1(1), 181–91.

Bucholtz, M. (1999). "Why Be Normal?": Language and Identity Practices in a Community of Nerd Girls. *Language in Society*, 28, 203–23.

Camarillo, A. (2004). Black and Brown in Compton: Demographic Change, Suburban Decline, and Intergroup Relations in a South Central Los Angeles Community, 1950 to 2000. In N. Foner & G. M. Fredrickson (Eds.), *Not Just Black and White: Historical and Contemporary Perspectives on Immigration, Race, and Ethnicity in the United States* (pp. 358–76). New York: Russell Sage Foundation.

Carr, E. S., & Lempert, M. (2016). *Scale: Discourse and Dimensions of Social Life*. Oakland, CA: University of California Press.

Casey, E. (1996). How to Get from Space to Place in a Fairly Short Stretch of Time: Phenomenological Protegomena. In S. Feld & K. Basso (Eds.), *Senses of Place* (pp. 13–52). Santa Fe: School for Advanced Research.

Cebreros, E. (2007). "Amigo Checking": Wave of Muggings Targets Immigrant Workers. *El Mensajero*, March 22, 2007. Retrieved from: https://www.indybay.org/newsitems/2007/03/23/18381934.php

Chavez, L. (2008). *The Latino Threat: Constructing Immigrants, Citizens, and the Nation*. Stanford: Stanford University Press.

Chiquiar, D., & Salcedo, A. (2013). *Mexican Migration to the United States: Underlying Economic Factors and Possible Scenarios for Future Flows*. Washington, DC: Migration Policy Institute.

Chishti, M., & Bergeron, C. (August 17, 2009). *New and Revised ICE Agreements with State and Local Law Enforcement Met with Criticism*. Migration Policy Institute. Retrieved from: https://www.migrationpolicy.org/article/new-and-revised-ice-agreements-state-and-local-law-enforcement-met-criticism

Clonan-Roy, K. (2018). Inappropriately Aggressive and Dangerously Submissive: Latina Girls Navigating and Resisting Racialized Sexualization in the New Latino Diaspora. In K. Mcqueeney & A. Girgenti-Malone (Eds.), *Girls, Aggression, and Intersectionality: Transforming the Discourse of "Mean Girls" in the United States* (pp. 153–73). New York: Routledge.

Clonan-Roy, K., Rhodes, C., & Wortham, S. (2013). Heterogeneous, Shifting Language Ideologies in the Schooling of Immigrant Mexican Children. Paper presented at the American Anthropological Association Meetings. Chicago. November.

Clonan-Roy, K., Rhodes, C., & Wortham, S. (2016). Moral Panic about Sexual Promiscuity: Heterogeneous Scales in the Identification of One Middle-School Latina Girl. *Linguistics and Education*, 34, 11–21.

Clonan-Roy, K., Wortham, S., & Nichols, B. (2016). Shifting Racial Stereotypes in Late Adolescence: Heterogeneous Resources for Developmental Change in the New Latino Diaspora. *Language & Communication*, 46, 51–61.

Coleman, M., & Kocher, A. (2011). Detention, Deportation, Devolution and Immigrant Incapacitation in the US, post 9/11. *The Geographical Journal*, 177(3), 228–37.

DeGenova, N., & Ramos-Zayas, A. Y. (2003). *Latino Crossings: Mexicans, Puerto Ricans, and the Politics of Race and Citizenship*. New York: Routledge.

Denner, J., & Guzman, B. L. (2006). *Latina Girls: Voices of Adolescent Strength in the United States*. New York: New York University Press.

Dick, H. (2011). Making Immigrants Illegal in Small-Town USA. *Journal of Linguistic Anthropology*, 21(S1), E35–E55.

Dixon, J., & Durrheim, K. (2004). Dislocating Identity: Desegregation and the Transformation of Place. *Journal of Environmental Psychology*, 24, 455–73.

Donato, K. M., & Rodriguez, L. A. (2014). Police Arrests in a Time of Uncertainty: The Impact of 287 (g) on Arrests in a New Immigrant Gateway. *American Behavioral Scientist*, 58(13), 1696–722.

Donoso, J. C. (December 8, 2014). *On Religion, Mexicans Are More Catholic and Often More Traditional than Mexican Americans*. Pew Research Center. Retrieved from: https://www.pewresearch.org/fact-tank/2014/12/08/on-religion-mexicans-are-more-catholic-and-often-more-traditional-than-mexican-americans/

Durand, J., & Massey, D. S. (Eds.). (2004). *Crossing the Border: Research from the Mexican Migration Project*. New York: Russell Sage Foundation.

Eckert, P. (1987). *Jocks and Burnouts: Social Categories and Identity in the High School*. New York: Teachers College Press.

Fairlie, R. W., Reedy, E. J., Morelix, A., & Russell, J. (August, 2016). *The Kauffman Index: Startup Activity, National Trends*. Ewing Marion Kauffman Foundation. Retrieved from: https://www.kauffman.org/wp-content/uploads/2019/09/kauffman_index_startup_activity_national_trends_2016.pdf

Flores, A. (September 18, 2017). *How the U.S. Hispanic Population Is Changing*. Pew Research Center. Retrieved from: https://www.pewresearch.org/fact-tank/2017/09/18/how-the-u-s-hispanic-population-is-changing/

Flores, R. D. (2014). In the Eye of the Storm: How Did Hazleton's Restrictive Immigration Ordinance Affect Local Interethnic Relations? *American Behavioral Scientist*, 58(13), 1743–63.

Friedrich, P. (1972). Social Context and Semantic Feature: The Russian Pronominal Usage. In J. Gumperz & D. Hymes (Eds.), *Directions in Sociolinguistics: The Ethnography of Communication* (pp. 282–95). New York: Holt, Rinehart & Winston.

Gallo, S., & Wortham, S. (2012). *Sobresalir*: Latino Parent Perspectives on New Latino Diaspora Schools. *International Journal of Multicultural Education*, 14(2), 1–17.

Gallo, S., Allard, E., Link, H., Wortham, S., & Mortimer. K. (2014). Conflicting Ideologies of Mexican Immigrant English across Levels of Schooling. *International Multilingual Research Journal*, 8, 124–40.

Gans, H. (2012). Against Culture versus Structure. *Identities: Global Studies in Culture and Power*, 19(2), 125–34.

García, L. (2009). "Now Why Do You Want to Know about That?": Heteronormativity, Sexism, and Racism in the Sexual (Mis)education of Latina Youth. *Gender & Society*, 23(4), 520–41. Retrieved from: http://doi.org/10.1177/0891243209339498

Gergen, K. J. (1973). Social Psychology as History. *Journal of Personality and Social Psychology*, 26(2), 309.

Gibson, M. (1988). *Accommodation without Assimilation: Sikh Immigrants in an American High School*. Ithaca, NY: Cornell University Press.

Glazer, N. (1993). Is Assimilation Dead? *The Annals of the American Academy of Political and Social Science*, 530, 122–36.

González, R. (2016). *Lives in Limbo: Undocumented and Coming of Age in America*. Oakland: University of California Press.

Gordon, D. (October 28, 2015). *Immigrants Bring Rejuvenation to Many Small Towns*. The Daily Yonder. Retrieved from: https://www.dailyyonder.com/immigrants-bring-rejuvenation-to-many-small-towns/2015/10/28/

Gordon, D. (September 2, 2016). *Want to Preserve American Small Towns? Embrace Immigrants*. Zócalo Public Square. Retrived from: https://www.zocalopublicsquare.org/2016/09/02/want-preserve-american-small-towns-embrace-immigrants/ideas/nexus/

Gordon, M. M. (1964). *Assimilation in American Life: The Role of Race, Religion, and National Origins*. New York: Oxford University Press.

Grey, M. A., & Woodrick, A. C. (2005). "Latinos Have Revitalized Our Community": Mexican Migration and Anglo Responses in Marshalltown, Iowa. In V. Zúñiga & R. Hernández-León (Eds.), *New Destinations: Mexican Immigration in the United States* (pp. 133–54). New York: Russell Sage Foundation.

Hall, Kathleen D. (2002). *Lives in Transition: Sikh Youth as British Citizens*. Philadelphia: University of Pennsylvania Press.

Hamann, E. T., & Harklau, L. (2010). Education in the New Latino Diaspora. In E. G. Murillo (Ed.), *Handbook of Latinos and Education* (pp. 157–69). New York: Routledge.

Hamann, E. T., & Reeves, J. (2012). ICE Raids, Children, Media, and Making Sense of Latino Newcomers in Flyover Country. *Anthropology & Education Quarterly*, 43(1), 24–40.

Hamann, E. T., Wortham, S., & Murillo, E. G. (2002). Education and Policy in the New Latino Diaspora. In S. Wortham, E. G. Murillo, & E. T. Hamann (Eds.), *Education in the New Latino Diaspora: Policy and the Politics of Identity* (pp. 1–16). Westport, CT: Ablex Press.

Hamann, E. T., Wortham, S., & Murillo, E. G. (2015). *Revisiting Education in the New Latino Diaspora*. Charlotte, NC: Information Age Publishing.

Hanchett, T. W. (1996). U.S. Tax Policy and the Shopping-Center Boom of the 1950s and 1960s. *The American Historical Review*, 101(4), 1082–110.

Haviland, J. (2005). "Whorish Old Man" and "One (Animal) Gentleman": The Intertextual Construction of Enemies and Selves. *Journal of Linguistic Anthropology*, 15(1), 81–94.

Herrera Lasso, C. Q., & Pérez Esquivel, D. (2014). The Mexican Reputation: A Strategy to Improve the Stereotype Mexico Shares with Its U.S. Diaspora. Cambridge: Harvard University, John F. Kennedy School of Government.

Hill, J. (1995). Mock Spanish: A Site for the Indexical Reproduction of Racism in American English. In D. Glick (Ed.), *Language & Culture, Symposium Two*. Retrieved from: https://language-culture.binghamton.edu/symposia/2/part1/.

Horsley, S. (July 28, 2010). *Under Obama, More Illegal Immigrants Sent Home*. National Public Radio. Retrieved from: https://www.npr.org/templates/story/story.php?storyId=128826285

Ignatiev, N. (1995[2009]). *How the Irish Became White*. New York: Routledge.

Jaynes, G. (2004). Immigration and the Social Construction of Otherness. In N. Foner & G. Fredrickson (Eds.), *Not Just Black and White: Historical and Contemporary Perspectives on Immigration, Race, and Ethnicity in the United States* (pp. 100–16). New York: Russell Sage Foundation.

Jencks, C., & Mayer, S.E. (1990). The Social Consequences of Growing Up in a Poor Neighborhood. In L. E. Lynn, Jr. & M. G. H. McGeary (Eds.), *Inner-City Poverty in the United States* (pp. 111–86). Washington, DC: National Academy Press.

Jones, J. A. (2012). "Blacks May Be Second Class, but They Can't Make Them Leave: Mexican Racial Formation and Immigrant Status in Winston Salem." *Latino Studies*, 10(1–2), 60–80.

Jordan, M. (November 8, 2012). *Heartland Draws Hispanics to Help Revive Small Towns*. The Wall Street Journal. Retrieved from: https://www.wsj.com/articles/SB10000872396390443696604577645500654098514

Kearney, M. (1995). "The Local and the Global: The Anthropology of Globalization and Transnationalism." *Annual Review of Anthropology*, 24, 547–65.

LaGumina, S. J. (1999). *WOP! A Documentary History of Anti-Italian Discrimination in the United States*. Toronto: Guernica.

Latour, B. (2005). *Reassembling the Social*. New York: Oxford University Press.

Lee, S. (1994). Behind the Model-Minority Stereotype: Voices of High- and Low-Achieving Asian American Students. *Anthropology & Education Quarterly*, 25(4), 413–29.

Lee, J., & Bean, F. D. (2007). Reinventing the Color Line Immigration and America's New Racial/Ethnic Divide. *Social Forces*, 86(2), 561–86.

Lemke, J. (2000). Across the Scales of Time: Artifacts, Activities, and Meanings in Ecosocial Systems. *Mind, Culture, and Activity*, 7(4), 273–90.

Levine, R. A. (July, 2004). *Assimilating Immigrants: Why America Can and France Cannot*. RAND Corporation. Retrieved from: https://www.rand.org/content/dam/rand/pubs/occasional_papers/2005/RAND_OP132.pdf

Link, H., Gallo, S., & Wortham, S. (2014). "gusame ka'lata!": Faux Spanish in the New Latino Diaspora. In A. Creese & A. Blackledge (Eds.), *Heteroglossia as Practice and Pedagogy* (pp. 255–73). London, UK: Springer.

Link, H., Gallo, S., & Wortham, S. E. (2017). The Production of Schoolchildren as Enlightenment Subjects. *American Educational Research Journal*, 54(5), 834–67.

Londoño, E., & Vargas, T. (2007, October 26). Robbers Stalk Hispanic Immigrants, Seeing Ideal Prey. The Washington Post. http://www.washingtonpost.com/wp-dyn/content/article/2007/10/25/AR2007102502740_pf.html

López-Sanders, L. (2009). Trapped at the Bottom: Racialized and Gendered Labor Queues in New Latino Destinations. In *Annual Meeting of the American Sociological Association*. San Francisco, CA.

Lukose, Ritty A. (2009). *Liberalization's Children: Gender, Youth and Consumer Citizenship in Globalizing India*. Durham, NC: Duke University Press.

Lundström, C. (2006). Okay, but We Are Not Whores You Know: Latina Girls Navigating the Boundaries of Gender and Ethnicity in Sweden. *Young*, 14(3), 203–18.

Mangual Figueroa, A. (2016). Citizenship, Beneficence, and Informed Consent: The Ethics of Working in Mixed-Status Families. *International Journal of Qualitative Studies in Education*, 29(10), 66–85.

Manning, M. (2000). Beyond Racial Identity Politics: Towards a Liberation Theory for Multicultural Democracy. In R. Delgado & J. Stefancic (Eds.), *Critical Race Theory: The Cutting Edge, 2nd Edition* (pp. 448–54). Philadelphia: Temple University Press.

Massey, D., & Denton, N. (1998). *American Apartheid*. Cambridge: Harvard University Press.

Massey, D., Alarcón, R., Durand, J., & González, H. (1987). *Return to Aztlan: The Social Process of International Migration from Western Mexico*. Berkeley: University of California Press.

Matza, M. (June 15, 2009). *Attacks on Mexican Immigrants often Go Unreported*. Philadelphia Inquirer. Retrieved from: https://www.inquirer.com/philly/news/homepage/20090615_Attacks_on_Mexican_immigrants_often_go_unreported.html

Mehan, H. (1996). The Construction of an LD Student: A Case Study in the Politics of Representation. In M. Silverstein & G. Urban (Eds.), *Natural Histories of Discourse* (pp. 253–76). Chicago: University of Chicago Press.

Mendoza-Denton, N. (2008). *Homegirls: Symbolic Practices in the Making of Latina Youth Styles*. Oxford: Blackwell.

Millard, A., Chapa, J., & Burillo, C. (Eds.). (2004). *Apple Pie and Enchiladas*. Austin: University of Texas Press.

Millard, A., Chapa, J., & Crane, K. (2004). E Pluribus Unum? Discussion, Conclusions, and Policy Implementations. In A. Millard, J. Chapa, & C. Burillo (Eds.), *Apple Pie & Enchiladas* (pp. 204–21). Austin: University of Texas Press.

Moll, L. (1992). Bilingual Classroom Studies and Community Analysis: Some Recent Trends. *Educational Researcher*, 21(2), 20–4.

Morawska, E. (2001). Immigrant-Black Dissensions in American Cities. In E. Anderson & D. Massey (Eds.), *Problem of the Century* (pp. 47–96). New York: Russell Sage Foundation.

Mortimer, K. S., Wortham, S., & Allard, E. (2010). Helping Immigrants Identify as "University-Bound Students": Unexpected Difficulties in Teaching the Hidden Curriculum. *Revista de Educacion* (353), 107–28.

Murillo, E., & Villenas, S. (1997). *East of Aztlán: Typologies of Resistance in North Carolina Communities*. Paper presented at Reclaiming Voices: Ethnographic Inquiry and Qualitative Research in a Postmodern Age, Los Angeles.

Murillo, E. G. (2002). How Does It Feel to Be a Problem?: "Disciplining" the Transnational Subject in the American South. In S. Wortham, E. E. Murillo, & E. T. Hamann (Eds.), *Education in the New Latino Diaspora: Policy and the Politics of Identity* (pp. 215–40). Westport, CT: Ablex Press.

National Commission on Asian American and Pacific Islander Research in Education. (2008). *Asian Americans and Pacific Islanders: Facts, Not Fiction: Setting the Record Straight*. The Asian/Pacific/American Institute at New York University and the Steinhardt Institute of Higher Education Policy at New York University. Retrieved from: http://care.gseis.ucla.edu/wp-content/uploads/2015/08/2008_CARE_Report.pdf

National Research Council. (1997). *The New Americans: Economic, Demographic, and Fiscal Effects of Immigration*. Washington, DC: The National Academies Press. https://doi.org/10.17226/5779

Newland, K. (2009). Circular Migration and Human Development. *Human Development Research Paper*, 42. United Nations Development Program.

Nichols, B., & Wortham, S. (2018). Black Flight: Heterogeneous Accounts of Mexican Immigration in a Diverse Community. *Language & Communication*, 59, 4–16.

Nunn, N., Qian, N., & Sequeira, S. (May 31, 2017a). Migrants and the Making of America: The Short- and Long-Run Effects of Immigration during the Age of Mass Migration. *Research Briefs in Economic Policy, 77*. Cato Institute. Retrieved from: https://www.cato.org/publications/research-briefs-economic-policy/migrants-making-america-short-long-run-effects?utm_content=buffer60b85&utm_medium=social&utm_source=facebook.com&utm_campaign=buffer

Nunn, N., Qian, N., & Sequeira, S. (January, 2017b). *Migrants and the Making of America: The Short- and Long-Run Effects of Immigration during the Age of Mass Migration*. Cambridge: Harvard University. Retrieved from: https://scholar.harvard.edu/files/nunn/files/nunn_qian_sequeira_immigrants.pdf

Oakes, J. (1985). *Keeping Track: How Schools Structure Inequality*. New Haven: Yale University Press.

Office of the Press Secretary. (July 10, 2009). *Secretary Napolitano Announces New Agreement for State and Local Immigration Enforcement Partnerships & Adds 11 New Agreements*. U.S. Department of Homeland Security. Retrieved from: https://www.dhs.gov/news/2009/07/10/secretary-announces-new-agreement-state-and-local-immigration-enforcement

Orellana, M. F. (2009). *Translating Childhoods: Immigrant Youth, Language, and Culture.* New Brunswick, NJ: Rutgers University Press.

Oropesa, R. S., & Landale, N. S. (1997). In Search of the New Second Generation: Alternate Strategies for Identifying Second Generation Children and Understanding Their Acquisition of English. *Sociological Perspectives,* 40(3), 429–55.

Parisi, D., Lichter, D. T., & Taquino, M. C. (2011). Multi-Scale Residential Segregation: Black Exceptionalism and America's Changing Color Line. *Social Forces,* 89(3), 829–52.

Passel, J. S., & Cohn, D. (February 11, 2008). *U.S. Population Projections: 2005–2050.* Pew Research Center. Retrieved from: http://www.pewhispanic.org/2008/02/11/us-population-projections-2005-2050/

PennWharton. (June 27, 2016). *The Effects of Immigration on the United States' Economy.* University of Pennsylvania. Retrieved from: https://budgetmodel.wharton.upenn.edu/issues/2016/1/27/the-effects-of-immigration-on-the-united-states-economy

Pew Hispanic Center. (2011). *The Mexican-American Boom: Births Overtake Immigration.* Washington, DC: Pew Research Center.

Pew Research Center. (January 31, 2008). *Do Blacks and Hispanics Get Along? Yes, but Not Always, and Not about Everything.* Retrieved from: http://www.pewsocialtrends.org/2008/01/31/do-blacks-and-hispanics-get-along/

Pew Research Center. (September 18, 2017). *Facts on U.S. Latinos, 2015: Statistical Portrait of Hispanics in the United States.* Pew Research Center, Hispanic Trends. Retrieved from: https://www.pewresearch.org/hispanic/2017/09/18/facts-on-u-s-latinos-previous-years-data/

Phillips, K. (1969). *The Emerging Republican Majority.* New Rochelle, NY: Arlington House.

Portes, A., & Rumbaut, R. G. (2001). *Legacies: The Story of the Immigrant Second Generation.* Oakland, CA: University of California Press.

Portes, A., & Zhou, M. (1993). The New Second Generation: Segmented Assimilation and Its Variants. *The Annals of the American Academy of Political and Social Science,* 530(1), 74–96.

Prieto, L., Sagafi-nejad, T., & Janamanchi, B. (2013). A Bourdieusian Perspective on Acculturation: Mexican Immigrants in the United States. *Administrative Sciences,* 3(4), 290–305.

Proshansky, H. M., Fabian, A. K., & Kaminoff, R. (1983). Place-Identity: Physical World Socialization of the Self. *Journal of Environmental Psychology,* 3, 57–83.

Quillian, L. (2002). Why Is Black–White Residential Segregation so Persistent?: Evidence on Three Theories from Migration Data. *Social Science Research,* 31(2), 197–229.

Rangel-Ortiz, L. X. (2011). The Emergence of a New Form of Mexican Nationalism in San Antonio, Texas. *Studies in Ethnicity and Nationalism,* 11(3), 384–403.

Rodríguez, N. (2012). New Southern Neighbors: Latino Immigration and Prospects for Intergroup Relations between African-Americans and Latinos in the South. *Latino Studies,* 10(1–2), 18–40.

Rolón-Dow, R. (2004). Seduced by Images: Identity and Schooling in the Lives of Puerto Rican Girls. *Anthropology & Education Quarterly*, 35(1), 8–29.

Rosa, J. (2019). *Looking Like a Language, Sounding Like a Race*. Oxford Studies in Anthropology of Language. New York: Oxford University Press.

Sampson, R. J., Morenoff, J. D., & Gannon-Rowley, T. (2002). Assessing "Neighborhood Effects": Social Processes and New Directions in Research. *Annual Review of Sociology*, 28, 443–78.

Santiago, A. M. (1996). Trends in Black and Latino Segregation in the Post-Fair Housing Era: Implications for Housing Policy. *Berkeley La Raza Law Journal*, 9(2), 131–53.

Saunders, J., Lim, N., & Prosnitz, D. (2010). *Enforcing Immigration Law at the State and Local Levels a Public Policy Dilemma*. RAND. Retrieved from: https://www.rand.org/content/dam/rand/pubs/occasional_papers/2010/RAND_OP273.pdf

Seligman, A. I. (2005). *Block by Block: Neighborhoods and Public Policy on Chicago's West Side*. Chicago: University of Chicago Press.

Shankar, S. (2008). *Desi Land: Teen Culture, Class, and Success in Silicon Valley*. Durham, NC: Duke University Press.

Short, J. R., Hanlon, B., & Vicino, T. J. (2007). The Decline of Inner Suburbs: The New Suburban Gothic in the United States. *Geography Compass*, 1(3), 641–56.

Silver, A. M. (2015). "Clubs of Culture and Capital: Immigrant and Second-Generation Incorporation in a New Destination School." *Ethnic and Racial Studies*, 38(5), 824–40.

Silverstein, M. (1985). Language and the Culture of Gender: At the Intersection of Structure, Usage, and Ideology. In E. Mertz & R. J. Parmentier (Eds.), *Semiotic Mediation: Sociocultural and Psychological Perspectives* (pp. 219–59). Orlando: Academic Press.

Silverstein, M. (1992). The Indeterminacy of Contextualization: When Is Enough Enough. *The Contextualization of Language*, 22, 55–76.

Silverstein, M. (2013). Discourse and the No-thing-ness of Culture. *Signs and Society*, 1(2), 327–66.

Small, M. L., & Newman, K. (2001). Urban Poverty after *The Truly Disadvantaged*: The Rediscovery of the Family, the Neighborhood, and Culture. *Annual Review of Sociology*, 27, 23–45.

Smith, R. C. (2014). Black Mexicans, Conjunctural Ethnicity, and Operating Identities: Long-Term Ethnographic Analysis. *American Sociological Review*, 79(3), 517–48.

Solorzano, D. G. (1997). Images and Words That Wound: Critical Race Theory, Racial Stereotyping, and Teacher Education. *Teacher Education Quarterly*, 24(3), 5–19.

Sontag, D. (December 11, 1992). *Across the U.S., Immigrants Find the Land of Resentment*. The New York Times. Retrieved from: https://www.nytimes.com/1992/12/11/nyregion/across-the-us-immigrants-find-the-land-of-resentment.html

Stanton-Salazar, R. D. (2001). *Manufacturing Hope and Despair: The School and Kin Support Networks of US-Mexican Youth*. New York: Teachers College Press..

Sulzberger, A. G. (2011, November 13). *Hispanics Reviving Faded Towns on the Plains*. The New York Times. https://www.nytimes.com/2011/11/14/us/as-small-towns-wither-on-plains-hispanics-come-to-the-rescue.html

Tolnay, S. E. (2003). The African American "Great Migration" and Beyond. *Annual Review of Sociology*, 29, 209–32.

Trevelyan, E., Gambino, C., Gryn, T., Larsen, L., Acosta, Y., Grieco, El, Harris, D., & Walters, N. (2016). *Characteristics of the U.S. Population by Generational Status: 2013. Current Population Survey Reports*. United States Census Bureau. Retrieved from: https://www.census.gov/content/dam/Census/library/publications/2016/demo/P23-214.pdf

Trouillot, M. (1991). Anthropology and the Savage Slot: The Poetics and Politics of Otherness In R. G. Fox (Ed.), *Recapturing Anthropology: Working in the Present* (pp. 17–44). Santa Fe, NM: School of American Research Press.

Valencia, R. (Ed.). (1997). *The Evolution of Deficit Thinking: Educational Thought and Practice*. Stanford Series on Education and Public Policy. New York: Falmer Press.

Valenzuela, A. (1999). *Subtractive Schooling: U.S.-Mexican Youth and the Politics of Caring*. Albany, NY: State University of New York Press.

Vandor, P., & Franke, N. (October 27, 2016). *Why Are Immigrants More Entrepreneurial?* Harvard Business Review. Retrieved from: https://hbr.org/2016/10/why-are-immigrants-more-entrepreneurial

Waters, M. C., Kasinitz, P., & Asad, A. L. (2014). Immigrants and African Americans. *Annual Review of Sociology*, 40, 369–90.

Wilson, W. J. (1987). T*he Truly Disadvantaged: The Inner City, the Underclass, and Public Policy*. Chicago: University of Chicago Press.

Wimmer, A. (2008). Elementary Strategies of Ethnic Boundary Making. *Ethnic and Racial Studies*, 31(6), 1025–55.

Winn, M. T. (2011). *Girl Time: Literacy, Justice, and the School-to-Prison Pipeline. Teaching for Social Justice*. New York: Teachers College Press.

Wortham, S. (2001). *Narratives in Action: A Strategy for Research and Analysis*. New York: Teachers College Press.

Wortham, S. (2005). Socialization beyond the Speech Event. *Journal of Linguistic Anthropology*, 15, 95–112.

Wortham, S. (2006). *Learning Identity*. Cambridge University Press, New York.

Wortham, S. (2012). Beyond Macro and Micro in the Linguistic Anthropology of Education. *Anthropology and Education Quarterly*, 43(2), 128–37.

Wortham, S., & Reyes, A. (2015). *Discourse Analysis beyond the Speech Event*. New York: Routledge.

Wortham, S., Mortimer, K., & Allard, E. (2009). Mexicans as Model Minorities in the New Latino Diaspora. *Anthropology and Education Quarterly*, 40(4), 388–404.

Wortham, S., Murillo, E., & Hamann, E. (Eds.). (2002). *Education in the New Latino Diaspora: Policy and the Politics of Identity*. Westport, CT: Ablex.

Yosso, T. (2002). Critical Race Media Literacy: Challenging Deficit Discourse about Chicanas/os." *Journal of Popular Film and Television*, 30(1), 52–62.

Zambrana, R. E., & Zoppi, I. M. (2002). Latina Students. *Journal of Ethnic and Cultural Diversity in Social Work*, 11(1–2), 33–53.

Zúñiga, V., & Hernández-León, R. (2005). Introduction. In V. Zúñiga & R. Hernández-León (Eds.), *New Destinations: Mexican Immigration in the United States* (pp. xi–xxix). New York: Russell Sage Foundation.

Index

Aaron 83, 100, 102
African Americans 1–8, 22–5, 27–9, 55–6
    church communities 78, 81, 101, 106
    negative stereotypes 205
    public spaces 147, 149–50, 152–4, 156–60, 164, 165–6, 168, 171, 173–8, 181, 184, 187–90, 192–6
    residential neighborhoods 110–11, 114–24, 127–30, 134, 136, 138–42, 143–4
    senior citizen 2
African Methodist Episcopal church 20
Allie, migrant history
    arrival in 2003 9, 11
    elementary school experiences 64–72
    family goal 41, 48, 64, 68, 72
    parents 64, 66–70
    positive narration 12
    school life 14–18, 38–9
American citizens 31, 68, 73, 168, 185
American culture 7, 85, 87–8, 97, 102, 208, 210–11, 230–1, 233
American schools 47, 67–9, 73
Anglo parishioners 92, 94, 98–101
Asian migrants 45–6

bilingual teachers 49, 69, 214
Black community 3, 22–4, 27, 60–1, 63
    Catholic 80–1
    interethnic conflict 142–6
    Mexican relations 4, 35, 37
    migrants 4, 22–3, 27–8
    politics 187–90
    public spaces 147, 149–50, 153, 155, 157, 159–61, 164, 170, 171–9, 184, 187, 189–96
    residential neighborhoods 110–16, 119–20, 123–4, 126–9, 131, 133–6, 138–9, 141–6
    residents and earlier migrants 28
    solteros and slumlords 126–9
    students 52–3, 55
    youth 54, 62–3

Black criminals 125, 143, 148, 151, 153, 157, 159, 223
Black flight 140–2, 205
Black Lives Matter movement 63, 217, 226, 244–6
Black students 52–3, 61–2
business
    exclusion 171–8
    Martínez family 165–9
    revitalization 169–71

Castro, Juan, migrant history
    childhood and migration 41–2
    cohort 44, 49, 51
    economic concerns 49–50
    English learning, challenges 49–50
    families, comparison with Americans 32–3
    generation 50–2, 62
    on migrants place 14
    reason to return Mexico 42–4
    school absenteeism 49
    student life 38–41
Catholic churches. *See also* St. Joseph's parish
    creating interethnic connections 98–102
    growing Mexican involvement 84–90
    history of St. Joseph's 79–84
    Mexican celebrations 95–8
    Polish and Italian communities 77
    Spanish at church 90–5
    stories and complex realities 102–7
Ciccone, Leo, migrant history
    childhood memories 21–2
    interethnic relations 22
    on Mexicans' pathways 35
    narratives of decline 25–8
    on social relationship 25–6
community organizations
    Arte, Tecnología, y Educación del Pueblo (ATEP) 201, 210, 226, 228–36, 238, 244, 247

Index

AYUDA 162, 166, 201–2, 206–11, 215, 226, 228–9, 232, 235, 247
Club de Padres 201–2, 210–12, 215–19, 228–9, 234–5, 243
Marshall Men for Progress (MMP) 201–2, 205, 210–11, 220–2, 224, 226–8, 232, 238, 247
Washington Community Center 179, 201–5, 220
Y-Achievers 201–2, 205, 211, 220–2, 224, 226–8, 232, 235, 244, 247
YMCA 24, 221
community pathways 8–11, 12, 15, 35, 37, 107, 109, 199–200, 250
contingent resources 10, 12–13, 34, 38, 73–4, 77, 90, 147, 185, 197, 200, 239, 246–8
cycle of migrant groups
   heterogeneous goals 253
   historical context, the Mexican 242–4
   individual pathways 245–8
   oversimplified stories 248–51

Darrell 121–3, 140–1, 144, 224–5
divergent pathways 34–5, 71, 73
Doreena, migrant history 121, 123, 126, 140–1, 172–3, 175–6, 197, 224
   ancestors 2
   childhood memories 24
   on Mexicans, characteristics 3, 5
   narratives of decline 25–6, 29
   on variability of generations 27

educators 10, 15–17, 37–8, 40, 45–7, 49–51, 53–5, 57, 59–62, 70, 73
elementary schools 1, 15, 38–40, 46, 52, 57, 64, 65, 69–70
English as a Second Language. *See* ESL
English language learners 15–16, 46, 49
English-speaking parishioners 82, 92, 94, 99
ESL 38, 52–3, 56
   classes 41, 48–9, 52–3, 69, 208
ethnic groups 22, 25, 34–5, 53

Faccone, Carlo, migrant history
   ancestors 21
   children's education 40
   dedication to Juana 28–9
   Mexican community's development, role in 32–3

Faccone, Juana, migrant history 64, 125–6, 148, 150, 157, 161, 164–6, 168, 180, 183–4, 212–16, 234, 243, 249–50
   children's education 40
   as first settler 28
   narratives of decline 31, 33
   siblings 30
Father Kelly 90, 99–106, 152, 161, 197, 217, 224, 235, 243–4
   church population 28
   first Catholic parish's history 19
   Mexican Celebrations 95–8
   on Mexicans, characteristics 3, 30
   reassignment 106
   Spanish-language events at church 90–5

generations 2, 21, 27, 68
Gloria 204–5
Good Hope Church 88–90, 94–5, 98, 105, 107

Harrison 122–3, 220–6
Hernán and Mariana (Allie's parents) 64, 66, 68, 71–2, 85, 93, 182, 251
high school 15, 37–41, 46–51, 55–6, 61–3, 66
Hispanics 27–8, 31, 63, 68–9, 71
   in politics 186–7 (*see also* Martínez, Edwin; Solis, Sandra)
   residential neighborhoods 131–3

individual migrants 6, 8–9, 17, 34
intact families 33, 39, 41, 61, 68, 78, 136, 250
interethnic connections 28, 62–3, 76, 78–9, 88, 98
interethnic relations 22, 37, 52, 55, 76–7, 81, 107, 156, 191, 194, 199–200, 239, 241, 245
Irish Americans 1, 35, 76, 80, 106, 109, 117, 191, 241, 243, 245
   church communities 76, 79–80, 88, 98, 103–4, 106
   public spaces 147, 150–1, 162, 169, 191–2, 195–6
   residential neighborhoods 109–10, 112, 114–19, 122–3, 138, 144
   stereotypical migrant pathways 145
Irish Catholic church 2, 5, 20, 29, 98
   Mexicans 77

Irish migrants 7, 17, 22, 28, 119, 237, 239, 244
Italian Americans 3, 7, 28–9, 34–5, 80–1, 110, 112, 117, 138, 147, 150, 169, 241
  church communities 80, 106
  priest at St. Joseph's parish 106
  public spaces 147, 150–1, 162, 169, 171–2, 185–6, 192, 195–6
  residential neighborhoods 110, 117, 119, 138–9
  stereotypical migrant pathways 145
Italian migrants 7, 17, 21, 28, 118, 237, 240, 245

Jamar 121–3, 144, 225
John 175, 203, 221–2, 224, 226–7

Keon 121, 123, 172
kindergarten 9, 50, 65, 243

Latina girls 51, 61
longstanding residents 2, 5–6, 13–14, 23–5, 49–51
López, José Luis 217

Marshall's history
  economic decline 25–8, 114–15
  first church 19
  housing ordinance 134–6
  material and ideological changes 26–8
  Mexican revitalization 28–34
  migration waves 20–4
  resources 18
  revitalization narratives 112–13, 124, 129, 136–8, 145–6
  slumlords 124–31
  solteros 124–40
  town's early history 19–20
  victims 124–36, 145
Martínez, Edwin 148, 151, 165, 167, 184–94, 197, 199–200, 217, 230, 242, 249
McCarthy, Meghan 80, 97, 103
Mexican children 6, 15, 47, 51, 56, 70, 101, 183, 204, 208, 224, 229, 232, 235, 243
Mexican community 9–10, 32, 37–9, 75–7. *See also* community organizations
  in politics 184–6, 190–7

  residential neighborhoods 109–15, 122–46
Mexican currency crisis 28
Mexican families 28–9, 32, 59, 69, 77
Mexican girls 55, 58–63, 246
Mexican migrants 1–3, 5–7, 27–9, 31, 33–4, 74, 76–9
  core claims 34
  in Marshall town 29–33
  trauma and dislocation 85–6
Mexican narrators 29, 144, 153, 155, 157–61, 171, 200
Mexicans' pathways 4, 8, 11, 35
Mexican students
  after-school jobs 45
  blue-collar jobs 40
  chronic absenteeism 48–9
  cohorts 38, 45, 51, 56, 71, 73
  derogatory characterizations of girls 58–63
  diverse pathways 73–4
  educational capacity 37–8
  ESL program 46, 49
  learning English 38–40
  ontogenetic pathways 39
  peer groups 38–40, 47
  teacher's view 46–7
Mexican youth 40, 54, 62–3
middle school 37–9, 41, 50–7, 59–61, 65–6, 69–70, 208
migrant groups 1–2, 4–5, 7, 11, 22, 27, 31, 37, 76
migration stories 6, 8, 13, 17, 28, 31, 34–5. *See also specific migrant history*
  religious conversion 102–7
MMS (Marshall Middle School) 51–6, 58–60
model minorities 45, 139, 149, 171, 237

Nancy, migration history
  cohort 39, 51
  ESL program 56–7
  family goal 48
  interethnic relations 52–6
  middle school experiences 50–2
  student life 38–9
narrators 2, 26, 118, 122, 125, 130–1, 136, 153, 156, 159. *See also specific narrators*

neighborhoods
  Black flight and stories 120–4, 126–9, 140–2
  conflict, and reconciliation 136–46
  Hispanic stories 131–4
  Housing Ordinance 134–6
  interethnic conflict 142–6
  nostalgia and decline 114–15
  slumlords and victims 124–34
  White stories 115–20, 129–31
networks 10, 12, 14, 17, 34–5, 63, 73–4
newcomers 5, 81, 84, 103, 104–5, 184, 187, 193–7, 207, 250–1
New Latino Diaspora community 33, 50, 104, 113, 138, 246
nuclear family 32, 48, 64, 85–6, 136

Obama, Barack 181–2, 189
Ortega, Raúl 85, 95, 106

Paco 168, 171, 183, 213
Pastor Dave 89, 93–5, 207
Patricia 212–13
payday mugging narratives
  Black 154–7
  Mexican 157–61
  White 152–4
peers 16, 38, 40, 42, 44, 47, 49–50, 52, 58, 62, 70, 73, 206, 246
police 31, 95, 142, 151–4, 179–83, 209, 241
politics
  Blacks in 187–90
  Edwin, Hispanic candidate 186–7
  "native" or "natural Marshallites" 191–7
poverty 6, 41, 51, 145, 154, 172, 222, 235, 239
powerful and limited stories 237–54
  community development 242–5
  cycles of migration 239–42
  future 252–4
  ideologies, and theories 248–52
  pivotal events 245–8
  timescales 239
properties 119, 123–4, 132, 138
  rental 26, 112, 123, 135
  residential 114, 141, 195
Protestant churches 77
public space

Black narratives 154–7
Martínez family's role 148, 151, 165–9, 184, 197
Mexican businesses 161–9
Mexican community 147–51
Mexican narratives 157–61
migration enforcement 150–1, 171, 178–84, 197
payday muggings 151–61
revitalization of commerce 169–71
White narratives 152–4
Puerto Ricans 28, 69, 82, 131–2, 137–8, 182, 201, 206–7, 209–10

Quakers 13–14

racism 6, 8, 28, 51, 55, 62, 70–2, 117, 118, 132, 172, 178, 184, 196, 204–5
residential neighborhoods 34, 109, 111–14, 119–20, 124, 135
resources, heterogeneous 12, 17, 71, 197, 200, 252
Rosa 90–1, 101, 170–1, 210

St. Joseph's parish 1, 35, 76, 106
  assimilation stories 84, 87–8, 104–5
  bilingual masses 100
  Blacks, exclusion 78
  ethnically diverse community 103
  history 79–84
  interethnic relations 76, 78–9, 88, 95, 98–102, 107
  longstanding residents 77–8, 87, 92, 98–100, 102–4, 106–7
  Mexican celebrations 90, 95–8, 99, 102
  Mexican involvement 77–8, 84–90
  Spanish-speaking priest 77
Sara, migrant history
  student life 59–62, 73
schooling 15, 38, 40, 43, 47, 66, 69
schools
  Allie in elementary school 64–72
  diverse pathways 73–4
  hypersexual Mexican girls 58–63
  interethnic relations 52–6
  Juan in high school 40–50
  language 56–8
  Nancy in middle school 50–63
sexual abuse 59

sexuality 59, 62
Sister Carmela 87, 101–2
   view of migration 102
Smith, James, migrant history
   ancestors 4
   career 23
   childhood memories 21
   family history 23–4
   migrant experiences 5
   narratives of decline 25–7
   on neighborhood 119–21
solidarity 8, 27, 62, 120, 133, 176, 196, 200, 202, 220, 225–6, 228, 235, 244, 253
Solis, Sandra 186
Spanish-speaking students 38, 46, 56, 69

teachers 10, 15–16, 39, 46–8, 54–9, 65, 69–70, 74
   elementary school 16, 39, 57, 65
Trent, Molly 81, 83, 99–101, 106

undocumented migrants 68, 125, 137, 152, 180–3
   status 150, 152–3, 178, 216, 248

United States. *See also specific migrants;* Marshall's history
   church's role 76
   economic crisis in 2008 33
   upward mobility 37, 72, 119–20, 141, 149, 183, 228

Valeria 204–6
Victor 95
violence 50, 153–4, 157–60, 181, 241, 250

White narrators 26, 110–11, 113, 115–16, 124, 126, 130–1, 145, 154, 161, 178
White parishioner 78, 80–4, 86–90, 92, 94, 96–7, 101
Whites
   interethnic conflict 142–6
   residential neighborhoods 109–10, 112–17, 119–25, 129, 133–4, 136–40, 144–5
   solteros and slumlords 129–31
White slumlords 129–31, 135
White stories 112, 115–16, 129, 196. *See also specific narratives*
White students 54–5, 61

www.ingramcontent.com/pod-product-compliance
Lightning Source LLC
Chambersburg PA
CBHW072129290426
44111CB00012B/1840